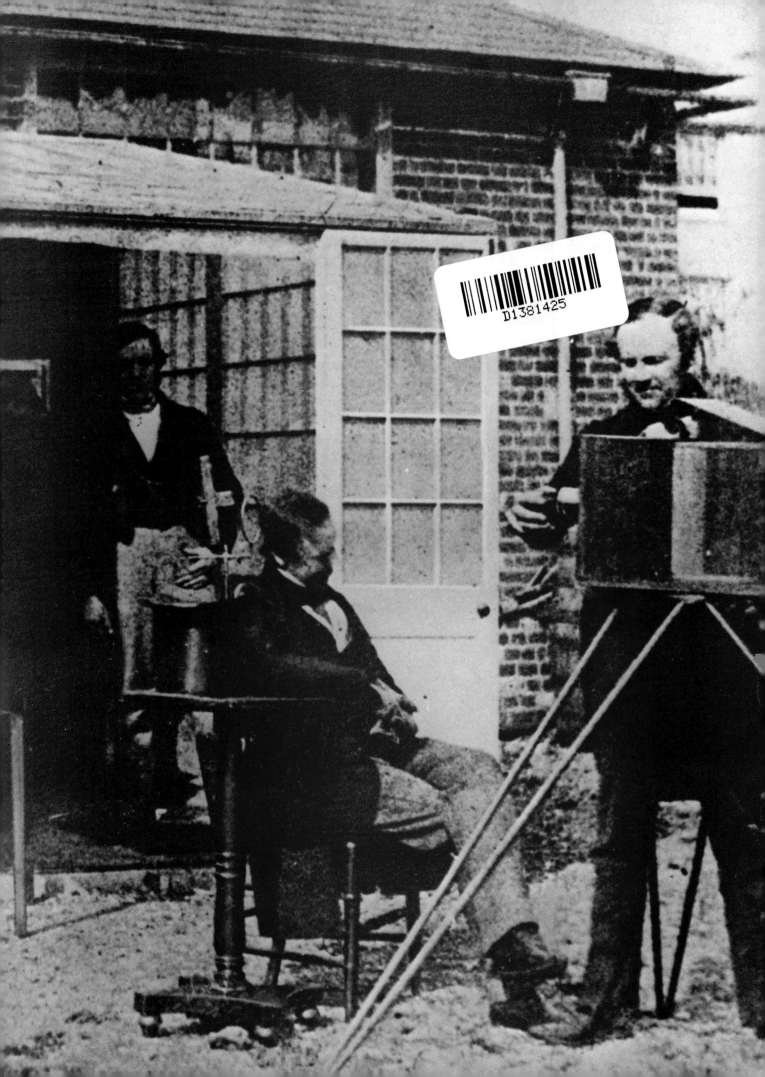

THE HOW IT WORKS ENCYCLOPEDIA OF
GREAT INVENTORS & DISCOVERIES

Marshall Cavendish London & New York

Published by Marshall Cavendish Books Limited
58 Old Compton Street
London W1V 5PA

First Printing: 1978
© Marshall Cavendish 1974, 1975, 1978

Printed in Great Britain

ISBN 0 85685 429 8

INTRODUCTION

When men began to make tools, they began to create a way of life which was worth recording, and historical time began. The inexorable process of invention and development was already under way in ancient times: man is the only animal who knows that he is not immortal. His curiosity about his earthly existence manifests itself in many ways: he is the only animal who writes novels, who practises religion, and who tirelessly tries to manipulate his environment by using it.

It is remarkable how many things which we take for granted had their origin in ancient times. What we usually refer to as the invention of printing was actually the invention of movable type: the Chinese had practised block printing for centuries before that. Much of the history of invention is also the history of economics, exploration, philosophy, and of human consciousness itself.

The flow of inspiration has crossed centuries and national boundries; it has often depended on the right person in the right place at the right time. Accidents have also resulted in discovery: dry-cleaning was invented when the owner of a French dye-works noticed that a tablecloth was cleaner where fuel from a lamp had been spilled on it.

Did you know that Robert Fulton, builder of the first commercially successful steamboat, was also an accomplished painter of miniature portraits who exhibited his work at the Royal Academy? Or that Benjamin Franklin never patented any of his ideas, believing that everyone should benefit equally from scientific knowledge? Or that Samuel Morse, inventor of the telegraph and the Morse code, once ran for public office on an anti-Catholic ticket? This book contains the biographies of more than a hundred people, from Agricola to Zworykin, who have changed the way we live; it contains the details of their personal lives, their habits and foibles, as well as the history of science from the ancient philosophers to television. Appended to some of the biographies are discussions of Newton's laws, Einstein's Theory of Relativity, and so forth. Well written, to be both informative and entertaining, illustrated with hundreds of colour pictures and diagrams, many of historical interest, the book will be a permanent source of fascination for curious people of all ages.

CONTENTS

AGRICOLA, Georgius (1494-1555)

Georgius Agricola was the first man to make a thorough study of mining and minerals. Although he was trained as a doctor, his books on mining were vastly influential.

Agricola was born Georg Bauer in the German town of Glauchau in the Erzgebirge hills. He grew up in an age when books were becoming widely available for the first time, and attended several schools in Glauchau and nearby Zwichau and Magdeburg.

His father was a dyer and woollen draper. Georg did not go to University until he was 20 — 12 to 15 was the usual age in those times. He graduated from the University of Leipzig in 1515 and stayed on to teach elementary Greek.

At about this time, Georg Bauer Latinized his name, as was then the fashion among scholars. Bauer means farmer or peasant, for which the Latin equivalent is Agricola.

To further his education, he went to Italy, where he read classical works on medicine and philosophy. He became fascinated by the possible healing powers of minerals, which were abundant in his native Erzgebirge.

He returned to Germany as an MD and took up a post as town physician at Joachimsthal, now Jáchymov, Czechoslovakia, a new town which had grown to be one of the principal mining centres of Europe and famous for its silver. Coins made from Joachimsthal silver were known as *thalers*, from which the word *dollar* is derived.

Its population of 10,000 consisted almost entirely of miners and smelters crowded together. Occupational diseases were widespread. Through his visits to mines and smoky smelting houses, Agricola soon had an excellent knowledge of mines and metallurgy.

Life in Joachimsthal was so demanding that Agricola eventually moved his practice to Chemnitz, a quieter mining town. Here he turned his knowledge to profit, and a judicious choice of mining shares made him one of the 12 richest men in the town.

Agricola's reputation won him an appointment as official historian but his scholarly regard for truth led him to uncover previous rulers' mistakes, and he fell into disfavour. His historical work was not published until 1963.

Agricola's fame rests on his publications on mining and geology. His most important work, *De Re Metallica*, went into minute detail about the techniques of mining in his time. It was published posthumously in 1556 in 12 volumes, and contained not only observations of what he saw around him but also original suggestions about metals and their ores. He gave clear interpretations of the importance of erosion in geology and the origins of ore, and increased by a third the list of known minerals.

The high regard for Agricola even in his own lifetime is revealed by the fact that although he was a Catholic in a fiercely Protestant town, he was several times elected mayor of Chemnitz.

At a time when it was common for industrial techniques to be closely guarded secrets, Agricola believed that processes and innovations should be published and made available to all. He wrote in Latin to gain wide circulation, but *De Re Metallica* was immediately translated into German and Italian. A century later, the British philosopher Robert Boyle called Agricola 'the most classick author we have about mines', and his work remained the standard for nearly two centuries.

Left: in this engraving Agricola wears a doctor's cap and holds a hammer, symbolizing learning and geology.

Below: from 'De Re Metallica': a mine drainage pump, powered by a treadmill, B, speed-increasing gearing, C and D, turns the ribbed wheel, E, pulling an endless chain of padded pistons, G, up a tube and back to its lower end in the mine. Water comes up between the pistons. This 'rag and chain' method was a primitive way of getting a waterproof seal, a severe problem in early engineering.

AMPÈRE, André Marie (1775-1836)

André Marie Ampère was a French mathematician and physicist with wide-ranging interests and a phenomenal memory. He made contributions to mathematics, mechanics, physics and philosophy, but it is mostly for his work on electricity that he is remembered. The basic unit of electric current, the ampere, is named after him.

Born near Lyons, Ampère was the son of a rich silk merchant who tutored him privately. The young André showed a precocious ability in mathematics, and by his teens he had read the works of the greatest mathematicians. His father was executed in 1793 during the Reign of Terror, and André gave private instruction in science to support himself.

He married in 1799 and became professor of physics at Bourg from 1801 to 1803. There he published a small but impressive treatise on the statistics of games of chance. He returned to Lyons, where his wife died, and then moved on to a lectureship in mathematics at the École Polytechnique in Paris. He taught there for the rest of his life, becoming a professor in 1809 and being elected to the French Academy of Sciences in 1814. Despite the loss of his father and his wife, which left him depressed for life, he had a warm and friendly personality.

In 1820 a meeting of the French Academy saw a demonstration of the discovery of Oersted (*q.v.*) that a compass needle is deflected by the passage of an electric current through a nearby wire. Inspired by this first basic step in electromagnetism, Ampère also began to experiment and in a few weeks was able to demonstrate further developments, among these was the so-called 'Ampère's rule', that a current flowing in a horizontal conductor or wire pointing north deflects a compass needle to the east.

Ampère went on to show that when current flowed in the same direction along two parallel conductors, the wires were attracted, but that if the current in one conductor was reversed, the wires would be repelled. He showed that the magnetic force round a conductor is inversely proportional to the square of the distance. This analogy with gravitation led him to be called the 'Newton of electromagnetism'. Ampère's laws were the foundations of the electromagnetic theory put forward by Maxwell (*q.v.*) in 1865.

In addition to the mathematical laws of electromagnetism, Ampère announced that a coil of wire with a current flowing through it acted in the same way as a magnet, and that a bar of iron placed inside such a coil became magnetized. He called such an arrangement a solenoid, a name that is still given to the electromagnets used in relays and other devices.

Ampère deduced from his experiment that permanent magnets operate by the circulation of small electric currents inside iron bars, and that the Earth's magnetism reveals the existence of electric currents inside the Earth. These advanced ideas foreshadowed modern ideas about matter.

Left: Ampère, from a book by Figuier.

Below: his apparatus to show the motion of a conductor in a magnetic field. The frame, pivoted and supplied with current at A and B, is a double loop to cancel out the Earth's magnetic field. The bar magnet acts mainly on the part nearest it, turning it at right angles to the magnet. Arrows show the (conventional) direction of current – later shown to go the other way.

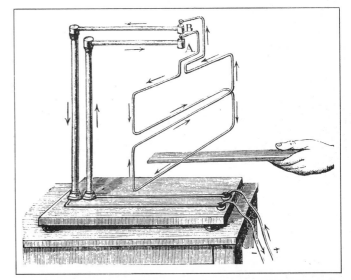

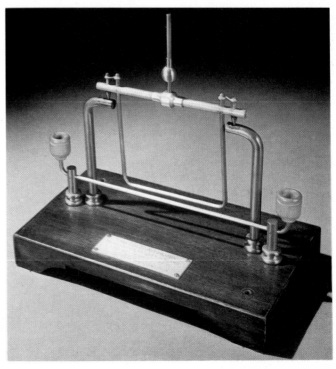

Right: reproduction of Amprère's 1820 apparatus to show the effect of currents passing through a pair of parallel conductors. The bar with connectors at each end is fixed; the other pivots in mercury filled recesses to give a good contact. The bars can be connected beneath the board so that current flows the same way in both, with the result that they attract each other, or in opposite directions in each of them, so that they repel each other.

ARCHIMEDES (287-212 BC)

Archimedes was born in Syracuse, Sicily, in 287 BC, and died there in 212 BC. Little is known about his life other than his discoveries, which were detailed in numerous published works. It is thought that Archimedes may have spent some time studying at Alexandria, which at that time was a centre of learning, returning later to Syracuse to carry out his researches into mathematics, mechanics and engineering.

His inventions were notable, though he probably did not invent the Archimedean screw for raising water from a river. But he did invent other devices, including compound pulleys, burning mirrors which worked like solar furnaces to set fire to the sails of invading ships, and a large catapult-type stone throwing machine which, it is said, prevented the Romans from conquering Syracuse for three years. Although these devices are of interest, Archimedes is more famous for his practical contributions to mathematics and hydrostatics.

In mathematics, he made discoveries in the field of plane and solid geometry. Perhaps his greatest achievement here was working out the ratio of the volume of a cylinder to a sphere placed in it. Archimedes himself considered this measurement so important that he asked for a sphere and a cylinder to be engraved on his tombstone. He also measured π, the ratio between the diameter and the circumference of a circle, by drawing a circle and then, inside it, a series of polygons (many sided figures, such as an octagon) increasing the number of their sides until they met on the circle. This 'method of exhaustion' provided a very close approximation to π, which he showed lay between $3^1/_7$ and $3^{10}/_{71}$.

Archimedes' work in hydrostatics involved a series of experiments on the relative density (also known as specific gravity) of substances. These were prompted by an accusation by King Hiero of Sicily that his metal workers had stolen some of his gold and, to hide their crime, had alloyed the gold with silver. Legend has it that while contemplating the problem in his bath Archimedes noticed that his body, immersed in the water, displaced a volume of water equal to that of his body. He was therefore able to distinguish between pure gold and the lighter gold–silver alloy by immersing equal weights of both in water and noting how far the water level rose in each case. The alloy, being less dense than the gold, was bulkier for its weight and displaced more water.

Archimedes is supposed to have been so elated by his discovery that he leaped out of the bath and ran naked through the streets shouting 'Eureka' (I've found it).

He also discovered the centre of gravity while working out his 'law of the lever'. In Archimedes' time the lever was used widely as a matter of course without any theoretical explanations given. He used its principle to show that if equal weights were placed at different distances from the point of support then the one further away would descend.

As a mathematician and physicist, Archimedes was undoubtedly a genius. His experiments in hydrostatics led to the development of the hydrometer for measuring the density of liquids. The methods he used for his mathematical calculations were the foundation of an important branch of mathematics—calculus, which is fundamental to solving complex problems in all types of science.

When the Romans finally managed to invade Syracuse, their general, Marcellus, gave orders that Archimedes should be treated with respect. He was killed by a Roman soldier because he didn't get out of the way fast enough while busy drawing a diagram on the sand.

16th century German engraving of Archimedes about to leap out of his bath. The two crowns represent the experiment for which the bath gave him the idea, and the spheres his geometrical work.

Below: the diagram shows that the Archimedean screw forms a series of chambers which move upwards as it turns. In this, the original type, the casing revolves in one piece with the screw, preventing leakage. In the modern type, seen in the photograph in a Cyprus grape press, the screw revolves in a stationary casing, but the effect is the same.

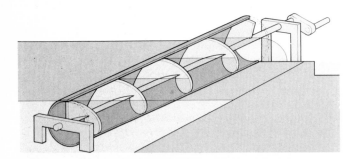

AVOGADRO, Amedeo (1776-1856)

Count Amedeo Avogadro was born in Turin and spent most of his life there. There was a legal tradition in his family, and in spite of his interest in practical science he studied law and qualified in 1796, being in part-time practice for a long time afterwards.

His serious study of physics began in 1800, and he became Professor of Physics at Vercelli in 1809, where he produced his famous hypothesis on the volumes of perfect gases. Between 1820 and 1850 he occupied the Chair of Physics at the University of Turin, and conducted research into the electrical properties of substances, as well as making investigations into thermal expansion and specific heat.

Of Avogadro's published works, the most important was his four-volume physics text book, *Fisica dei corpi ponderabili*, which appeared between 1837 and 1841.

Avogadro's fame rests on his proposal that equal volumes of all gases, under the same conditions of temperature and pressure, contain the same number of molecules. This hypothesis was published in 1811 in the French *Journal de Physique*, soon after Gay-Lussac's discovery that the volumes of combining gases bear a simple ratio to each other and to the volume of the new compound.

Avogadro's hypothesis, in conjunction with Gay-Lussac's law, should have allowed the molecular formulae and atomic weights of gases to be determined experimentally, but his paper attracted little attention because it was supported by so little experimental evidence. Avogadro also proposed that the simple gases, such as hydrogen and oxygen, might exist as molecules containing two atoms instead of one, a suggestion that seemed to conflict with the widely-accepted 'indivisible' atomic theory of John Dalton (*q.v.*). Avogadro continued to publish papers on the subject, as well as on other chemical research.

The vindication of Avogadro's hypothesis came after his death, when in 1860 Stanislao Cannizzaro presented a system of atomic weights determined using Avogadro's work. Since then his hypothesis has been accepted without question, and his ideas on the molecular nature of the simple gases have also proved to be correct.

Avogadro's hypothesis has given rise to the concept of 'gramme-molecular weight' (a mass of a substance equal to its molecular weight expressed in grammes), and to Avogadro's Number, which is the number of molecules contained by the gramme-molecular weight of a substance. Avogadro's Number, usually denoted N, was not accurately determined until 1941 when R T Birge evaluated it to be 6.02486×10^{23}.

Because of the volume of the molecules themselves, Avogadro's hypothesis is not strictly obeyed by real gases, but the difference is very slight except under conditions of high pressure.

Below: bust of Avogadro; the lack of paintings shows that he was not famous during his lifetime.

BABBAGE, Charles (1791-1871)

Charles Babbage was born at Totnes, Devon, the son of a wealthy banker. After a succession of private tutors, he entered Trinity College, Cambridge, in 1810. At this time, mathematical instruction consisted mainly of the study of the works of Newton (*q.v.*), neglecting the more recent investigations of Euler, Lacroix and other European mathematicians. To encourage reform, Babbage and his contemporaries founded an Analytical Society.

In 1816, Babbage, John Herschel (*q.v.*) and others translated Lacroix's treatise on the calculus (an important way of solving many mathematical problems), followed in 1820 by a joint work, *Examples to the Differential and Integral Calculus*. It was while working on these projects that Babbage wondered if machinery could be used to do some of the calculation.

Babbage married in 1814, and thereafter lived in London, but his married life was tragic. He was too engrossed in his work to be a good father, and of his eight children only three survived. Furthermore, his wife died in childbirth in 1827.

In 1822, Babbage made a model of a calculating machine that could add six-figure numbers. Encouraged by this success, he designed a far more elaborate machine or 'difference engine' for the calculation of tables, which would automatically set printing type to eliminate the chance of human error, and in 1823 the Government advanced £1500 towards the cost of making the engine. He hoped that such a machine would prevent errors occurring in mathematical and astronomical tables.

The work, however, went very slowly. By 1827, when it should have been finished, there was little to show, and rumours that he had put the money to his own use caused a nervous breakdown. More money was advanced, but in 1834 his skilled foreman resigned, and the machine was left unfinished.

Between 1835 and 1848 he worked on a new calculator, the 'analytical engine', paying for it entirely from his own fortune. This, too, remained unfinished at his death. In all, he had spent £20,000, a considerable amount in those days, on these projects.

Among his more lasting inventions were the heliograph, a signalling device using mirrors in sunlight, and the ophthalmoscope, the device still used for examining the interior of the eye. He was also an expert in ciphers. In 1832 he published *Economy of Manufacturers*, a widely circulated book dealing with the organization of labour. In 1827 he was appointed Lucasian Professor of Mathematics at Cambridge, but did not give a single lecture during his ten-year term.

An over-sensitive and tactless person, Babbage was unpopular with many of his contemporaries; the Astronomer Royal, Sir George Airy, called his first machine a 'humbug'. Babbage replied by writing a book attacking prominent Fellows of the Royal Society. He was born far ahead of his time, and only in an age of digital computers can his understanding of the problems of automatic calculation be appreciated.

Babbage's difference engine, below left, was partly completed when he argued with his chief instrument maker and work stopped. The Stockholm firm of Scheutz completed a working machine in 1855. The photograph, below, taken by Mackie, shows Charles Babbage aged 69.

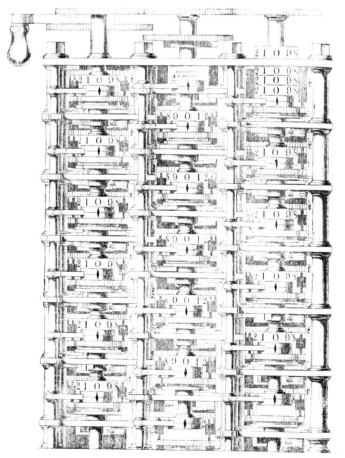

BACON, Roger (c1220-1292)

Roger Bacon, philosopher and scientist, was probably born at Ilchester in Somerset, England. He studied at Oxford and later at Paris, enjoying early training in the *quadrivium*: geometry, arithmetic, music and astronomy.

At Paris in about 1237 he became regent master, teaching elementary arts and science. At this time the works of Aristotle were banned in France on religious grounds, but when the ban was lifted, around 1240, Bacon was one of the first to lecture on his philosophical writings. He was particularly impressed with the popular book *Secret of Secrets*, thought to be Aristotle's guide to kingship written for Alexander the Great. Inspired by this work, he envisaged a system of universal knowledge far beyond the limited academic scope of his time, and in 1247 he took the decisive step of returning to Oxford to study the work of Robert Grosseteste (about 1175–1253), a Franciscan physicist and mathematician. For the next twenty years he devoted himself to the study of languages, mathematics, optics, alchemy and astronomy, training assistants and cultivating the friendship of savants, as well as spending more than £2000 on equipment.

By 1257 he had joined the Franciscans, to whom Grosseteste had bequeathed his library, and an unfortunate period followed. Restricted in his experimental facilities, and cut off from the other researchers of his time, his intolerance of others made him very unpopular. Finally, he was sent to Paris and forbidden to publish further.

In 1266, Pope Clement IV asked Bacon for a secret copy of his great encyclopedia of the sciences. This vast project had long been in Bacon's mind, and, in the hope of gaining funds for its publication, he wrote three preliminary volumes in only 18 months. Unfortunately, his prospective patron died before the third book had reached him. This ended Bacon's hopes of producing a complete encyclopedia, which he had hoped would help to bring science into the curriculum of the universities and encourage experimental research.

Bacon is best known today as a reformer of experimental science rather than for producing any significant and original work himself, although he was far ahead of his time in arguing that light travels in pulses and is not instantaneous. He also performed fundamental researches into the working of the eye, and experimented with mirrors and lenses. As an outcome of this he described a telescope but did not actually make one. Bacon's interests extended to mechanical innovations, and he foresaw the possibility of mechanically powered ships, carriages and even flying machines.

Unfortunately, his eccentricities prevented his reformist ideas from receiving the attention they deserved.

Below: the invention (or introduction into Europe from China) of gunpowder was attributed to Bacon.

Right: Bacon's geometrical diagrams showing the working of the eye. Everything is drawn spherical; it was a mediaeval convention that the sphere was a perfect shape.

BAIRD, John Logie (1888-1946)

John Logie Baird was the first man to demonstrate that television was a practical possibility. The son of a minister, he was born at Helensburgh, near Glasgow on 13 August 1888. He served as an apprentice engineer in a Glasgow factory, and studied at Glasgow University and the Royal Technical College (now the University of Strathclyde).

Dogged by ill-health, Baird was declared unfit for military service in 1914, and soon decided to leave his work as an electrical engineer and set himself up as an inventor. In 1923, exhausted by his various enterprises and ordered to recuperate after a complete breakdown, he concentrated on the idea of sending pictures by radio waves.

In that year he produced his first crude apparatus, using a scanning disc pierced with holes, in which the shadow of a cross was recorded and transferred to a screen. The following year, in a small workshop in Hastings, he gave the first demonstration of television, and in 1925, with a capital of £500 he formed a company called Television Limited. He approached the Marconi organization with his ideas, but was told that they were not interested in developing television.

Baird achieved a breakthrough in 1926, when the BBC (British Broadcasting Corporation) agreed to broadcast a picture from his transmitter to a receiver, the first wireless transmission of television. In 1927 the Baird Television Development Company was formed, and in 1928 a short wave television transmission was sent from London to New York. A year earlier, in Glasgow, Baird had demonstrated his first colour television set.

It was clear to all concerned that television, to be a success, needed the cooperation of the BBC, and several experiments were arranged. The first public transmission was made on 30 September, 1929, with a speech by Sir Ambrose Fleming (*q.v.*), the inventor of the radio valve [vacuum tube]. At this time there were fewer than 30 television sets in the country capable of receiving it, but as news of the invention spread, and test transmissions continued, the Baird Company received orders for thousands of receivers. On 14 July, 1930, the first television play was transmitted, and soon afterwards an audience in the Coliseum Theatre, London, saw a live programme from the Baird studios displayed on a large screen.

By this time the Marconi–EMI company, in association with the Radio Corporation of America, had produced cathode ray receivers along the lines of modern sets and were posing a serious challenge to Baird's mechanical scanning method. For his part, Baird saw no future in the cathode ray tube system. Anxious to score some more 'firsts', Baird televised the Derby horserace in 1931 and 1932. The second transmission was seen by 5000 people in the Metropole Theatre, London, on an improved large screen, and was reported as 'the most thrilling demonstration of the possibilities of television yet witnessed'. In 1934, however, the BBC decided to adopt the Marconi–EMI system, and Baird never forgave them for this decision.

Baird died at Bexhill on 14 June 1946, while working on colour and stereoscopic (three dimensional) television systems. Although his mechanical scanning method was abandoned commercially in his own lifetime, it was later adapted by Peter Goldmark (*q.v.*) for his colour system. (*See also* Vladimir Zworykin.)

Above: John Logie Baird, undeterred by the commercial failure of his mechanically scanned television system, continued research into other aspects of TV, including colour. In this 1943 picture, he is on the left.

Below: scanning section of his 1925 experimental apparatus, which gave pictures of 30 lines at a rate of 10 pictures a second.

BECQUEREL, Henri (1852-1908)

Henri Becquerel is famous for his discovery of radioactivity — the radiations given off spontaneously by certain atoms with unstable nuclei. He was born into a family with a tradition for original scientific research and it was while continuing research begun by his father that he stumbled upon this new and exciting phenomenon.

Becquerel's grandfather, Antoine César (1788–1878), had been a pioneer in electrochemistry and had experimented with telegraphy and magnetism, while his father, Alexandre Edmond (1820–1891), had studied light and phosphorescence. Born in Paris, Becquerel studied at the École Polytechnique, entering the École des Ponts et Chaussées in 1874. In 1878 he became an assistant at the Musée d'Histoire Naturelle, often taking his father's place.

For his doctorate, bestowed in 1888, he submitted a thesis on the absorption of light by crystals, which he investigated while carrying on the work begun by his father into phosphorescence and fluorescence. (Phosphorescence is a glow emitted by a substance, which unlike fluorescence continues long after the source of excitation, for example sunlight, is removed.)

By the late 1880s academic accolades were beginning to fall upon Becquerel. In 1889, he was elected a member of the Académie des Sciences, and in 1892 he became Professor of Physics at the Musée d'Histoire Naturelle, as his father and grandfather had been. From 1895 he was a professor at the École Polytechnique and at the same time chief engineer in the bridges and roads department.

The work for which Becquerel is best remembered, the discovery of radioactivity, was brought about by the discovery by Röntgen (q.v.) in 1895 of X-rays, which he first noticed because of their ability to make certain materials fluoresce.

Fascinated by this discovery, Becquerel wondered if the natural luminescence, or glow, of certain minerals might be accompanied by similar X-ray emission. He took a thin, transparent crust of crystals of potassium uranyl sulphate (a uranium salt) and placed it on a photographic plate wrapped in lightproof paper. Both plate and crystals were exposed to sunlight for several hours. When developed, an outline of the crystals appeared on the photographic plate. To exclude the possibility of a chemical reaction caused by vapours, a variation of the experiment was tried using a thin sheet of glass to separate the uranium salt from the paper covered plate, and again the outline appeared. Subsequently, Becquerel found that in a similar experiment where some uranium crystals had been left, unexposed to light, in a dark drawer together with a photographic plate, they left an even stronger outline on the developed plate. So, accidentally, it was discovered that the photographic effect of these crystals was not tied up with any fluorescence arising from exposure to sunlight or X-rays. Further research proved that the uranium in the salt was the active agent.

During the following years, Becquerel became engrossed in his work on this strange radiation. He discovered that it was not, like visible light, subject to the laws of reflection, and he also found that it could discharge an electroscope, a device for storing static electricity. Together with Ernest Rutherford (q.v.) he realized that more than one type of radiation was involved, and in 1900 his experiments on the influence of electric and magnetic fields had proved that one component consisted of beta particles, or high speed electrons, which, because of their velocity, have a certain power of penetration.

Becquerel failed to identify the alpha particles, or helium nuclei, in the radiation, but in 1903 he confirmed that a third component was particularly penetrative, being able to pass through several inches of lead. Now known as gamma rays, they were formerly called Becquerel rays, although the original discovery was made in 1900 by P Villard. Becquerel's enthusiasm for his research into radioactivity influenced his friends Pierre and Marie Curie (q.v.), and they discovered new radioactive elements, more powerful than uranium. In 1901, the three suggested that radioactivity might be caused by changes occurring within an atom.

For their researches into radioactivity, these three scientists were jointly awarded the Nobel Prize for Physics in 1903. In appreciation of his important findings, Becquerel was made a foreign member of scientific societies in many different countries, and a Fellow of the Royal Society, London, shortly before his death at Croisac in Brittany.

Below: Henri Becquerel in his laboratory with a large electromagnet; in fact, in this scientific family, it was his grandfather who had been interested in magnetism.

BELL, Alexander Graham (1847-1922)

Alexander Bell was born in Edinburgh, into a family that was keenly interested in the study of sound. His grandfather, also Alexander Bell (1790–1865), was an actor who became concerned with clear pronunciation, so that his words could be plainly distinguished by all his audience. After perfecting his own speech, he went to teach elocution in London. His son Alexander Melville Bell (1819–1905) studied how the lips, tongue, mouth, throat and breath work together to form words. He drew pictures of how the mouth formed different sounds, and from this devised a pictorial code called *visible speech* which was used to teach the deaf and dumb to speak.

The third Alexander in the family, who called himself Graham to avoid confusion, was educated by his mother, who was an artist and musician, before he went to high school. It was said that he could manipulate his pet dog's throat to turn its growls into speech-like sounds. From the age of 16, Graham taught elocution, and in 1865 he conceived the idea of transmitting speech electrically. This idea came after reading Herman Helmholtz's book *The Sensations of Tone*, which taught him the principles and theory of sound.

In 1867 Graham Bell went to assist his father in his school

Below: Alexander Graham Bell's original telephone, which first transmitted sound on 3 June 1875.

Right: Bell lecturing on sound at Salem, Mass., in 1877. He used slides and practical demonstrations; the blackboard shows the motion of sound waves.

Below right: the phonautograph, which used a membrane and stylus to trace sound waves on a moving sheet of smoked glass.

of elocution in London, and in his spare time studied anatomy and physiology at University College, London. His brothers both died of tuberculosis, and Graham was also showing signs of the disease. In 1870 his father decided to move what remained of the family to the cold, dry climate of Canada. Graham's health quickly improved after they set up home in Ontario, and the immediate acceptance of the visible speech system by North American instructors of the deaf ensured the family's success. Before the Bells arrived, few people had attempted to teach the deaf how to speak.

Graham went to Boston to set up a speech training school, where his patience and kindness with children became as renowned as the visible speech system. In 1873, he was appointed professor of vocal physiology at Boston University. While at Boston he met a wealthy American lawyer whose daughter had become deaf in childhood. He taught the girl, and the two became so attached that they married in 1870. The girl's father became one of Graham's financial backers.

Graham Bell had seen queues of people waiting at telegraph offices in Boston for a free line, and he devised a

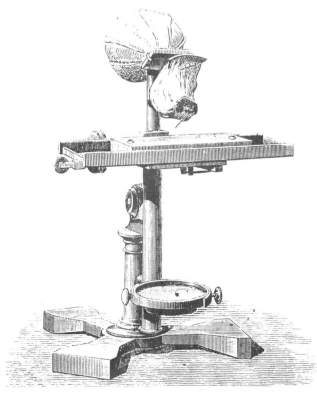

method for sending as many as six or eight telegraph messages along the same line. This method, called the harmonic telegraph, was patented in 1874. It worked by sending several different tones along the same wire, each of which could be interrupted by a morse key. But there were problems in the system, largely due to the difficulty of accurately tuning each receiver, and while solving these Bell realized how sound waves in the air could be made to vary the strength of an electric current in a wire. This was the breakthrough he needed for the telephone.

At the Massachusetts Institute of Technology, Graham Bell had found a device called a phonautograph. This had a mouthpiece in front of a stretched membrane, which had a bristle attached. Sound waves from speech made the membrane vibrate, and the bristle drew a pattern of the sound on smoked glass. From a study of how the human ear used the same principle, Bell learned how to make a microphone and a simple receiver that would translate a varying current back into sound. Bell's patent for the telephone was granted in 1876, while he was still experimenting to perfect the system.

On March 10 that year, while setting up his equipment, he accidentally spilled battery acid on his trousers and automatically called out to his assistant: 'Mr. Watson, come here—I want you'. Watson was waiting at the other end of the telephone circuit on another floor of the same building—but he heard the message, the first words transmitted by telephone.

The telephone was exhibited in Philadelphia that same year, and impressed many leading scientists. The Brazilian emperor picked up the telephone and said in amazement:

'It talks!' Bell's fame was from then on ensured, and he set up the Bell Telephone Company to exploit his invention. By the end of 1876, telephone conversations between New York and Boston were possible. Despite legal battles over his patent, which was contested by Elisha Gray among others, the courts upheld Bell's claim to priority every time.

In 1880, Bell was awarded the Volta prize of 50,000 francs by the French government, and he used this to set up a laboratory in Washington, DC. There he made the staggering advance of using selenium crystals to transmit sound waves by means of a beam of light. This was the first true 'wireless' transmission, and anticipated many later developments in electronics.

At his new laboratory, Bell and his assistants produced the graphophone, an improvement on Edison's phonograph, which used wax records, both cylindrical and disc-shaped. With money from these patents, Bell set up the Volta Bureau for research into deafness. He never forgot his original calling of teaching the deaf.

In 1881, as President James A Garfield lay mortally wounded by an assassin's bullet, Bell invented a locator to detect metal objects in the body. It did not save the Presi-

Below left: Bell's liquid transmitter, which transmitted the first speech on 10 March 1876. Vibrations changed the depth of a rod in water, varying the electrical resistance. The receiver used an electromagnet.

Below: Bell is here making the first telephone call from New York to Chicago in 1892.

Bottom: his HD-4 hydrofoil reached a world record 114km/h on 9 September, 1919.

dent, partly because the metal of his bedsprings spoiled the readings. The next year Bell became an American citizen and set up a laboratory on Cape Breton island, Nova Scotia. His fertile mind was fascinated by the idea of flight, and he designed and built man-carrying kites as well as a vertical take-off propeller, which anticipated the helicopter rotor. Bell supported the aviation work of Samuel Langley, and formed the Aerial Experimental Association, whose members included the aviation pioneer Glenn Curtiss.

Bell's ingenuity and range of interest knew no bounds. When his study in Washington became too hot, he rigged up an air cooling system. Bell worked on sheep breeding for 30 years in an attempt to produce more lambs each season, and his work is continued to this day. He was a founder of the National Geographic Society, and also set up the learned journal *Science*.

Bell's interest in flight led him to examine the possibility of getting a flying machine airborne from water. He began to investigate hydrofoil boats, whose underwater foils provide lift in the same way as an aircraft's wings. Although he never succeeded in making a seaplane, Bell saw how the speed of a boat could be improved by lifting its hull out of the water, and with his assistant Casey Baldwin produced the HD-4, then the fastest boat in the world—in 1918 it reached a top speed of over 70 mph (112 kph).

But many of Bell's ideas were too advanced for the available technology. In his lifetime, the one invention that did

have radical social consequences was the telephone. Bell participated in the opening of the first transcontinental telephone line in 1915. From the east coast he again commanded his old assistant, who was on the west coast: 'Mr. Watson, come here—I want you'. His invention, which at first had linked two rooms, now linked a nation—and was soon to link the world.

BENZ, Karl (1844-1929)

Karl Benz, a German engineer, was a pioneer of automobile construction. He was the son of a railway engineer, who died when Karl was only two years old. But Karl seemed to have inherited a flair for engineering, and studied mechanical engineering at his home town of Karlsruhe. He left his studies to work in a locksmith's, and made designs for a 'horseless carriage' in his spare time. Originally, he thought of adding an engine to his bicycle, but soon decided that a three-wheeled vehicle would be a better idea.

Benz designed a simple two-stroke engine on the principle used by the French engineer Etienne Lenoir, whose engine

Karl Benz built several versions of his original three wheeled car, trying out various improvements and modifications. This one had a single cylinder 0.9 horsepower engine, giving a top speed of 15 km/h, and ran on solid rubber tyres.

ran on coal gas. He risked his life savings to build a prototype engine, but the result was so successful that a backer put up money for Benz to establish a small manufacturing plant at Mannheim, which opened in 1879.

Meanwhile, the German Nikolaus Otto had produced an engine working on the four-stroke Otto cycle, and Benz turned to this as the power source for the automobile he still hoped to build. By 1885, Benz had produced a prototype horseless carriage. This was a three-wheeled vehicle using a four-stroke engine with a horizontal cylinder. The engine ran on benzine, a highly volatile petroleum derivative based on aliphatic hydrocarbons, not to be confused with the aromatic compound benzene.

This was the first practical petrol-driven engine, and it introduced many features. To vaporize the fuel, Benz designed a small carburettor. He invented an electrical ignition instead of the flame ignition that had been used before, and he covered the engine with a jacket through which cooling water could flow. In 1886, Benz patented a simple radiator to cool the water again for recirculation.

The engine ran at 250 to 300 rpm, more than twice as fast as his gas engines, and developed about $\frac{3}{4}$ hp. The drive was transmitted by two chains to the rear axle via a primitive clutch.

On 29 January 1886, Karl Benz received a patent for the Patent Motor Car. Its top speed was less than 10 mph. He exhibited an improved version at the Paris Exhibition in 1887, but it was not until he drove through the streets of Munich the following year that his orders grew. In another model, his two teenage sons drove their mother for 125 miles—then the longest automobile journey.

His original backers were not impressed with the idea of motor vehicles, so Benz had to find alternative financial

handbrake

petrol tank under seat

brake block

chain

Above: despite its more primitive wooden wheels with iron tyres, this is a later version of 1888. It does not yet have a radiator, though Benz had introduced and patented the idea earlier; cooling water boils away at 4.5 litres an hour. The coil and spark plug ignition is of the modern type, unlike many later competitors' systems. The brakes press directly on the tyres.

Left: Benz in old age, with one of his firm's cars.

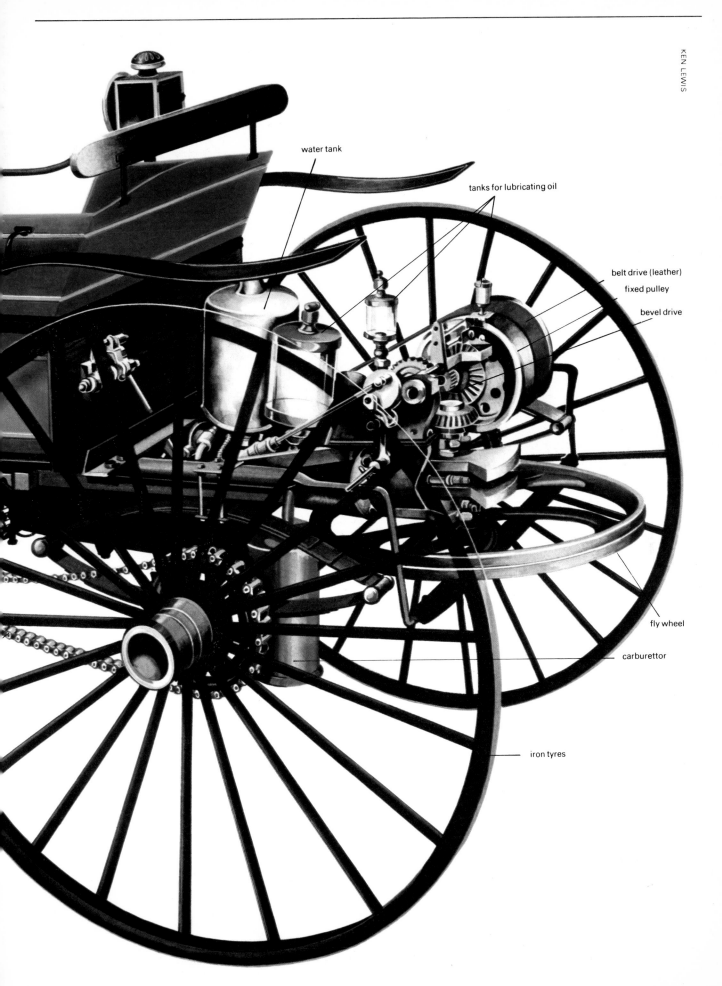

water tank

tanks for lubricating oil

belt drive (leather)

fixed pulley

bevel drive

fly wheel

carburettor

iron tyres

support and start a new factory. In 1890 he built his first four-wheel car, and a Benz car exhibited in Chicago, in 1893, influenced American motor pioneers. Two years later, Benz built the world's first bus.

By 1900, 4000 three-gear 'Comfortable' models, with a 3-horsepower engine, had been sold, and the Benz company was the largest automobile manufacturer in Europe. Benz retired from the management in 1903, and in 1926 the firm merged with the Daimler company to form Daimler-Benz AG, the makers of Mercedes-Benz cars.

BERZELIUS, Jöns Jacob (1779-1848)

Berzelius was a Swedish chemist who is credited with founding modern chemistry. In his lifetime he carried out thousands of experiments which showed that there were two fundamental branches of chemistry, inorganic, concerning minerals, and organic, which dealt with the chemical compounds found in living matter. But his most remarkable observation was his theory that atoms combined with each other because of electrical forces.

Berzelius was the son of a clergyman schoolmaster. Both parents died while he was young and his education was arranged by his stepfather. He studied at Uppsala, graduating in 1802. The thesis which he presented was on the therapeutic effects of electricity, which he showed to be negligible. Berzelius took a research position at the School of Surgery in order to pursue his chemistry experiments, and later spent two years as physician to the poor before he was appointed Professor of Medicine and Pharmacy in 1807.

Over a ten-year period Berzelius analyzed some 2000 simple compounds. He was especially interested in finding

Above right: Berzelius' 1827 apparatus for measuring the carbon and hydrogen content of organic compounds, behind an improved version (by Liebig) of 1830. The compound, heated with potassium chlorate, gave off water (absorbed by calcium chloride in the white tube) and carbon dioxide (collected in the jar).

Right: Jöns Jacob Berzelius as a young man.

out about the way chemicals combined and found that no matter how a compound was prepared it always consisted of certain proportions of each element. He became an early supporter of the atomic theory of Dalton (*q.v.*), that atoms from different elements have different weights.

Soon after the discovery by Volta (*q.v.*) of the electric cell, Berzelius and his colleague W Hisinger (1766–1852) experimented with passing electric currents through chemical solutions. From this Berzelius evolved his dualistic electrolytic theory, in which he proposed that atoms form themselves into electrically charged positive or negative groups. He believed that compounds were formed by the regrouping of these oppositely charged parts during chemical reactions. In 1819 he published the *Essay on Chemical Proportions* linking his atomic and electrochemical theories.

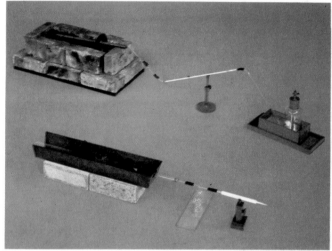

Berzelius went on to measure the atomic weights of all the known elements, and in 1828 published the first accurate atomic weight table. He used the atomic weight of oxygen as his standard. During this work, Berzelius realized the need for the abbreviation of each element's name and some notation for representing the number of atoms present in a chemical compound. He introduced the system still used today for chemical formulae based on the Latin or Greek abbreviation for each element's name together with subscript to show the number of atoms in each compound, for example H_2SO_4.

Berzelius discovered the elements selenium and thorium, and his assistants found lithium and vanadium. In the course of his experiments Berzelius made many improvements in laboratory techniques, introducing the desiccator to keep samples free from moisture, which distorts results when accurate weights are needed, and perfecting gravimetric analysis. His biochemical experiments included the analysis of blood, bile, parts of the eye, milk and muscle tissue. But his interests were widespread and he also studied geology. A useful tool, used in the laboratory by Berzelius for analyzing rock samples, was the blowpipe. The sample was placed in a cavity in a block of charcoal which was held above a candle flame. Compressed air was blown continuously through the blowpipe to give a localized hot flame which reduced or oxidized the sample.

In 1835 Berzelius was created a baron. Late in his life he wielded such great power over chemistry that at times his influence became obstructive. When modifications to his theories were proposed he became upset, and his previous good nature turned into an irate reaction against criticism or change. But this has not obscured his real contribution to the growth of chemistry which, like any other branch of science, must progress by continual modification and revision.

BESSEMER, Sir Henry (1813-1898)

Until the mid-nineteenth century, steel was an expensive metal produced only in small quantities and used in the manufacture of such items as swords and springs, while much larger quantities of cast iron were used in bridges, towers and buildings. As the size of these structures increased, it became necessary to use steel in place of cast iron, which was too brittle and liable to fracture under heavy loads. The growth of the railways also created a large demand for high quality steel for the rails and the rolling stock.

In the late 1840s important developments in steelmaking were made by two men working independently on either side of the Atlantic. In 1847, William Kelly, at his iron works in Eddyville, Kentucky, noticed that some molten iron lying in a hearth used to refine pig iron into wrought iron began to glow when a current of air passed over it. He realized that the carbon content of the iron was being converted to carbon monoxide, releasing heat and at the same time reducing the carbon content. By controlling the amount of this reduction, he could produce quantities of steel much more cheaply than had previously been possible.

In England, Henry Bessemer was proceeding on similar lines, although he kept the metal liquid at a very high temperature, while Kelly worked at lower temperatures without completely liquefying the metal.

Bessemer's immediate objective in making cheaper steel was making stronger barrels for cannon, so that they could be rifled inside. Rifling not only meant spinning the projectile so that gunnery could be more accurate, but keeping more of the explosive power behind the projectile in order to increase its range. Cast iron barrels were not strong enough to withstand the added pressure.

On 11 August 1856, Bessemer described his process at a meeting of the British Association for the Advancement of Science, and he subsequently received considerable financial support to develop his experimental work into a large scale steel making unit. Unfortunately, although he did not know it at the time, Bessemer's experimental work was carried out using pig iron (the crude iron produced in a blast furnace) with a low phosphorus content. Phosphorus is present in most of the iron ores exploited in Europe, and its presence in steel renders the metal brittle, so when Bessemer began large scale production using these ores, the steel was of very poor quality. Bessemer described the first practical results of his conversion method as 'most disastrous'. His financial backers agreed and he decided to finance his own work by investing in a steel works in Sheffield, which eventually produced large amounts of steel for the railway industry.

The operating principle of a Bessemer converter was simply the removal of impurities from molten pig iron by forcing a blast of air through it. The purified iron was then turned into steel by adding the required amounts of carbon and other additives. The main impurities in pig iron are carbon, silicon, manganese, sulphur and phosphorus, which combine with the oxygen in the air to form oxides. These oxides are

Photograph of Sir Henry Bessemer, whose converter process for steelmaking, after initial setbacks, finally succeeded at his Sheffield works in 1860.

either burnt off as gases, as in the case of carbon (which forms carbon monoxide and dioxide), or they are absorbed, as in the case of silicon and manganese, into slag which forms on top of the molten metal. No external heating is needed, as the chemical reactions taking place produce sufficient heat to keep the metal molten.

Converters lined with silica refractory bricks, known in the trade as 'acid' bricks, produced steel known as acid Bessemer steel from low-phosphorus pig iron. In 1878 the 'basic' Bessemer process was introduced, in which the converter was lined with bricks containing dolomite (a carbonate of magnesium and calcium). By adding lime to the molten iron, phosphorus and silicon were removed as calcium phosphate and calcium silicate, which formed a slag, so pig iron containing a high proportion of phosphorus could be used. Lime could not be used in a silica lined converter because it would react chemically with the lining, so the acid process was not suitable for converting pig iron with a high phosphorus content.

When most of the impurities had been removed, and the molten iron was relatively pure, controlled amounts of a manganese and iron alloy (spiegel), ferro-silicon and aluminium were added to remove iron oxide and excess oxygen. To finally convert the iron into steel, carbon in the form of coke or anthracite was added to bring the carbon content to the correct proportion for the type of steel required.

Bessemer's converter design became one of the mainstays of the steel industry for over one hundred years. A large iron barrel, typically of about 40 tons capacity, shaped like a concrete mixer and lined with refractory bricks, was supported on two trunnions (triangular frames) between which it could be tilted from a horizontal to a vertical position. The air was blown in through vents known as *tuyères*, which were situat-

ed either in the bottom of the barrel, or in the side just above the level of the molten metal, in which case the air was blown across the surface of the iron. With the barrel in the horizontal position, it was loaded with scrap iron, molten pig iron, and (in the basic process) lime. It was then tilted to the vertical position and the air was blown through. After the 'blow' the spiegel was added, and the metal was poured into a ladle to which the correct amount of carbon had been added to produce the finished steel. The conversion process took between 15 and 30 minutes, and the metal was poured carefully into the ladle so that the slag was left in the converter to be removed later. The slag from the basic process was very rich in soluble phosphoric acid, and was ground up to make fertilizer.

The progress of the conversion process was judged by inspection of the flare of flames and gases coming from the mouth of the converter. This originally depended on the skill of the ironmaster in estimating the state of the metal according to the type and colour of the flare, but more accurate methods were evolved using spectrographs, photoelectric cells and thermocouples to analyze the contents and temperature of the flare and the metal.

The Bessemer process was a fast method of making good quality steel, although there was a high loss of iron carried away by the air blast.

In 1879 Bessemer was accepted as a Fellow of the Royal Society and knighted by the British government.

Below: the cross section shows how air is blown in through the hollow trunnion and passes to the tuyères via the wind box. The three small diagrams show the stages of the conversion process.

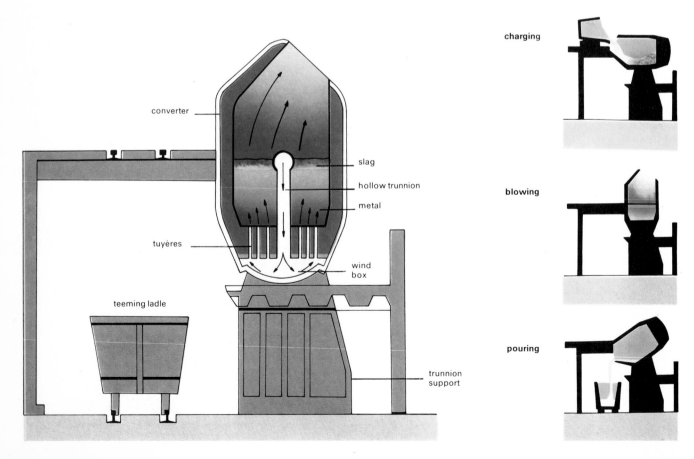

converter

slag

hollow trunnion

metal

tuyères

wind box

teeming ladle

trunnion support

charging

blowing

pouring

Below: the two Bessemer converters at the British Steel Corporation's steelworks at Workington, Cumberland, were the last in use in Britain. They operated until 1977. Now bulk steel production is by the open hearth or basic oxygen processes.

BETHE, Hans (1906-)

Hans Bethe's work lies behind many of the nuclear physics discoveries of the 20th century. Born in Strasbourg, now part of France, he studied physics at the universities of Frankfurt and Munich, where he gained his doctorate in 1928.

His early work was on the behaviour of electrons passing through crystals—solid state physics. The quantum theory provided a new interpretation for this work, and through this, Bethe gained a better knowledge of the way the fundamental particles in matter behave.

Shortly after receiving his PhD, he married a senior colleague's daughter, Rose Ewald. Between 1930 and 1933, he worked with Rutherford (*q.v.*) and Fermi (*q.v.*), studying collisions between atomic particles, further improving his knowledge of nuclear physics. By then it was becoming clear that Germany was no place for someone with Jewish parents, so he moved to England and then, in 1935, to Cornell University in New York State. He became an American citizen in 1941.

In the late 1930s Bethe made his name as a nuclear physicist by writing a review of all that was known about the subject at the time. In 1938 he went to a Washington conference on Theoretical Physics, and became intrigued by problems in astrophysics. A story is told that on the train back to Cornell he decided to try and work out the nuclear reactions which might go on inside stars to produce their energy. He began scribbling equations on a sheet of paper and, according to his close friend George Gamow, 'had the correct answer at the exact moment when the dining car steward announced the first call for dinner'.

It took several months more work before the details could be published, but this is the discovery for which Bethe is best known. Independently in Germany, Carl von Weizsäcker came up with the same solution.

Bethe's reputation as a theoretical physicist made him a natural choice to organize this side of the work at Los Alamos during World War II, which led to the development of the atomic bomb. Rose, his wife, was put in charge of housing the people on the project. He was given the nickname 'The Battleship' because of his approach to problems: weighing them up, then ploughing straight through them without hesitation. His encyclopedic grasp of the subject made problem solving seem easy.

Although nuclear physics was his main interest, Bethe's work during the war covered a wide range of topics, from the effects of artillery shells to the development of microwave radar.

Having helped to create nuclear weapons, Bethe became a leading advocate of disarmament. In 1958 his expert ability at problem solving and his reputation for integrity made him invaluable at the Geneva test ban discussions. Among his many scientific awards is the 1967 Nobel Prize in Physics, for 'contributions to the theory of nuclear reactions, especially his discoveries concerning the energy production in stars'.

Below: Professor Hans Bethe, well known both for his integrity and his views on nuclear proliferation, lecturing on wave physics at Cornell in 1967.

BLÉRIOT, Louis, (1872-1936)

The French aviator Louis Blériot was the first man to make a sea crossing by air. He made his historic flight in July 1909 across the English Channel in a small monoplane. Born in Cambrai, France, Blériot became a wealthy man by making motor accessories, particularly car headlamps, before turning his interest to flight. Around 1899 he built a model aircraft with wings that flapped like a bird (an *ornithopter*); then in 1905 he collaborated with the French aviation pioneer Gabriel Voisin in the building of a glider constructed like a box-kite. It was·fitted with floats and towed by boat to launch it from the river Seine. Blériot experimented with powered biplanes during 1906 but soon turned to the monoplane design which was to influence European aircraft development strongly.

Of the early Blériot monoplanes, the most successful was airborne for 20 minutes but lacked manoeuvrability. This was a common failing in European aircraft at that time because they were not usually as carefully thought out as the Wright brothers' pioneer aircraft. In contrast to some of the weird arrangements of the time, the seventh Blériot design introduced a layout for light aircraft that is still used today: monoplane, enclosed fuselage tapering to the tail, front-mounted engine and propeller, rear tailplane and rudder, two-wheel main undercarriage and a small tail wheel. Blériot's eighth plane made a pioneer cross country flight of 17 miles (27 km) in 1908. But it was his number XI design that proved to be his greatest success.

The London *Daily Mail* newspaper had put up a prize of £1000 for the first person to cross the English Channel. The initial attempt was made on 19 July 1909 by the Englishman, Hubert Latham, incidentally the first man to successfully roll and light a cigarette in an open cockpit. But Latham's plane suffered engine failure and came down in the sea. While he struggled to build a replacement, on July 25 Louis Blériot took off from near Calais at 4.41 AM and landed at Dover 37 minutes later, where he was soon greeted by a customs officer. Blériot's monoplane was powered by a three cylinder Anzani engine of only 25 horsepower. It was controlled by a simple joystick which warped the wings to provide control, as ailerons were not then in general use.

In World War I Blériot set up a successful aircraft factory that built 10,000 military planes for the French government, including the famous SPAD fighter. He was awarded the first flying licence of the International Aeronautical Federation, and set up flying schools at Pau, France, and in Hendon, England. In a Blériot monoplane, the chief instructor at the Hendon school made the first non-stop flight from London to Paris on 12 April 1911—fifty years to the day before the first manned space flight. Louis Blériot died in Paris on 2 August 1936, following a heart attack.

Near right, top: Louis Blériot at the age of 37, photographed on the day after *his historic Channel crossing on 25 July, 1909 (which explains his haroic pose).*

Centre: this picture was taken immediately after his landing; he looks more relieved. His wife is with him; their subsequent doings at a London hotel were the subject of a poem by Max Beerbohm (later censored).

Bottom: Blériot's monoplane on display.

Right: in Blériot's time, any pasture could serve as an airfield and a magnet for the curious.

Below right: a Blériot monoplane in a garage on King Street in Brighton.

BOHR, Niels (1885-1962)

Niels Bohr, the Danish physicist, formulated revolutionary theories of atomic structure, making him one of the foremost scientists of the century. He was born into a scientifically brilliant family in Copenhagen, and as a student distinguished himself in physics. After obtaining his doctorate in 1911, Bohr went to work in England, first with J J Thomson at the Cavendish Laboratory, Cambridge, and in 1912 with Rutherford (*q.v.*) at Manchester University. Rutherford's group had recently performed some experiments that led to a new concept of the atom.

According to Rutherford's concept, the atom consisted of a positively charged nucleus, with negatively charged electrons orbiting it. According to classical theory, however, such orbiting electrons would emit radiation as they moved, causing them to lose energy and to slowly spiral into the nucleus. But this did not appear to happen.

To explain this, Bohr made a bold theoretical step that has guided all further thinking about the atom. He linked events in the atom with the discovery in 1900 by Max Planck (*q.v.*) that energy is not continuous, but comes in little packets, or *quanta*. Bohr maintained that electrons *could* orbit the atomic nucleus without radiating energy, but that only certain orbits were possible, each corresponding to a different energy state. An electron would emit or absorb a specific packet of radiation—a quantum of energy—only as it jumped between one orbit, or energy state, and another.

This theory explained the odd dark lines that crossed the spectra of bright objects at particular wavelengths. Scientists knew these as *Fraunhofer lines* but were unable to understand them. Notable among such lines was the Balmer series that were emitted or absorbed by hydrogen atoms. In 1885 the Swiss mathematician Johann Jakob Balmer found that the wavelengths follow a simple mathematical progression. Bohr showed that the frequency of the absorbed or emitted radiation corresponded to the energy difference between electron orbits.

This idea introduced the quantum nature of matter. Though Bohr's atomic theory was later modified by other scientists who introduced elliptical electron orbits, orbits at varying inclinations, and finally the concept of the electron not as a particle but as a wave, the Nobel Prize in physics for 1922 was awarded to Bohr for this work.

Bohr returned to the University of Copenhagen as a professor in 1916, and in 1920 an institute of theoretical physics was created there especially for him. Here he began to regard the nucleus of the atom as a liquid drop, which absorbed particles when bombarded, and then re-emitted other particles. In the case of heavy nuclei, the nucleus might split into two parts.

In 1938 the German physicists Otto Hahn and Fritz Strassmann split uranium this way. (Hahn received the Nobel Prize in 1944.) Lise Meitner and Otto Frisch, who had been forced out of the country by Hitler, called the process fission, and concluded that a great deal of energy would also be released. Bohr received news of this development in 1939, just as he left for the United States, where at Princeton with John A Wheeler he calculated that it was the isotope uranium-235 that was being split. This work, performed on the eve of World War II, ushered in the age of atomic energy.

During the war Bohr remained in Copenhagen until 1943, when he faced imprisonment because of his patriotism. He fled to Sweden with his family in an overcrowded fishing boat, and from there he managed to fly to England. Later he went to the USA where he made some technical contributions to developmental work on the atomic bomb. Bohr, however, was very concerned about controlling such enormous destructive power. He advocated a policy of openness in which no one country could gain a secret advantage.

During the 1950s Bohr helped to found CERN—the European Centre for Nuclear Research at Geneva, and took an active interest in its work until his death. In 1957 Bohr was awarded the first Atoms for Peace prize.

Below: Niels Bohr and many other eminent scientists at a conference in Brussels in October, 1927.

Bottom: Professor Bohr at the particle accelerator of the Copenhagen Institute of Theoretical Physics, of which he was the director.

BOYLE, Robert (1627-1691)

Robert Boyle, philosopher and scientist, was born at Lismore Castle in County Cork, Ireland, on 25 January 1627, the fourteenth child and seventh son of the first Earl of Cork. He was a gifted child with a very good memory, and when he was sent to Eton school at the age of eight he already had a good command of Latin and French. At the age of eleven he left Eton to travel and study in Europe with a private tutor, and by the time he was fourteen he was in Florence, Italy, studying the work of Galileo (*q.v.*).

Returning to England in 1645 he spent seven years at Stalbridge, Dorset, where he continued his studies into philosophy, theology and science and began some early experimental work. After two years in Ireland he went to live in Oxford, where he met several members of the 'Invisible College', a group of independent scientific investigators who held discussions and conducted experiments in London and Oxford. This group became the basis of the Royal Society, founded in 1660 under the patronage of King Charles the Second. Boyle was a founder member of the Society, but when he was offered the post of president in 1680, he did not accept, as his religious views prevented him from taking oaths.

While he was in Oxford he repeated the air pump experiments of von Guericke (*q.v.*), assisted by Robert Hooke (*q.v.*), and with his improved version of the apparatus conducted further experiments of his own. He published the results in his *New Experiments Physico-Mechanical* of 1660, a later edition of which included the famous gas law that bears his name. This law, which states that the pressure of a given mass of gas is inversely proportional to the volume, was actually discovered by one of his assistants, a Mr Towneley. Another result was the discovery that the boiling point of water is lower under reduced pressure.

Boyle believed that all matter was made up from extremely small particles, which were combined together in varying ways to form the different chemical substances. In 1661 he published the *Skeptical Chymist*, in which he set out his views on this subject and attacked the old theories of the alchemists. These had either followed the ideas of Aristotle, in which everything is made from various combinations of the four 'elements', earth, fire, air, and water, or the later theory of Jabir (also called Geber) who held that the main elements were mercury and sulphur.

Boyle's views on the atomic composition of matter were influenced by the work of other philosophers such as Gassendi, Descartes, and Democritus. In fact, much of his work was based on that of other people.

His researches covered most of the branches of science then known. In addition to his work on air and atoms, he investigated the nature of light, electricity, magnetism, crystals and chemical compounds, and pigments derived from plants.

In 1668 he moved to London where he lived with one of his sisters. Frequent ill health may have encouraged an interest in medicine and diseases, on which he wrote a series of books between 1684 and 1691. His research into biology and physiology was somewhat hampered by his dislike of having to dissect specimens for investigation.

He was a devout Christian and wrote many articles on theology. He died in London on 30 December 1691, and in his will endowed the Boyle Lectures, to defend Christianity against atheists, pagans, and other 'notorious infidels'.

Boyle is remembered as an experimenter of genius, who lent important weight to the atomic theory of matter and encouraged practical experimental research in the manner advocated by his predecessors Galileo and Bacon (*q.v.*).

Left: this picture of Robert Boyle reflects his rank.

Below left: air pump apparatus used by Boyle and Hooke at Oxford to investigate von Guericke's work.

Below right: Boyle's second air pump, with an improved water seal.

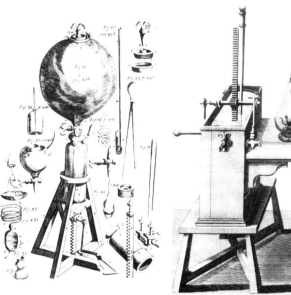

BRAHE, Tycho (1546-1601)

Tycho Brahe, the greatest astronomical observer of pre-telescopic times, was born into a noble Danish family. At the age of 14 he was attracted to astronomy when he witnessed a partial eclipse of the sun and was intrigued by the fact that such a phenomenon could be predicted.

At that time, planetary positions were still calculated from observations and work of Greek astronomers, Hipparchus and Ptolemy in particular. These predictions were in need of improvement, a situation impressed upon Tycho in 1563, when a close approach (*conjunction*) of Jupiter and Saturn occurred a month away from the predicted time. As a result he began building sighting instruments on an unprecedented scale, including a quadrant 19 feet (5.8 m) across. Using the quadrant, he could measure positions accurately to one arc minute (a sixtieth of a degree). By this time Tycho had abandoned all previous thoughts of a political career: he had sufficient wealth to maintain an observatory and assistants.

The turning point in his life came in 1572, when, on 11 November, he independently discovered an exploding star, or *supernova*, in the constellation of Cassiopeia. This brilliant star, which for a few weeks was visible in broad daylight, conflicted with the widely accepted principle of stellar immutability. Some people claimed that the 'star' moved, suggesting an atmospheric origin, a theory which did not offend the classical concept of the 'perfection' of the heavens. Tycho, however, with his superb instruments, proved in his book *De Nova Stella* (1573) that the star was stationary in the sky.

Impressed by Tycho's achievements, King Frederick II of Denmark bestowed on him the island of Hveen in the Oresund near Copenhagen. The king also supplied Tycho with the means for building a great observatory there. From 1576 to 1596, Tycho was virtual dictator on the island, living in luxury in his famous observatory of Uraniborg. He built increasingly more elaborate instruments in his workshops and created a magnificent library, as well as possessing his own printing press. His rule of Hveen terminated after quarrels with the new king, Christian IV. Eventually Tycho went to Prague, where he died in exile.

During the 20 years spent at Uraniborg, Tycho and his assistants measured with great accuracy the positions of 777 stars, as well as making many observations of the Sun, Moon and planets. Tycho was the first observer to apply corrections to his raw observations, making allowances for instru-

Tycho Brahe, left, claimed to have invented many of his instruments, though most were just improved, such as the armillary below. A star was sighted along one of the moveable arms, EF; then the instrument was turned over and the other arm used to reduce errors.

mental inaccuracies, observational errors, and even atmospheric refraction. Through such refinements of observation, he was able to prove that the parallax (apparent change in position of a celestial object when viewed from different points on Earth) of the comet of 1577 was smaller than that of the Moon, proving that it was further away. This revelation refuted the popular belief that comets were atmospheric phenomena.

With the exception of his researches into the supernova and the comet, Tycho was concerned with amassing observational data. He believed that the planets moved around the Sun, but that the Sun moved around the Earth, carrying the planets with it. Johannes Kepler (*q.v.*), however, who stayed with Tycho during the last year of his life and obtained the manuscript observations, used them to prove that the Earth and planets all revolve around the Sun, and that their orbits are elliptical, not circular, as previously thought.

Right: silver medal commemorating the 1577 comet. Tycho's nose was also silver; he lost the original in a duel.

Below: Tycho's concept of the solar system: the planets orbit the Sun, but the Sun and Moon orbit the Earth. This 1661 version, made after his death, shows four moons of Jupiter which Galileo had discovered telescopically.

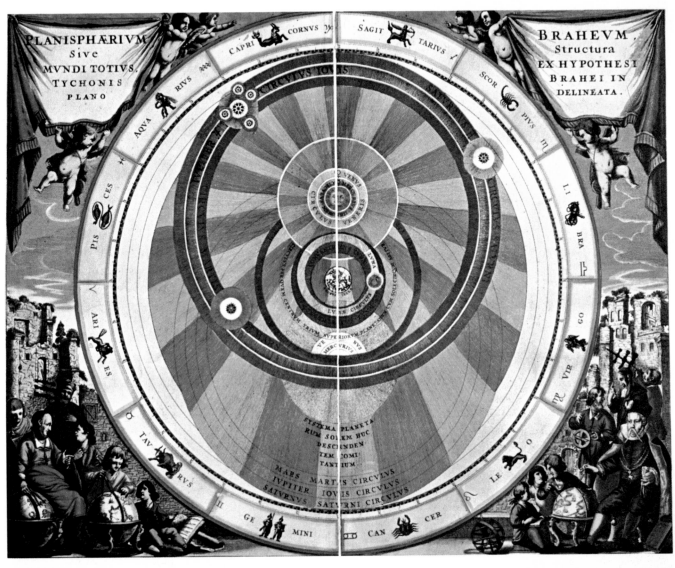

BRAUN, Wernher von (1912-1977)

Wernher von Braun, the German-American rocket pioneer, designed the world's first successful long-range missile (the V2) and was in charge of the team that built the Saturn 5 launcher used in the Apollo moon flight.

Von Braun became interested in astronomy and the idea of spaceflight while still in his teens, when he was presented with a telescope by his parents. The son of a German baron, he studied engineering as a boy and was an early member of the German Rocket Society in the late 1920s, helping the rocket pioneer Hermann Oberth with his engine experiments. The German Rocket Society moved into an abandoned munitions dump on the outskirts of Berlin in 1930, and began to build prototype rockets. The group launched some of the first successful European liquid-fuelled rockets, and their design called the Repulsor reached a height of one mile (1.6 km) in 1931.

In 1932, the German army took over rocket development, and von Braun went to the artillery range at Kummersdorf, south of Berlin, to do experimental work on rocket propulsion for his doctorate. Here he developed new rocket designs, and in December 1934 flew two small rockets to a height of $1\frac{1}{2}$ miles (2.4 km). This brought increased funds and an enlargement of his research group. In 1937 the work was moved to Peenemünde on the Baltic coast, where von Braun became technical director. Part of the money for the Peenemünde move had come from the Luftwaffe (the German air force), whose aircraft development chief Major von Richthofen (cousin of the World War I 'Red Baron') had

Left: Dr Wernher von Braun when he was director of the George C. Marshall Space Flight Center at Huntsville, Alabama, where he worked from 1960 to 1970.

Below left: von Braun (arm in plaster) in the Austrian Alps after his surrender to Allied troops in 1945; he was taken to the USA to continue his rocket design work and took US nationality in 1955.

Below: after an air raid in August 1943 killed over 800 at Peenemünde, V2 production was moved to several places; this one is at Nordhausen. On 10 April 1945, the town was captured by the US First Army, who took over the huge underground factory and liberated the adjacent slave labour camp.

Above right: cutaway of the A4 rocket, later called the V2.

1. Internal carbon guide vanes.
2. External control vanes.
3. Electro-hydraulic servomotors.
4. Turbine exhaust.
5. Stabilizing fins.
6. Hydrogen peroxide tank.
7. Liquid oxygen tank.
8. Shell construction.
9. Servo operated alcohol valve.
10. Front jointing.
11. Conduit.
12. Warhead.
13. Central exploder tube.
14. Control and radio equipment.
15. Alcohol tank.
16. Double walled alcohol delivery pipe to pump.
17. Rear joint ring.
18. Air bottles.
19. Tubular frame. supporting turbine and pump assembly.
20. Alcohol distribution pipe.
21. Combustion chamber.
22. Chain drive to external control valves.
23. Venturi nozzle.

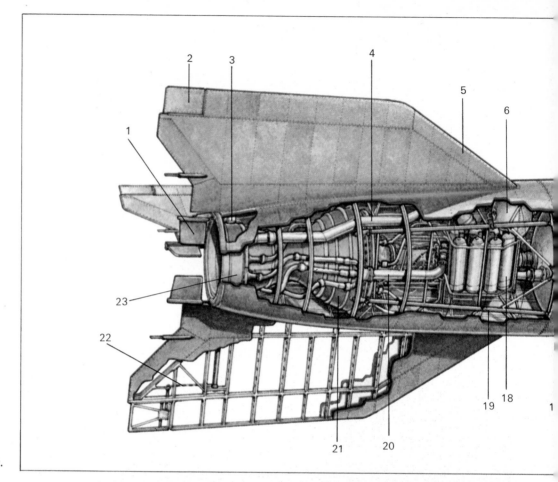

Below, near right: the scientists and engineers with the invading American army showed great interest in the assembly lines for the rocket. Here at Kleinbodingen, Germany, a partly completed rocket shows the unfinished engine compartment at the base.

Far right: scarcely less ingenious than the rocket itself were the rapidly deployed mobile launchers developed after Allied air reconnaissance and bombing had made static launch sites unusable.

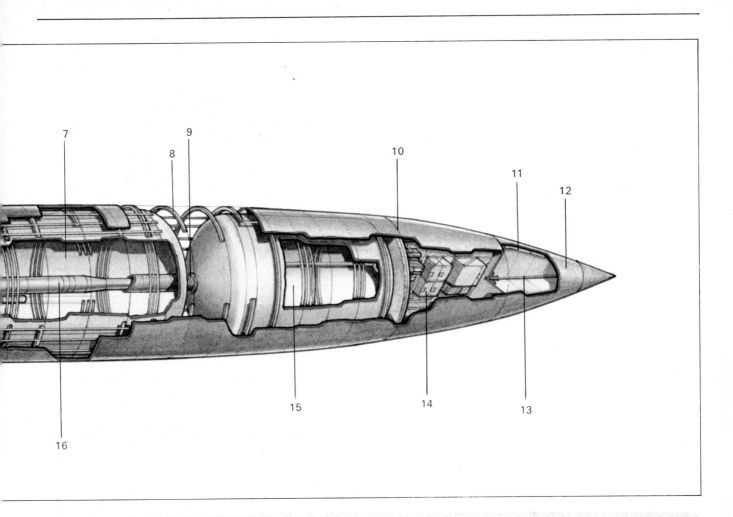

enlisted von Braun in developing jet-assisted take-off for aircraft.

At Peenemünde the von Braun team tested a new design, a 21 ft (6.4 m) long rocket called A3, developing a thrust of 3300 pounds (1500 kg). Problems with the guidance system caused tests to fail. Meanwhile, as German troops moved into various parts of Europe, the Army Ordnance Department specified their need for a long range missile, capable of carrying a one ton warhead. This rocket was called the A4, later known as the V2. The guidance problems with the earlier design had to be ironed out, and this was done with the A5 test vehicle which in 1939 reached $7\frac{1}{2}$ miles (12 km).

The success of the A5 smoothed the development of the A4, the largest and most advanced weapon in the world at the time of its first successful flight in October 1942. The 46 foot (14 m) long, 27,000 pound (12,240 kg) rocket rose to a height of 60 miles (96 km) and flew a distance of 120 miles (193 km) at 3000 mile/h (4800 km/h). It was the world's first guided missile, and by the end of World War II over 5000 had been built. Several thousand of these were fired at England and other European targets, although by that time von Braun had been arrested and briefly imprisoned by the SS on a charge that he was developing rockets for space flight, and had no interest in their use as weapons.

This was partly true: by the end of the war the group had developed designs for an improved and piloted V2, a two stage rocket capable of carrying a payload of 2500 pounds (1130 kg) and a three stage launcher for manned orbital flights. They had also designed a four stage vehicle with a minimum $2\frac{1}{2}$ million pounds (1.2 million kg) of thrust capable of putting heavy satellites into orbit.

At the end of the war, von Braun and his group surrendered to advancing American troops. The German technicians and rocket components were captured by US and Soviet forces, and all major rockets in use today are descendants of the German V2. Von Braun moved to the White Sands Proving Grounds in New Mexico, where numerous upper atmosphere soundings were made with the V2. In 1950 von Braun and 130 of his original Peenemünde team moved to Huntsville, Alabama, with the army ballistic missile programme. Here he developed the Redstone rocket, later used as a booster for US sub-orbital manned launches. From the Redstone were developed the Jupiter and Juno rockets, which launched early American satellites.

In 1960, the von Braun group became part of the civilian NASA organization, and he was made director of the George C Marshall Space Flight Center at Huntsville. From their experience with Redstone and Jupiter rockets, the group developed the Saturn series. The first of these, the two stage Saturn 1, was used for test flights of dummy Apollo capsules. Its improved successor, the Saturn 1B, was used to launch manned Apollo capsules into Earth orbit. The culmination of the Saturn programme was the development of the three stage Saturn 5, capable of orbiting a 140 ton payload or sending 47 tons to the Moon. The total thrust of its first stage was $7\frac{1}{2}$ million pounds (3.4 million kg), developed by five engines each with a thrust equal to the first stage of a Saturn 1.

In 1972 von Braun retired from NASA to take up a post in private industry working on the applications of satellites to the world's problems.

Early development suffered from repeated failures; this V2 fell over as it was being launched at Peenemünde.

BRUNEL, Isambard K (1806-1859)

Isambard Kingdom Brunel was an English engineer who made revolutionary advances in the fields of railway and ship engineering. His father was Sir Marc Isambard Brunel (1769–1849), a French-born engineer who practised his profession in New York and later in England, where he designed machines for cutting and shaping timber. Sir Marc also built the first tunnel (designed for foot passengers and later used by the London Underground railway) under the River Thames between Rotherhithe and Wapping, as well as designing the tunnelling 'shield' (excavating machine) which completed the construction of the tunnel in 1873.

Isambard K Brunel inherited his father's engineering ingenuity and daring. Joining his father in building the Thames tunnel, Brunel was seriously injured when water broke into the diggings. To recuperate, Brunel went to Bristol where he prepared designs for a suspension bridge over the River Avon. One of his designs led to the construction of the Clifton suspension bridge, which was only completed after Brunel's death.

Right: Isambard Kingdom Brunel and the chains of the stern checking drum used to control the launching of the Great Eastern in 1857.

Below: his father's Thames tunnel is still in use by the London Underground railway.

After recovering from his injuries, Brunel continued his engineering work in the Bristol docks. In 1833 he became chief engineer to the Great Western Railway. During this time Brunel promoted a 7 ft (2.1 m) wide, broad gauge track, which gave great stability at high speed. Although the broad gauge was eventually abandoned, it helped to promote the progress of the railways.

Having built over 1000 miles of railway line in Britain, Brunel also produced numerous advanced bridges to carry the lines over the rivers. To help in the construction of a bridge at Chepstow in 1852, he invented the compressed air caisson which allowed men to work on the bridge foundations on the river bed. The same technique was used in 1859 for building the Saltash bridge which took the railway over the river Tamar in two 455 ft (139 m) spans, 100 ft (30 m) above the river at high water.

In spite of his achievements in the railway, Brunel is chiefly remembered for his three historic ships. Each ship was far in advance, both technically and in size, of anything that had gone before. His first ship, the *Great Western*, was built to continue the Great Western Railway from England over the Atlantic to the United States. Launched in 1837, the *Great Western* was 236 feet (72 m) long—28 feet (8.5 m) more than any previous ship—and displaced 2300 tons. The first regular steamship service between England and the United States began with the *Great Western* which made the crossing in the remarkably short time of 15 days.

Brunel was still resolved to build a larger sister ship to the wooden, paddle driven *Great Western*. A special dry dock was constructed at Bristol for what was to become Brunel's finest ship, the *Great Britain*. She was 322 feet (98 m) long and weighed 3300 tons. The most remarkable feature about her, though, was that she was the first large ship to be made of iron and to be driven by a propeller. She was, in fact, the forerunner of all modern ships.

The success of the *Great Britain* led Brunel to plan another ship which would be four times larger and designed for the Australian run. The outcome was the *Great Eastern*, which was made with a double skin of iron and was unique in having both propellers and side paddlewheels for propulsion. It had 10 boilers, five decks, and was to accommodate 4000 passengers. Her trials, however, showed that she burned twice as much coal as Brunel had anticipated and that she would never be able to make the long run for which she had been designed.

Although a commercial failure, the *Great Eastern* made history by laying the first Atlantic submarine cable and remained the largest ship in the world for 40 years. The financial and technical problems of building the mammoth vessel broke Brunel's health and he died of a stroke the year after her launch.

Plans of the Great Britain, now recovered from the Falkland Islands and restored for display in Bristol.

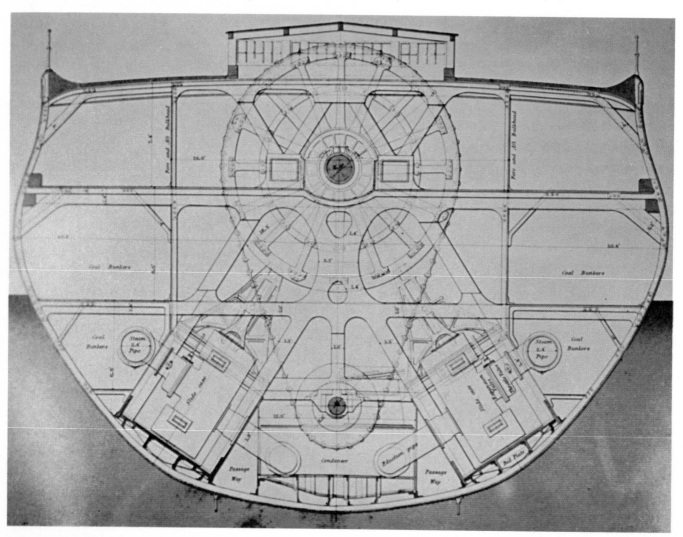

Below: when Brunel's broad gauge railway gave way to the standard gauge in 1892, over 620 broad gauge locomotives had been built; all were scrapped.

Bottom: the 19,000 tonne, 212m Great Eastern had to be launched sideways; she was checked too much and stuck fast for three months.

CARLSON, Chester (1906-1968)

Chester Carlson was the American inventor of the xerography method of photocopying. Carlson's parents, who were of Swedish origin, were both invalids, his mother dying from TB when he was seventeen. Although he had to work part-time to support his family, Carlson successfully studied chemistry at school and, in 1930, gained a degree in physics from the California Institute of Technology.

He joined Bell Telephone Laboratories in New York, first as a researcher and then in the patent department. It was here that he realized the immense labour involved in copying documents, which often had to be entirely retyped. In 1935 he decided to design a quick, clean copying machine.

Carlson realized that ordinary photographic techniques were out; the market was dominated by major companies, and the techniques were time-consuming and messy. He turned instead to an age-old discovery — static electricity, the same force that makes a comb which has been vigorously rubbed pick up scraps of paper.

By 1937 he had made a copy of a celluloid ruler on a charged plate, and filed his first patent for this new technique which he called 'electrophotography'. In 1938 he rented a small room to use as a laboratory, and brought in an unem-

ployed German physicist, Otto Kornei, to assist him. Together, they produced the world's first xerographic print on 22 October of that year. A metal plate coated with sulphur was charged by rubbing it with a handkerchief, and exposed to a glass slide bearing the words '10–22–38 Astoria'. Dark powder was pressed against the plate and the image, in the form of the dark powder, was successfully transferred.

Carlson then had the problem of selling his invention to a firm which could develop and market it. After many frus-

The first xerographic copy, made in Astoria, NY, on 22 October 1938 by Carlson and Otto Kornei.

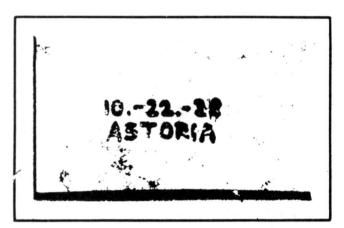

Below: Chester Carlson with one of his early machines. He went on to found the hugely successful Xerox Corporation, now Rank Xerox.

trating years, during which he improved the process by using more sensitive plates and a powder that would stick to ordinary paper, Carlson joined forces with the Battelle Memorial Institute at Columbus, Ohio. They took on the development work in return for a share in the profits.

On 1 January 1947, a photocopying firm called the Haloid Company of Rochester, New York, signed an agreement for rights to the new dry-printing process. This firm named the process xerography, meaning 'dry writing'. Eventually they became the Xerox Corporation. In 1950, the first Xerox machines were marketed, using plates coated with light-sensitive selenium (a non-metallic element of the sulphur-tellurium group) and entirely new ways of charging and powdering the plates.

One problem was that someone was still needed to do the operations that in later designs became mechanized. Only in 1960 with the introduction of the self-contained 914 machine, was Chester Carlson's dream fully realized—perfect copies delivered automatically at the touch of a button. And the profits from that dream made him a multi-millionaire.

CARNOT, Sadi (1796-1832)

Sadi Carnot was a French physicist who founded the science of thermodynamics, which literally means 'heat movement'. His early death from cholera at the age of 36 was a great loss to science in the 19th century.

Carnot came from one of the most prominent families of his day. He was the son of Lazare Carnot, the French minister for war, and elder brother of Hippolyte Carnot, a French politician whose son, Marie François Sadi Carnot, was president of the French Third Republic. Hippolyte's second son, Marie-Adolph, was a mineralogist after whom the uranium ore carnotite is named.

Carnot was educated at the École Polytechnique, noted for its science teaching. Although he was nominally trained to be a military engineer, his main interest was in the harnessing of heat energy, as in steam engines. Carnot has been called the most profoundly original French physicist of his day—a reputation based on his sole publication, a book called *Réflexions sur la Puissance Motrice de Feu*. In this book, published in 1824, Carnot set out to find whether the motive power of heat is unbounded, and whether possible improvements in steam engines have a limit or whether these improvements may be carried on indefinitely.

Although steam engines were becoming common, no one fully understood the principle on which they worked. The engines were also very inefficient—none of them turned more than 10% of their heat energy into work. Carnot found that there was a relationship between temperature and work done in the engine, which was a glimpse of what was later to become the first law of thermodynamics: that energy is never destroyed, only changed from one form into another.

More importantly, he found that the efficiency of an engine depended on the temperature difference between the heat source (in the case of a steam engine, the boiler) and the heat sink, or receiver (the condenser for the steam engine). Carnot saw that the boiler and condenser were two essentials for a heat engine; without the temperature gradient that they gave, the engine would not work at all. The third and last essential was a working fluid to transfer the heat, which in this case was steam.

Sadi Carnot, who lived to only 36; his vital work on thermodynamics was rediscovered years later.

Carnot reached his conclusions by visualizing an ideal engine in which the processes of heating steam—using it to push a piston, and letting the piston return by condensing the steam—all took place in a repeatable cycle. This so-called *Carnot cycle*, which is theoretically reversible, can never be obtained in practice because in a real engine some energy is always lost through friction.

Carnot showed that the nature of the working fluid does not matter, and neither does the way the temperature drops between the heat source and the heat sink. The maximum efficiency of the engine is governed purely by their temperature difference. This work is the basis for the so-called second law of thermodynamics, which, in its simplest form, states that heat only flows spontaneously from a hotter body to a colder one. Although other scientists, such as Clausius and Kelvin (*q.v.*), later developed Carnot's work, his was the first clear analysis of the processes occurring in heat engines.

CAVENDISH, Henry (1731-1810)

Henry Cavendish is mainly known for his investigations into physics and chemistry. Although he wrote many important papers, it was not until the contents of his notebooks were published, many years after his death, that the true breadth of his work became known.

A grandson of the 2nd Duke of Devonshire, Cavendish was described as 'the richest of the learned, and the most learned of the rich'. He was born at Nice on 10 October 1731, and spent his life in private scientific pursuits in the style of other 'gentleman scientists' of the period. His retiring habits made him a mystery, almost an object of fun, in his own lifetime.

Cavendish had a notorious aversion to women, and it is not surprising that he never married. His social activity, in fact, was confined to the regular Thursday dinners of the Royal Society, of which he became a Fellow in 1760. At home his female household staff were under threat of dismissal if they ever crossed his path. It is related that once, having met a housemaid on the stairs, he ordered a separate staircase to be built for his private use.

Cavendish lived in an age when chemical research was beginning to emerge from the restrictions of Aristotelian dogma and alchemical positivism. His greatest achievement in this field arose from his discovery of hydrogen in 1766. Cavendish called it 'inflammable air', and produced it by the action of acids such as sulphuric or hydrochloric on metals such as iron or zinc. Itself an event of major importance, it led in 1784 to his synthesis of water from a mixture of hydrogen and air, fired by a spark. This experiment proved conclusively that water could not be the fundamental element the ancient philosophers had claimed.

Cavendish analyzed other gases in the air, particularly carbon dioxide, or 'fixed air' as it was then called. He also discovered that about 1 % of atmospheric air consisted of an unknown substance, identified a century later by Sir William Ramsay (1825–1916) as being mainly the inert gas argon.

His investigations into electricity were also of a fundamental nature. He studied the electrostatic forces between charged bodies, proving that they obey an inverse square law, and also examined the phenomenon of electrostatic capacitance, which would have application in electronics more than 100 years later.

In 1798, Cavendish published perhaps his greatest experiment, in which he arrived at a value for the mass, and consequently the average density, of the Earth. By measuring the movement of a small pellet when it was gravitationally attracted by a large mass of lead, the ratio of the mass of the Earth to that of the lead could be calculated. An experiment of this nature, involving such microscopic measurements, could be successfully carried out only by the most painstaking work. The figure Cavendish obtained was within 1 % of the true value (5.52 times the density of water), and his classic method, with refinements, is still used today.

Cavendish died at Clapham on 24 February 1810. His name is now commemorated in the Cavendish Laboratory at Cambridge, although the funds for this establishment were provided by Spencer Compton Cavendish.

Above right: Henry Cavendish, chemist and physicist.
Right: his magnetic variometer recorded variations in the Earth's magnetic field between two points.

COLT, Samuel (1814-1862)

Samuel Colt, American gunsmith and inventor, designed what are probably still the most famous pistols in the history of firearms.

Colt's father was a businessman of varying fortunes who made an early start in the silk weaving trade in Ware, Massachusetts. Samuel Colt, who was brought up to be familiar with firearms, had a scientific bent, and was impressed with the mechanization of all the processes of making textiles from silk thread. He demonstrated his ability to 'blow a raft skyhigh' on nearby Ware pond, and was saved from the wrath of drenched spectators by a local mechanic, Elisha Root, who was fascinated by Colt's underwater explosion. Having been sent to Amherst Academy, Colt damaged part of the school through his interest in explosives, and left before he was expelled. At the age of 16 he ran away to sea, sailing from Boston.

In Calcutta, Colt saw an early revolving pistol made by Elisha Collier. The mechanism was primitive and unsatisfactory. Back on board ship, watching the ratchet and pawl mechanism which drew up the anchor, Colt whittled a wooden model pistol that worked better than Collier's version. On returning home he persuaded his father to back the making of a prototype pistol. To get more money for development work, the ingenious young man staged a travelling show in which he demonstrated laughing gas.

By 1835 he had a workable design for a revolver which he patented in England and on the Continent, and the following year in America. At Patterson, New Jersey, he set up the Patterson Arms Manufacturing Company, which turned out a .36 calibre five-shooter. Colt had hoped to manufacture this weapon on the basis of mass production, but he failed to get enough backing for the massive initial investment which was necessary for production machinery. Consequently the guns, made by hand, were expensive and attracted only limited orders. The company went bankrupt in 1842.

Colt then worked on underwater mines for the government. He developed the first successful underwater cables for firing them, but the government lost interest despite successful tests. In association with Samuel Morse (*q.v.*), he adapted this invention to establish the first underwater telegraph links between New York and Coney Island in 1843.

By now the Mexican War had begun, and the Texas Rangers in 1847 ordered 1000 Colt pistols, as they had been impressed with the rapid-firing capability of the first models. Since his original production equipment had been sold, Colt had to hire Eli Whitney's arms company to make up a new design. When the order was completed, he set up Colt's Patent Firearms Company in Hartford, Connecticut, and began his own assembly line manufacture in connection with his old friend Elisha Root.

Colt is sometimes credited with the invention of the revolver, but the concept preceded him by many years. He perfected the design based on the mass production by precision machinery of interchangeable parts, and this is his important contribution. In this connection, the contribution of Root was invaluable; as an engineer, he designed machine tools and especially jigs and fixtures in unprecedented numbers. Together the two men successfully established the principle of interchangeable parts once and for all. Since American industry was booming and labourers were in short

Below: Samuel Colt, who based his revolver mechanism on that of a ship's anchor, patenting it in 1835.

Bottom: an 1838 model. Improvements continued up to 1850; Colt pistols were used in the Mexican War.

supply, the new kinds of machinery were adopted with enthusiasm.

Colt's guns attracted world-wide attention, and he set up a larger company which made him a wealthy man and which still survives on the same site. He died during the Civil War, when his factory was working harder than ever, but the guns survived, in particular the .45 calibre single action revolver produced for the Army and nicknamed the Peacemaker. This weapon linked Colt's name with the Wild West.

COPERNICUS, Nicholas (1473-1543)

Nicholas Copernicus, the son of a Polish merchant, was born at Torun, on the Vistula, on 14 February 1473. Ten years later his father died, and he went to live with his uncle, Lucas Watzenrode, Bishop of Ermland. After studying in Bologna and Padua, where he acquired knowledge of medicine, mathematics and astronomy, he returned to Poland. His uncle, to whose retinue he had been attached, died in 1512, and Copernicus then took up the post of Canon of Frauenburg Cathedral.

The duties associated with this post were minimal, and Copernicus devoted the rest of his life to a study of the planetary motions. At that time the positions of the planets in the sky were computed from observations made centuries previously, on the basis of the Ptolemaic theory, according to which the Sun and planets all moved around the Earth, in circular orbits. At an early age, however, Copernicus realized that the predicted and observed planetary positions were in considerable disagreement.

In order to explain the movements of the planets even approximately, Ptolemy had proposed that each one moves in a small circle or *epicycle*, the centre of which revolves in a circular orbit around the earth. As errors crept in, fresh epicycles were introduced on an arbitrary basis; in Copernicus' time the system contained 80 epicycles and still was not providing accurate positions. Copernicus realized that a much simpler, and therefore more acceptable, explanation of the planetary motions arose from supposing the Sun to be at the centre, with the Earth and planets revolving around it.

By 1530, he was sufficiently satisfied with his proposition, which had been put forward before but never backed by observational evidence, to write a pamphlet, the *Commentariolus*, which he sent to several scholars. The reaction was discouraging, however, for an Earth-centred universe was desirable theologically, and this consideration was more important than the accuracy of the predictions. Copernicus had no doubt that his Sun-centred system provided a more accurate explanation of planetary movements, even though he was forced to invoke epicycles, as Ptolemy had done. In a sense, the systems of Ptolemy and Copernicus are both incomplete because they make no attempt to explain why the celestial bodies move as they do.

By the time he circulated his pamphlet, Copernicus had already written a full length book, *De Revolutionibus Orbium Coelestum* ('On the Revolutions of the Heavenly Bodies'), dealing with the whole subject. His reluctance to publish this work has never been explained, and it was not until George Joachim Rheticus (1514–1576), his energetic disciple, undertook the printing that the book finally appeared. Tradition has it that Copernicus received the first printed copy on his deathbed. He died on 24 May 1543.

Although Copernicus had shown that a Sun-centred system was plausible, the Ptolemaic theory was not universally abandoned for another century, by which time Kepler (*q.v.*) had explained the movements of the planets perfectly by supposing them to move around the Sun in elliptical orbits, and Newton (*q.v.*) had provided the theory of gravity, which justified Kepler's explanation.

Only in 1835 was Copernicus' book taken off the list of those banned by the Catholic Church. When in 1839 a statue to Copernicus was unveiled in Warsaw, no Catholic priest would consent to officiate.

Below: Nicholas Copernicus – a portrait made a century after his death; there are no surviving contemporary likenesses. Copernicus was not the first to suggest the Sun-centred theory: Aristarchus had done so in the 3rd century BC; but Ptolemy's Earth-centred theory was too entrenched to challenge. Even Copernicus held to the classical notion that orbits were perfect circles.

Bottom: armillary spheres demonstrating the Copernican (left) and Ptolemaic systems. It is clear which one is simpler.

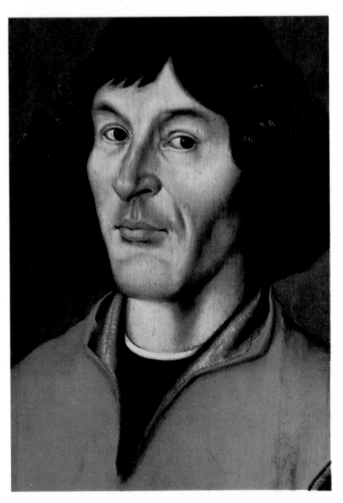

COULOMB, Charles (1736-1806)

Charles Augustin de Coulomb was a French scientist after whom a unit of electricity is named, in honour of his most important researches. (A *coulomb* is the amount of electricity conveyed in one second by current of one ampere.)

Coulomb came from a noble family who ensured that he was well educated. He showed a particular aptness for mathematics, and trained in engineering to join the Royal Corps of Engineers. After service in Martinique for several years, he returned to Paris in 1779, and was elected to the Academy of Sciences in 1781. Upon the outbreak of the Revolution he was forced to leave Paris, retiring to Blois with his friend and fellow scientist J C Borda (1733–1799). He continued his experiments and was eventually made an inspector of education in 1802.

Coulomb's early experiments involving the stresses required to break a substance (1773) led to the modern science of the strength of materials. The work on electricity and magnetism for which he is most famous was published in a series of papers between 1785 and 1789.

Experimenting with the magnetic compass, he saw immediately that the friction of the needle on the pivot must lead to errors. He designed a compass which suspended the needle from a fine thread, and saw that the amount of twisting of the thread must be directly related to the force applied to the needle by the Earth's magnetic field. This led to the invention of the torsion balance, for measuring very small weights. (The English geologist John Michell had independently invented the torsion balance about 1750, but was not successful in his attempts to use it to measure the Earth's gravitational field.)

The torsion balance led Coulomb to his most important discoveries. By moving two electrically charged spheres in the presence of a torsion balance, he was able to demonstrate that the force between them varied as they moved apart. He made studies of the effects of friction on machines and worked out a theory of lubrication. All this together with his views on magnetism was published in *The Theory of Simple Machines* in 1779.

From 1784 to 1789, while working in various government departments, he continued his work on electrostatics and magnetism and in 1785 came the full statement of what is now called Coulomb's law: that the electrical attraction or repulsion of two charged bodies depends on the product of their charges and the inverse square of their distance. This formula was very similar to the gravitational equation devised by Newton (*q.v.*).

At Blois, Coulomb examined the nature of static charges on bodies and found that they lay at the surface. He found that magnetic forces follow the same inverse square law as electrostatic forces. (Some of his work was duplicated by Henry Cavendish (*q.v.*), but Cavendish's work was not published until 1879.) Coulomb's discoveries, which confirmed the relationship between electricity and magnetism, were later proved by Oersted (*q.v.*) and Poisson, and led to the research into electrodynamics by Ampère (*q.v.*). All his work showed great originality backed up by careful experiment.

Charles Coulomb, right, invented this torsion balance, shown below in use for an experiment on electrostatics. The glass case kept out air currents.

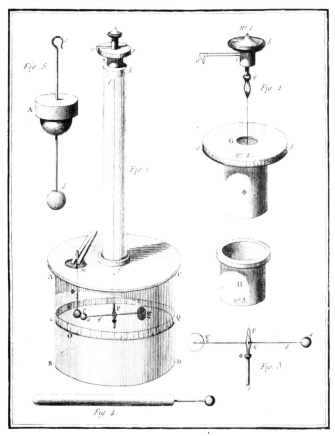

CROOKES, William (1832-1919)

William Crookes, a Londoner, became famous for his investigations into chemical and physical processes. He lived in an age when men of science did not specialize as much as they do today: after graduating from the Royal College of Chemistry he became superintendent of Oxford's Radcliffe Observatory meteorological department, and then became a lecturer in chemistry at Chester. Throughout his life he had varied interest in both chemistry and physics, and until an episode in later life was highly regarded as a scientific authority. In 1856 he married and settled down in London for the rest of his life, financing his private laboratory in Kensington Park Gardens with the fortune inherited from his father.

He was involved in scientific journalism all his life. In 1857 he contributed to one of the first photographic periodicals, the journal of the London Photographic Society, and at that time attracted considerable interest in astronomical circles by taking some of the best photographs of the Moon then achieved, receiving a grant from the Royal Society to help him in his work. In 1864 he became editor of the important *Quarterly Journal of Science*: but most important of all was his founding of the *Chemical News* in 1859, which he continued to edit until 1906.

Crookes' first major experimental success was the discovery in 1861 of the element thallium, which he detected, using a spectroscope, by its characteristic green line.

Crookes was consulted at commercial and government levels on a number of applied scientific matters. He advised upon sewage disposal, dyeing, and calico printing; in 1898 he aroused widespread concern at the amount of nitrogen that undisciplined cereal planting was taking from the soil; the tinted glass that still bears his name is used in welders' and glass-workers' goggles to absorb both heat and ultraviolet rays; and he made early attempts to synthesize diamonds.

The work which earned Crookes lasting fame, though, was his research into vacuum and radiation phenomena, and the Crookes tube is still a standard piece of laboratory equipment. This is a sealed glass tube, with positive (anode) and negative (cathode) electrodes at opposite ends, connected to a pump so that the amount of evacuation can be adjusted. The appearance of bright glows and dark spaces in the partially-evacuated tube indicates the density and speed of the electrons (cathode rays) as they journey from the cathode towards the anode.

Crookes used his device to study the behaviour of cathode rays. In the hands of Röntgen (*q.v.*), in 1895, the tube was used to identify X-rays, and Ernest Rutherford (*q.v.*) used it in his pioneer work on the nature of electrons.

By coating a patch of zinc sulphide on the interior of the tube, the impact of an electron could be seen as a brief flash. Crookes called this new instrument the *spinthariscope*, and with its aid he and other investigators observed the effect of a magnetic field on the direction of a beam of electrons. He was also able to reveal traces of radium salts by their phosphorescent effect on the screen. A similar principle is used today in the cathode ray tube of a television receiver.

Crookes also studied the radiant energy of hot objects, and he invented his radiometer to detect minute quantities of heat. The device is frequently seen today in classroom demonstrations or as a conversation piece. A lightly-constructed cross, with a vane at the end of each arm, rotates freely on a vertical pivot inside an evacuated glass globe.

Below left: Sir William Crookes.

Below right: his radiometer, rotated by infra-red rays.

Bottom: the focus tube demonstrated that cathode rays travel in straight lines.

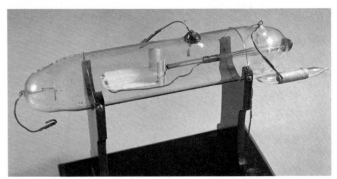

The opposite sides of each vane are painted white and dull black so that alternate faces are of opposite colour. When placed near a source of heat, the cross revolves with the white faces of the vanes leading.

Since dark surfaces absorb and radiate more heat than light coloured ones, Crookes believed that the rotational effect was due to radiation pressure from the black faces of the vanes. Radiation pressure is now known to have too feeble an effect to explain the phenomenon, which is due to an accumulation of the remaining air molecules in the globe at the warmer faces exerting a force against the vanes.

Crookes' distinguished scientific career was jeopardized when he began investigating psychic phenomena. During the period 1870 to 1874 he experimented with paraphysical effects, and claimed to be convinced by the manifestation of a deceased woman in the presence of the well known medium Florence Cook. Investigations by Crookes and other reputable scientists, in an attempt to assemble rational evidence, were viewed with wide suspicion and even contempt, and some of them were accused of faking demonstrations in order to convince their more sceptical colleagues. Crookes never fully recovered from the stigma associated with this episode.

Crookes received a knighthood in 1897, in addition to many other honours. He died in London on April 4, 1919.

CURIE, Pierre (1859-1906) and Marie (1867-1934)

Marie and Pierre Curie made fundamental discoveries about the radioactivity of atoms, and discovered the radioactive elements polonium and radium.

Pierre Curie was born in Paris, the son of a physician. He was not a rapid learner, having something of the dreamer in him, but he took readily to mathematics and was particularly at home with geometry. He later applied this talent to the study of the geometrical forms in crystals.

Pierre became a physics teacher in Paris at the age of 19. He collaborated with his elder brother Jacques on studies of crystals, which culminated in 1880 with the discovery of piezoelectricity. This is the production of an electric charge by pressure on certain crystals, a principle which is now used in microphones and ceramic record player pickups.

Pierre became director of laboratory work at the School of Industrial Physics and Chemistry in Paris, where he worked for the next 22 years. Here, he extended his researches on crystals, and deduced from them one of the most basic principles of modern science, that there is an underlying symmetry to the physical world.

Because Pierre had no laboratory of his own at the school, he had to set up his experiments in a corridor outside a classroom. Starting in 1891, he began the studies on magnetism that led to his doctor's thesis. He discovered the Curie point, a temperature at which ferromagnetic substances lose their magnetism.

He presented his thesis in 1895. Although he was shy and reserved, and not one to press for his own advancement, he was promoted to a professorship in belated recognition of his scientific ability. The previous year, he had met a Polish girl student named Marie Sklodovska. She had left her native Warsaw in 1891 to study at the Sorbonne, and lived, penniless, in a tiny room, fainting on one occasion from hunger in class. But she graduated at the top of her year.

Pierre Curie wrote, in his letters to Marie, of 'our dream for humanity, our dream for science'. They were to form the closest of personal and scientific partnerships.

After their marriage in 1895, Marie began to work with Pierre. In 1897 she decided to investigate the strange rays that Henri Becquerel (*q.v.*) had discovered coming from uranium. She found that the amount of radiation depended on the amount of uranium in the sample, and discovered that thorium compounds emit similar rays to uranium. Marie termed this effect 'radioactivity'.

But she found that some ores gave out more radioactivity than could be explained by the presence of uranium and thorium. She realized that traces of a new radioactive element must exist in these ores. Pierre laid aside his own researches to help in the study of pitchblende, a mineral with four times as much radioactivity as uranium oxide.

They found that radioactivity occurred in two chemically separate parts of the pitchblende, showing that there were

Above right: Pierre and Marie Curie in the early 1900s.

Right: pitchblende contains between 50 and 80% uranium oxide, but because of its high radioactivity the Curies suspected the presence of a new radioactive element. This sample shows a freshly fractured black pitchblende crystal.

45

Above: the Curies' radiation detector: a gold leaf electroscope with a microscope trained on the leaf to detect the slightest movement. The leaf, previously charged, is held out at an angle by electrostatic repulsion from the similarly charged vertical rod. A radioactive substance placed between the electrodes on the right would cause ionization of the air, resulting in charge leakage and movement of the leaf.

and introduced the new technique of radiation therapy into medicine. In 1903, Henri Becquerel and the Curies shared the physics Nobel prize for their work on radioactivity.

But tragedy was soon to mar their finest hour. Pierre died instantly when hit by a wagon in a Paris street in 1906. Marie, although with two daughters to raise, continued her work. She was appointed to Pierre's professorship, and a special institute was set up for her to continue her work. In 1911 she won her second Nobel prize, in chemistry this time, for the discovery and study of radium. But she also accepted it posthumously on behalf of Pierre.

Marie's first daughter, Irène, joined her mother to work in the Radium Institute. In 1926 she married Frédéric Joliot, one of her mother's assistants. Under the combined name Joliot-Curie, they were to continue the work of the Curies, winning a Nobel prize of their own in 1935, for the discovery of artificial radioactivity.

With advancing years, Marie Curie's health began to fail. Her hands had been damaged by exposure to radioactive substances. Although by then the dangers of radium were known, she ignored the health hazards. By 1933, it was clear that she was dying from the physical damage of continued exposure to radiation. On 4 July, 1934, she died of leukemia. The same disease later claimed her daughter Irène.

DAGUERRE, L J M (1757-1851)

Louis Jacques Mandé Daguerre, the inventor of the first workable photographic process, was born at Cormeilles-en-Parisis on 18 November 1787, the son of a magistrate's court official. He showed early talent for drawing, and at the age of 16 began studying under the designer at the Paris Opera. Three years later he became the assistant of the panorama painter, Pierre Prevost. In 1816 he became independent.

Having acquired enough money to set himself up as an artist, he graduated to painting panoramic views for the indoor 'in the round' displays that were then very popular in the capital. To achieve perfect accuracy of representation, he drew the outlines of the views using a *camera obscura*, a light-tight box with a lens at one end to cast an image of the view on to a sheet of paper.

In 1822, by using the same means, he introduced the Diorama. In this device, huge transparent and opaque painted screens were set up on a stage. By varying the lighting on the screens, so that one or the other or both were illuminated, he was able to produce the illusion of day and night passing over a scene such as a mountain view or the interior of a church.

Parisian audiences were stunned by the reality of the Diorama, and Daguerre became famous. In 1823, a second Diorama was opened at Regent's Park, in London.

In 1826, Daguerre began experiments to see whether the view projected on the screen of the camera obscura could be recorded on a plate by some chemical means. He had heard of the experiments of a fellow-countryman, Joseph Niépce (q.v.), who had already succeeded in recording the outlines of transparent objects on light-sensitive plates, and began a correspondence. Niépce was reluctant to divulge details of his method, but in 1829 they signed an agreement to undertake joint research. Niépce, however, died before any workable process had been developed, and Daguerre acquired his materials and continued the experiments.

two new radioactive elements to be found. One of them had properties similar to bismuth. Marie named this polonium, after her native land. The other, even more radioactive, was hard to separate from barium. She called it radium. The Curies announced these new elements in July and December 1898 respectively.

But they had to produce pure samples to study. Working in a poorly heated wooden shed with a leaky glass roof, Marie Curie began to boil down tons of pitchblende to find usable amounts of the new elements. Even in the worst weather they had to work with the windows open to let out the choking fumes. They often ate as they worked, and drank tea to warm themselves. Marie wrote afterwards that they were preoccupied, as in a dream. If they returned at night to continue the work, they saw the radium samples glowing with a green colour from the shelves.

By 1902, Marie had produced 0.1 grammes of radium chloride from over a ton of pitchblende. It took another eight years before she had grains of pure radium in her hand. The Curies published their results openly, with no attempt to patent their process or profit from it in any way.

They became international celebrities for their discoveries, which revolutionized the understanding of atomic structure,

Copy of the earliest known daguerrotype still in existence, taken by Louis Daguerre in 1837.

In Niépce's original process, a silvered copper plate was coated with white bitumen, a weakly light-sensitive substance which hardens upon long exposure, becoming insoluble in turpentine. The light parts of the object were therefore represented by bitumen, while the dark areas appeared as bare silver revealed by the solvent. Niépce darkened the silver by exposing the plate to iodine vapour, producing silver iodide. In 1826, Niépce managed to take a photograph of the view from his window, but exposure took eight hours on a sunny day.

In 1831, Daguerre discovered that a silver iodide plate was also sensitive to light, but still failed to produce an image in the camera obscura in a reasonable time. The breakthrough came after four more years of work. Having put an unsuccessful plate away in a cupboard, intending to re-coat it for later experiments, he was amazed to take it out a few days later and find a strong image impressed on it. By a process of elimination of the bottles in the cupboard, he discovered that the 'developing' agent was a few drops of mercury from a broken thermometer. The mercury vapour attached itself to the silver iodide affected by light, producing a picture with brilliant highlights.

Daguerreotyping spread rapidly round the world; even in America, the first photograph was taken in September of the same year. In defiance of his government's decision to publicize his process freely, Daguerre had previously managed to get patent rights in England, where the potential for profitable commercial exploitation was very great. The process, however, never became widespread in that country.

By modern standards, the daguerreotype process was very slow. Outdoor scenes in bright sunlight required an exposure of several minutes using the lenses then available, and sitters having their portraits taken had to rest their head in a special clamp. At that time there were no sufficiently strong sources of artificial light, and portrait studios, which could operate only on sunny days, had large windows and glass roofs, making them very hot and uncomfortable.

Daguerre spent the last decade of his life in retirement at Bry-sur-Marne, apparently content to let other experimenters improve his process.

He died in 1851, the year when the English sculptor Frederick Scott Archer (1813–1857) introduced the far superior collodion photographic process.

DALTON, John (1766-1844)

John Dalton was a chemist and meteorologist. He is now famous for the atomic theory, and for his law of partial pressure. These two apparently unrelated ideas stem from the love of meteorology Dalton acquired as a boy.

John Dalton was born on 6 September, 1766. His father was a Quaker woolweaver in Eaglesfield, near Cockermouth in Cumberland. He went to school until he was 12, when he began teaching, first at a school which he opened himself and then at a school in Kendal. Throughout his life he remained a Quaker.

Dalton acquired an interest in meteorology from a teacher, Elihu Robinson. From 1787 until he died he kept a meteorological diary and he wrote a book on meteorology which was published shortly after leaving Kendal in 1793. In that year he went to Manchester to be a tutor at New College, a position he was to hold for six years. After arriving in Manchester, Dalton published a description of his peculiar eyesight; his complaint is now called Daltonism or colour blindness. The description was the first good account of the affliction and brought it to general attention. To Dalton leaves appeared to have the same colour as red sealing wax, and the sky appeared pink.

In June 1800 John Dalton resigned from New College so that he could concentrate on his researches, supporting himself by giving private lessons. Dalton was a man of regular habits and meticulous about his dress. He usually wore knee breeches, grey stockings, buckled shoes, and a white neck cloth, and he carried a gold tipped cane. Every day, except

John Dalton's symbols for atoms and compounds. There are errors, but it was a start in the right direction.

Sundays and Thursdays, he worked in the laboratory from 8 am until 9 pm. On Thursday afternoons he went for a game of bowls at the 'Dog and Partridge'. After work he had supper and would then light his pipe and discuss the day's affairs with the Johns, the family in whose house he rented a room. Dalton was a silent, rather undemonstrative man and he never married.

His interest in meteorology led him to experiment with water and gases. In 1801 he read a series of papers to the Manchester Literary and Philosophical Society of which he was to become president in 1817. In one of them Dalton announced the law of partial pressures. This states that the pressure of a gas in a mixture is equal to the pressure it would exert if it occupied the same volume alone at the same temperature. The total of these partial pressures gives the pressure of the gas mixture. He also described a hygrometer he had designed to measure the humidity and argued that air is a mixture of gases, including water vapour, and not a single compound.

On his birthday in 1803, Dalton made an entry in his notebook in which he derived a list of atomic weights. On the next few pages he wrote out the atomic theory. There has been considerable debate as to how Dalton arrived at this but it was probably the solubility of gases that led him to the theory. Dalton's notebooks and other documents were destroyed during World War II, but they had been well examined by then. He did not publish the theory straight away, but mentioned it to another chemist, Thomas Thomson, who described it in a book. The next year Dalton described the atomic theory in his own textbook, *A New System of Chemical Philosophy*, using his own chemical symbols. The main postulates were: matter consists of indivisible atoms; all atoms of a given element are identical in weight and in every other property; different elements have different kinds of atoms of different weight; atoms are indestructible and merely rearrange themselves in chemical reactions (this was the basis of his law of multiple proportion).

The theory made him famous. He was invited to lecture in most of the learned centres, and when he visited Paris he was greeted by numerous eminent French scientists and shown the apparatus for demonstrating electromagnetic phenomena, devised by Ampère (*q.v.*). In 1822 he was elected a Fellow of the Royal Society and later became their first Royal Medallist. The French Academy of Science, in 1830, elected him one of its eight foreign associates, a great honour.

Dalton's daily routine did not change after he became famous. He published some more work on chemistry and meteorology, and republished his meteorological book. The first serious illness in Dalton's life occurred in 1837 when he suffered a paralytic attack. In May 1844 he had an apoplectic attack and on 27 July he was found dead in his bed, having just made an entry in his diary about the weather. Forty thousand people filed past his coffin and there was a 100 carriage funeral procession.

According to his own account Dalton was not brilliant, but won his achievements by perseverance. His school record shows this to be true. He published 140 papers but very few are remembered. The atomic theory, however, was a triumph. By 1800 there existed numerous rules and laws about chemical reactions. In a delightfully simple way the atomic theory explained them all and led to the discovery of more. It is for this reason that Dalton is best remembered. A statue was erected to his memory in Manchester.

Below: diagram Dalton used to explain why the curbed appearance of the aurora was due to the Earth's curvature. Vertical distances are exaggerated; in fact it occurs at a height of 100–800km.

Bottom: Dalton stirring a pond to release marsh gas.

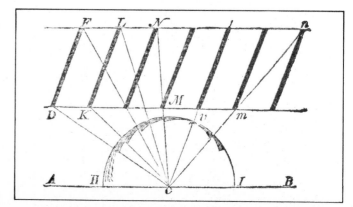

DARWIN, Charles Robert (1809-1882)

Charles Darwin was born in Shropshire, the son and grandson of famous doctors. His other grandfather was Josiah Wedgwood (*q.v.*), maker of the finest English porcelain.

Darwin studied medicine, but surgery horrified him, performed as it was in those days without anesthesia. He considered a career in the Church, but could not go in that direction either. His hobby was natural history, and his interest grew in this subject while at Cambridge.

He participated in a geological field trip led by Adam Sedgwick (1785–1873) who was the first to recognize the young Darwin's scientific ability, and who later was unalterably opposed to the theory of evolution. Then he was offered the post of ship's naturalist on a voyage of scientific exploration, aboard HMS *Beagle*. Despite some opposition from his father he accepted, and went to sea from December 1831 until October 1836, visiting South America, Australia, South Africa and many places in between. He suffered greatly from seasickness and permanently damaged his health. He may have been infected by a *trypanosome*, any member of a group of parasites of the blood, usually transmitted by insects, and causing such diseases as African sleeping sickness. Later in life he was considered, probably unfairly, a hypochondriac. In any case, the voyage was certainly the most important in the history of science.

He had already read some of the work of Sir Charles Lyell (1797–1875), a Scottish geologist whose theories were controversial. Lyell estimated the age of the oldest fossil-bearing rocks at 240 million years—unheard of then, but less than half the figure accepted today. Some idea of the truly great age of the earth was one of the necessary foundation stones of the theory of evolution.

Darwin originally accepted the orthodox theory of the fixity of species, but travelling down the coast of South America, he noticed how species gradually changed. The Galapagos Islands, several hundred miles off the coast of Ecuador, are famous for their giant tortoises, but what impressed Darwin was the variety of finches, later called Darwin's finches. There were fourteen different species of these birds on this little group of islands, species which existed, as far as anyone knew, nowhere else in the world.

There were two lines of Darwin's inquiry: the replacement of species in nearby areas by different but very similar species and the similarity between fossil types and living creatures in the same continent. Various facts fell into place if it were assumed that species were not fixed, but had been modified by descent. This explained otherwise inexplicable phenomena in the fields of comparative anatomy, embryology and palaeontology, as well as geographical distribution.

Darwin decided that the finches must have originally colonized the Galapagos Archipelago from the mainland, and then evolved into fourteen new species, some eating one kind of seed and some another, others eating insects, and so forth. As he had not had any systematic scientific training, it is a tribute to the quality of his mind that he understood the importance of discovering how and why these evolutionary changes took place. The French naturalist Lamarck (1744–1829) had believed that animals *tried* to change themselves: that an antelope became a giraffe by trying to reach higher leaves. But this was unacceptable, because it could not explain protective colouring: an animal

Charles Darwin thought clearly and wrote what he thought; he never wished or intended to start a controversy.

could not try to have stripes or spots.

Returning to England, Darwin read in 1838 a famous book on population written by Malthus (*q.v.*), which stated that mankind was doomed to poverty and starvation because population increase would always outstrip the increase in the production of food. Malthus' argument is probably wrong in the case of man, who shows remarkable ingenuity in finding food, but Darwin immediately had one of the keys to a theory of evolution: animals could not increase their food supply. He reasoned that the finches, which were kept in bounds by competition from other birds on the mainland of South America, must have found a relatively empty land when they colonized the Galapagos Islands, and multiplied unchecked until food became scarce, whereupon the weaker birds died without producing offspring. But if a heritable change occurred which allowed individual birds to find new food, these birds would be able to survive and propagate, encouraging change in the direction of the original, probably accidental, variation. Similarly, a giraffe born with a slightly longer neck could reach more food, thus living longer and producing more offspring.

He published his *Journal of the Voyage of the 'Beagle'*, and various other research results, such as his theory that coral reefs were formed by the accumulating skeletons of corals. Finally he began to write a book on species. Two years later he was thunderstruck to receive what amounted to a *precis* of his own work from Alfred Russel Wallace (1823–1913), another English naturalist.

Wallace, like Darwin, had experimented with various

A contemporary cartoon; the Victorians were outraged at the idea that their ancestors were apes.

planned; for the rest of his life he regarded it as an abstract of the book he should have written.

The theory of evolution immediately started a controversy that went on for decades. The implication was that what could apply to animals could also apply to man, and that therefore the theory was destructive of religion. Even scientists tried to make a separate case for mankind apart from animals, or to separate man's body from his soul. Darwin himself was too gentle and kind a man to take much part in the controversy; the reason he had wanted to write such a long book was to tie up all the loose ends in a vain attempt to avoid the controversy. In *Origin of Species* he had avoided the issue of man, but he went on to write at least ten more epoch-making books, including *The Descent of Man* (1871), and books about plants and worms as well as animals, anticipating modern genetics and explaining animal behaviour, sexual selection, the advantages of cross-pollination, and much else.

By the time of Darwin's death, his theory was triumphant, among scientists at least: religious bigots still refuse to believe the evidence today, but they have had no effect on the study of biology. Honours were showered on Darwin from all over the world, but the only recognition he received from the government of Queen Victoria was burial in Westminster Abbey.

Unknown to Darwin and to the rest of science, the weakest part of the theory of evolution was being strengthened even as his most important book was published, by the monk Mendel (*q.v.*) and his careful experiments with peas.

DAVY, Sir Humphrey (1778-1829)

Sir Humphry Davy was a brilliant and impetuous scientist who made discovery after discovery while still a very young man, and died exhausted at fifty. He invented the miner's safety lamp, which is still in use today, and discovered the chemical elements sodium, potassium and boron.

Davy was born in Penzance, Cornwall, the elder son of a well-to-do local family, and was given a thorough education in the hope that he would become a doctor. Even at an early age, he showed a keen intelligence and a great love of nature, and was liked and encouraged by everybody.

After an early interest in poetry, the young Davy turned his attention to science. His actual knowledge of the subject was rather sketchy, but this was less of a disadvantage at the end of the eighteenth century than it would be today, and it also allowed him to make up his own mind about theories that a more thoroughly educated man would have believed unquestioningly.

In 1797 he made friends with an older scientist, Davies Gilbert, who got him a job in the Medical Pneumatic Institution in Clifton, Bristol, a strange establishment which existed to make experiments on the effect of various gases on health. He had already performed his own experiments with nitrous oxide (laughing gas), later to be the first anaesthetic, and he encouraged his friends to try it too. Those who agreed included the poets Coleridge and Southey.

Davy experimented with ammonia and nearly killed himself inhaling water gas, a highly poisonous blend of carbon monoxide and hydrogen made by passing steam over red hot charcoal. In 1800 he published his first major work, *Researches Chemical and Philosophical*, which described his

vocational ambitions, had gone on long cruises as ships' naturalist, and had read Malthus. He had done nothing like Darwin's research, but had simply written down his opinions and sent them to the older, more famous man for his opinion. He immediately recognized the prior claim as well as the superior research of Darwin, and the two men read a joint paper to the Linnean Society in London, in 1858. In 1859 Darwin published *The Origin of Species*, one of the most important publishing events of the 19th century. It was a long book, but only a fraction of the length Darwin had

Above: Sir Humphry Davy was a man with the widest possible interests. Not only did he discover three chemical elements, he also contributed to physics, agriculture, mining, ship construction, zoology – and salmon fishing.

Right: some of Davy's apparatus for gas analysis, in which he made his earliest important discoveries.

Below right: his most famous invention, the miner's safety lamp. The gauze surrounding the flame prevented it from igniting explosive 'firedamp' – methane, the same as Dalton's marsh gas.

experiments. It was an instant success, and he became well known in scientific circles.

While still only twenty-two, Davy was invited to lecture in London at the Royal Institution. He was a naturally good lecturer and his talks on various topics were attended by the rich and famous; in 1802 he was made a professor. At this time, he was studying such widely different subjects as electric batteries and new methods of tanning leather.

In 1803 he was made a Fellow of the Royal Society; in 1805 he received the Copley medal, and in 1807 he became secretary of the Royal Society. Meanwhile, his research into electrolysis led him to discover sodium and potassium (both in 1807), and as a result of his experiments with potassium, another element, boron. In 1808 he invented the electric arc, still used today for welding. He found out the composition of hydrochloric acid and various important facts about the element chlorine; at the same time he was carrying on research into agriculture that led to the publication in 1813 of his book *Elements of Agricultural Chemistry*, the standard work on the subject for many years. A book he published a year earlier, *Elements of Chemical Philosophy*, was to have been the first of a series covering the whole of chemistry, but this was too much even for Davy, and he never got any further with the project.

During most of this time, England was at war with France, but such was Davy's fame that this did not stop the Institut de France from awarding him their Bonaparte prize in 1806. Other honours included a knighthood, which he was awarded in 1812.

Shortly after this, he married and set off on a European tour with his wife, in spite of the Napoleonic war. He took with him the young scientist Michael Faraday (*q.v.*), originally hired as a laboratory assistant but soon to be a famous scientist in his own right. During the course of his journey, he used portable scientific equipment to study chlorine compounds and to lay the groundwork for the discovery of the element iodine.

When Davy returned to England in 1815, the Society for Preventing Accidents in Coal Mines commissioned him to study mine explosions and how to prevent them. The result of these researches was the Davy miner's safety lamp, an oil lamp whose flame was encased in metal gauze, which allowed light and air through but prevented the heat of the flame from starting an explosion by conducting it away. The flame changes colour in the presence of explosive gas; this lamp is still used as a backup to more advanced equipment in detecting gas today.

For this vital invention, Davy was awarded the Royal Society's Gold Medal. The mine owners sent him a lavish set of silver plate, which he later sold to found a trust for awarding the Davy Medal for scientific discoveries. In 1818 he was made a baronet, and in 1820 president of the Royal Society.

His later work included help with the foundation of the Zoological Society and Regent's Park Zoo, and research into the corrosion problems of the copper bottoms of wooden ships. But he was already a prematurely old man and his health was decaying fast. In 1827, he set out for a final tour of Europe, resigning his presidency of the Royal Society to his early friend Davies Gilbert. Apart from a short visit to England in 1828–29 he spent the rest of his time in Europe, dying in Geneva in 1829.

Davy was as far from an academic, narrow-minded scientist as it was possible to be. He maintained a lifelong interest in poetry and literature, fishing and geology. He was a fair artist and illustrated one of his own books, *Salmonia*, a work on salmon fishing, published in 1828.

DEWAR, Sir James (1842-1923)

Sir James Dewar, famous for the invention of the vacuum-insulated flask (Thermos bottle), was a pioneer in low-temperature research. The son of a Scottish wine shipper, he was born at Kincardine-on-Forth on 20 September 1842. A prolonged bout of rheumatic fever caused his schooling to be scanty, but he graduated to Edinburgh University in 1858 where he studied under Lyon Playfair (1818–1898), professor of chemistry.

In 1869 he became lecturer in chemistry at the Royal Veterinary College. In 1875, however, he moved to Cambridge on his appointment to the Jacksonian Professorship of natural experimental philosophy, and in 1877 he became Fullerian Professor of chemistry at the Royal Institution in London. He held both posts until his death, although nearly all his important work was conducted with the superior facilities at the Royal Institution, where many of his contemporaries were invited to spend convivial evenings in his rooms.

Dewar's early papers, commencing in 1867 with a proposed molecular structure for benzene, covered varied fields including the measurement of high temperatures, the chemistry of the electric arc, and the way the eye responds to light. In 1872, during experiments into the specific heats

of substances at very low temperatures, he was troubled by the problem of insulating the sample from extraneous sources of heat. His solution was to enclose the experiment inside a vacuum jacket, so that heat transfer by conduction and convection through the surrounding air was eliminated. Twenty years later he used this principle to construct the Dewar flask, in which liquid gases could be stored at very low temperatures for long periods.

Dewar flasks are still used for this purpose, and the domestic vacuum flask was quickly developed commercially. It is curious that Dewar took no steps to patent the device, which could have made him a wealthy man.

It was at this point that Dewar took up the low-temperature studies with which his name is generally associated. In 1874 there appeared two important papers: *The Latent Heat of Liquid Gases*, read at the British Association, and *A New Method of Obtaining Very Perfect Vacua*. The subject of the second paper was the absorptive powers of charcoal, which could be used, Dewar discovered, to remove the last gaseous molecules from a high vacuum produced by the usual mechanical pump methods. Later, after he had produced liquid air, he found that charcoal cooled in this medium had its absorptive powers tremendously increased, and the very high vacua obtained through its use were of great importance to physicists working with elementary atomic particles. Charcoal was also used in gas masks issued during the First World War.

The physicist L P Cailletet (1832–1913) achieved the

Some early Dewar flasks; the final form, today's 'Thermos', is in one piece with double, silvered glass walls with a partial vacuum between them.

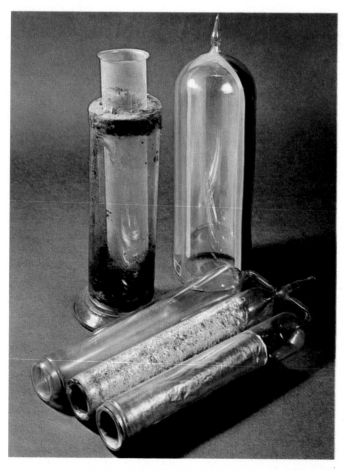

Sir James Dewar in his laboratory. His main achievements were in the field of cryogenic (low temperature) chemistry, and would not have been possible without the insulating flask he invented.

partial liquefaction of oxygen in 1877 by compressing it to a pressure of 300 atmospheres (4400 psi) and obtaining a vapour. Dewar, in 1884, was the first person to collect true liquid oxygen, and he demonstrated the process before an audience at the Royal Institution. The principle employed was to compress the gas, and then to allow it to expand through a valve into an evacuated chamber, at which point a sharp drop in temperature occurred. Solid oxygen was obtained two years later, and in 1895 he succeeded in collecting hydrogen vapour. Liquid hydrogen was obtained in 1898, but he failed in his attempt to liquefy helium because of the presence of neon, which froze relatively easily and blocked the valves of his apparatus. The success of his attempts, where others had failed, was largely due to his vacuum insulating jacket.

During the period 1888–1891 he was a member of a government committee on explosives, and during this time, in conjunction with Sir Frederick Augustus Abel (1827–1902), he invented the propellant explosive, cordite. Another committee on which he served concerned itself with the purity of the London water supply, and, like his contemporary Sir William Crookes (*q.v.*), he was consulted on sewage disposal.

Married with no children, a gourmet, and a lover of music and fine arts, Dewar was generally acknowledged as a poor teacher, a good lecturer, and a magnificent experimentalist. A great many honours came his way. He was President of the Chemical Society in 1897, and of the British Association in 1902. Elected a Fellow of the Royal Society in 1877, he was awarded its Rumford Medal in 1894, and was knighted in 1904. He died in London on 27 March 1923.

DIESEL, Rudolf (1858-1913)

Rudolf Christian Karl Diesel was an engineer who perfected the type of internal combustion engine that is named after him. He was born in Paris, the son of a German leather worker from Augsburg. Diesel's parents were strict, and the family was very poor. A harsh, insecure upbringing gave Diesel the drive to accomplish great things, but also had its effect on his mental stability.

Diesel was a brilliant student. As a boy he spent many hours in the Paris Museum of Arts and Crafts, where he made drawings of machines, including Cugnot's steam wagon of 1769. At the outbreak of the Franco-Prussian war of 1870, the Diesel family moved to London, where Diesel was fascinated by the machines in the Science Museum. Then he was sent to Augsburg to live with an uncle who was professor of mathematics at the Augsburg trade school. While in Augsburg he saw a pump which created heat by the compression of air, and his later success began to take form.

In 1875 he began attending lectures at the Munich Technical University. Among the lecturers was Carl von Linde, whose research in thermodynamics had led to the invention of refrigeration techniques. After graduating from the university with the most brilliant record in its history, Diesel went to work for von Linde in his refrigeration company, soon rising to the post of factory manager.

At university Diesel had found that existing engines were not very efficient, and had studied the theories of Carnot (*q.v.*) on the efficient transmission of energy in the form of heat. He resolved to build a more efficient engine. In his capacity as von Linde's plant manager, he became interested in the possibility of replacing steam with ammonia vapour, but gave that up in favour of the idea of using the heat from compressed air to ignite a fuel mixture in the cylinder. He patented designs in 1892 and 1893. At first he wanted to use coal dust in his engine, as the cheapest fuel available, but his design required a fluid which could be sprayed into the combustion chamber, so he settled on petroleum oil. His first successful engine was a 25 horsepower single cylinder

Rudolf Diesel: 1898 portrait by Alexander Fuks.

54

four stroke model built in 1897. It was displayed at a Munich exhibition in 1898, and the inventor soon became a millionaire.

A diesel engine needs no spark plugs because the fuel is ignited by the heat of the atmosphere in the combustion chamber, which is compressed by the upstroke of the piston. It will run on cheaper fuel than other internal combustion engines. In 1902 it was first used to generate electricity, and in 1903 the first diesel-powered ship was afloat.

Diesel's engine was not the first compression-ignition engine, and some of his patents were contested. A factory he built in Augsburg failed. Some of his early engines broke down; because of the tremendous pressures required, the earliest designs were not reliable. Diesel was a suspicious, difficult man who insisted that the engines be built to his original specifications, delaying improvements which could have been made. In spite of all this, his ability as an engineer was widely recognized, and there was some talk of a Nobel prize.

In 1913 he disappeared during a trip from Antwerp to Harwich on the mail steamer *Dresden* to discuss the sale of his engines to the British Admiralty. There was some speculation that he had been kidnapped or murdered by government agents in the tense atmosphere of pre-World War I Europe, but in fact he had made special preparations at home before leaving, and had spoken of suicide by jumping off a ship.

Below: early diesel engine, showing massive construction.

EDISON, Thomas Alva (1847-1931)

Thomas Alva Edison was the most famous and prolific inventor of all time. During his life, over 1000 patents were issued to him or his associates; he was rightly known as 'the wizard of Menlo Park', a town in New Jersey where he set up his first 'invention factory'. Yet he was not really a scientist, having no theory or mathematics, and most of his success came from perfecting ideas or already existing inventions by the trial and error method. It was Edison who said that genius was one per cent inspiration and 99 per cent perspiration.

Edison's inquiring mind showed itself early in life. He was full of questions, and refused to accept anything unless he could test it for himself. This attitude, together with the fact that he was not good at mathematics, got him expelled from school with the remark from his teacher that his brain was 'addled'. Thereafter he was taught by his mother, a former schoolteacher herself.

By the age of ten, he had set up a chemical laboratory in the basement of his home. When he needed more money to buy supplies for his experiments, he went to work selling newspapers and confectionery on the Grand Trunk Railroad. By the time he was twelve, he had set up a laboratory and a printing press in a baggage car on a train, to continue his self-education and to make more money by selling his own paper.

He learned telegraphy on the railway, and his services as a telegrapher were in demand during the Civil War, when he travelled all over the country, incidentally studying electricity. In 1868 came his first invention: a machine to record votes in Congress. Congress turned it down, because they

Below: Thomas Alva Edison in the early 1900s, in the chemistry laboratory of his West Orange plant, where he worked out a method of synthesizing carbolic acid.

were not interested in speeding up matters. Edison then resolved to work only on inventions that were commercially viable.

His first such invention was an improvement on the ticker machine which transmitted stock market prices. At this particular time in American history, when Wall Street was more powerful than the government and an enormous economic expansion was under way, this invention was so successful that Edison set up a small factory to build ticker-tape machines, which he later sold at a profit. This was the first instance of Edison's ability to see what needed to be invented before inventing it. Next he made improvements to the telegraph, culminating in a system which allowed four messages to be sent on one wire. He also made improvements to the typewriter.

By 1876 Edison was rich and famous. He quit manufacturing and set up his first 'invention factory', with a staff to help him develop ideas to a saleable state. Their first inventions were improvements to the telephone of Alexander Graham Bell (q.v.), including a microphone. These inventions got Edison involved in the struggle over who was going to exploit Bell's invention, and established once and for all the concept of inventing to commercial order which has dominated twentieth century technology.

In 1877 Edison produced his most celebrated invention, certainly his own favourite. This was the phonograph. Edison's device used a tinfoil-covered drum which was hand cranked while a stylus traced a groove on it. The first recording ever made was of Edison's own voice reciting 'Mary Had a Little Lamb'. Typically, Edison had written out a list of ten uses for a sound recording machine before he built it; he saw it as a useful office machine, and did not foresee the multi-million-dollar record industry of today, which has survived competition from radio, television, and Edison's own motion pictures.

Above right: Edison's first light bulb, with carbon (charred cotton) filament and air valve in the base.

Below, left and right: his first phonograph, with tinfoil cylinder, and two later cylinders made of wax.

Opposite page: Thomas A. Edison, from a portrait by Silvette.

Improvements were immediately made on the phonograph by others. Phonograph companies were set up with reciprocal rights to patents. The groove on the cylinder was cut so that the varying depth of the groove represented the sound, the so-called 'hill-and-dale' method. Later, Emil Berliner built a device called the gramophone which cut the groove on a flat disc using a lateral method; that is, the sound was registered according to the sideways wiggle of the groove. Berliner's system was eventually adopted universally, but to this day the record player is called the gramophone in Europe and the phonograph in the United States.

In 1878 Edison, using his trial and error method, began research towards the development of an incandescent light bulb. He made thousands of experiments before achieving success with a charred cotton thread, sealed in a vacuum so that it would glow without being consumed. His staff then worked out the principles of the modern generating and distributing system that made electric lights for every home practical. In 1882 the first generating station was opened at Pearl Street in New York. Edison used a direct current system; a former associate of his named Tesla developed an alternating current system for a rival company, Westinghouse, which eventually dominated. The Edison Electric Light Company, however, grew by mergers to become the General Electric Company.

While working on the light bulb, Edison made one of his few real scientific discoveries, the principles of the thermionic valve, or vacuum tube. At the time however, there seemed to be no use for its properties; not until 1900 did Fleming (q.v.) discover and develop its potential for wireless telegraphy.

He moved to a larger laboratory in West Orange, New Jersey, in 1887. In 1889 he built a motion picture camera and later set up a small studio for making films for peep-show machines. Once again, however, the entertainment aspects of his invention did not really appeal to him, and it was finally left to others to develop the motion picture industry. He did not even bother to patent his motion picture camera design outside the United States, so that there were numerous infringements when imported machines appeared.

Edison character was complex, and his reputation during his own lifetime was enormous. In 1896 Henry Ford (q.v.) went to Edison to ask his advice, and Edison told him that in his opinion the internal combustion engine was a practical source of power for a horseless carriage. Ford went on to develop the automobile industry, and idolized Edison for the rest of his life; Ford eventually built a restoration of one of Edison's laboratories on his estate in Michigan. In 1912 Edison would have been awarded the Nobel Prize with his former associate, Tesla, for their work on electrical generation and supply, but such was the animosity between them that Tesla refused to have his name linked with Edison's, and so neither won the award.

The flow of ideas continued until Edison's death in 1931.

Below: early electricity generating station, showing the generators with their square iron magnets. A shaft leads to a steam engine beyond the right hand wall.

Bottom: recording a concert with an electrically driven (but not, of course, amplified) phonograph. Note the batteries on the floor, the huge, ear trumpet-like 'microphone' and the box of spare cylinders.

EINSTEIN, Albert (1879-1955)

Albert Einstein, the theoretical physicist famous for his theory of relativity, was born in 1879 at Ulm, Germany, to parents of German-Jewish descent. His early education, at first in Munich and later in Switzerland, did not mark him out as any kind of genius at all. He found the pedantic methods of the German education system totally uninteresting, and he used often to miss lessons in order to indulge his voracious appetite for reading. At 17, he entered the Swiss Federal Polytechnic in Zürich after rapid cramming of a subject he had somewhat neglected—mathematics. The more liberal and easygoing atmosphere of Switzerland was much more in keeping with his own reflective ways, and in 1901 after graduating, he took out Swiss citizenship. Years later, in the winter of 1932–3, while Einstein was on a fortuitous visit to the California Institute of Technology, Hitler came to power in Europe, and Einstein decided to stay on in the United States, becoming an American citizen in 1940.

He had entered the Polytechnic with the idea of becoming a teacher but had difficulty in finding a post and ended up in the patent office in Berne. In 1905 he received his doctorate in physics from the University of Zürich. That year saw the publication of three of his papers, any one of which would have earned him a doctorate. Many of his ideas were only intelligible to a small minority of physicists and recognition did not come immediately.

Albert Einstein and the Trifid Nebula; without his theory of relativity it would be impossible to understand much of what happens in outer space.

Albert Einstein and Robert Oppenheimer. Oppenheimer worked on the atomic bomb; as a result of his concern with the debate about the social consequences of nuclear power, his security clearance was revoked in 1954. Einstein was one of the first to realize the great social responsibility of the scientist.

In each of these papers, however, Einstein had managed to combine the principle of sound empirical science—that any explanation must make as few unproven assumptions as possible—with an acute insight of new ideas. One of these papers was on the Special Theory of relativity, which was to appear in its final form in 1915 as his General Theory of relativity. It literally overturned the then accepted basis of physics.

Experiments had been conducted in an effort to prove or disprove the existence of the ether, an invisible substance which had been supposed to 'conduct' light and other electro-magnetic forces, such as radio waves. The idea was to measure the difference in the speed of light caused by the Earth's motion through the ether. The very failure of these experiments revealed something inexplicable by classical or Newtonian physics: that the speed of light is always the same, regardless of the relative motion of the observer. Hendrik Lorenz in Amsterdam was able to show that the motion through the ether could not be detected, and Henri Poincaré in Paris claimed that indeed it could never be detected. It was Poincaré (1854–1912) who coined the term 'relativity' and pointed out the consequence that nothing could travel faster than the speed of light. The young unknown clerk in the Swiss patent office resolved the contradictions in the work of the two older men.

The momentum of a body (its mass times its velocity) is what changes when a force acts upon it. But the addition of two velocities must always be lower than the speed of light. Since velocities do not simply add together, as in the pre-relativistic Newtonian physics, and because the continued application of a force cannot accelerate a body to beyond the speed of light, its mass must vary, with its velocity be-

Above: Henri Poincaré, who coined the term 'relativity' in 1904, and also pointed out that nothing can travel faster than light. But the theory was Einstein's own.

Below: Einstein in a classic lecturer's pose at the Carnegie Institute of Technology in 1934.

coming larger as the speed of light is approached. The correction is negligible at speeds below half that of light, but increases rapidly thereafter.

Of all the ramifications of this, the most difficult to understand is that time itself slows down at these high velocities. Thus, scientifically speaking, we can never know exactly when an event occurs, or to put it another way, time as measured by a moving observer must go at a different rate to that measured by a stationary observer.

There is now a wealth of experimental data which supports the slowing down of moving clocks, or time *dilatation*, as it is called. The simplest comes from particles called *mu mesons*, which are produced about six miles (10 km) up in the Earth's atmosphere where particles from outer space known as cosmic rays hit the atoms of the atmosphere. These mu mesons are well known from laboratory experiments, and they are unstable, only living about two millionths of a second before they split up into other particles. Even travelling at the speed of light they could only travel about one third of a mile before decaying, yet we see them at the Earth's surface; as they do travel with velocities close to the velocity of light, their ageing is slowed down. If their speed were three-fifths that of light, they would live for 20% longer, but if they were moving at 99.9% of the speed of light they would live more than twenty times longer, enough for them to penetrate down to the Earth's surface.

Einstein's Special Theory involved a new interpretation of mechanics, which resulted in the essential equivalence of mass and energy. Matter, said Einstein, was a form of energy, and energy a form of matter, with their interrelationship expressed by the famous equation $E = mc^2$, where $E =$ energy, $m =$ mass, and $c^2 =$ the square of the speed of light.

Here, he is more relaxed at an informal seminar.

When a minuscule amount of mass is annihilated, it is replaced by an immense amount of energy: this is the principle behind atomic power.

The other papers published in 1905 dealt with his explanations of the photoelectric effect, for which he was awarded the Nobel Prize in 1922, and of Brownian motion. The former was a turning point in modern physics. It not only provided the first clear and qualitative account of the ionization of metals by a beam of light, but it also showed that light came in discrete 'packets', which he called photons. Light was therefore shown to be 'quantized', just as matter was known to be. Five years previously Niels Bohr had shown a similar quantizing of the energy of the electrons in the atom, and so the stage was now set for the development of the quantum theory. Relativity and the quantum theory are two of the most important contributions to twentieth-century physics.

Brownian motion, the small zigzagging movements executed by dust particles immersed in a fluid, had baffled scientists since its discovery by the Scottish botanist Robert Brown in the nineteenth century. Einstein's paper explained it in terms of the millions of collisions that take place between the molecules of the fluid and immersed microscopic particles. This also had important ramifications for the advancement of physics, for it was the first occasion that the atomic theory was shown capable of producing explanations of observed phenomena.

Einstein spent the following years working through his conceptions of space and time, supporting himself and his family in a number of teaching posts in various European universities. After teaching at the University of Berne he moved, in 1909, to the University of Zürich and in 1910 to the German University of Prague, returning to the Swiss Polytechnic in Zürich in 1912. Finally in 1913 he settled in

Berlin to become a professor at the University of Berlin and a member of the research institute, the Royal Prussian Academy of Sciences, as well as a director of the prestigious Kaiser Wilhelm Institute. While there, his General Theory of relativity was published. This work, of enormous intellectual and philosophical elegance, developed the concepts he had outlined in the Special Theory into a new interpretation of the Universe. In it, the laws of physics were reduced to those of the geometry of a space-time continuum.

The General Theory is a theory combining gravitation with electro-magnetics, developed by Einstein with the help of his mathematician friend Marcel Grossman. Einstein realized that a gravitational field produced effects equivalent to acceleration, and by studying the effect of acceleration in special relativity was led to generalize the theory to include gravitational fields. As acceleration affects the measurement of time and distance in special relativity, so too do gravitational fields. As a result of this the geometry found near gravitating bodies is not quite the classical geometry of the ancient Greeks.

Light rays no longer follow straight lines: a gravitational field causes them to bend. The slowing down of clocks in a gravitational field has also been checked and again is in good agreement with the prediction of general relativity. This prediction can be tested to very great accuracy by sending a clock up into space on a rocket and comparing its time with a similar clock on Earth. The theory also predicts slight changes in the motion of the planets in the solar system, particularly for the closest planet, Mercury, which again agrees with observations. The first proof of the General Theory was observed during an eclipse of the Sun, when the light from distant stars was seen to be bent as it passed close to the gravitational pull of the Sun.

In his personal attitudes Einstein reflected the growing realization within the scientific community that the scientist, by virtue of both his intellect and the nature of his discoveries, has a special responsibility towards society. World War I affected him deeply, and made him very conscious of the outside world and the social injustice and folly that abounds there. Yet he was too much of a genius to ever live completely outside the rarefied atmosphere of his own mind. He was notoriously absent-minded, and anecdotes about him are to be found in abundance in his biographies. One day, for example, a student pointed out to him that he had forgotten to put on any socks. Einstein observed that, since he had not noticed it beforehand, socks must be a quite expendable article of clothing. From that day he is supposed never to have worn socks.

In 1921 he visited America to speak on behalf of the Zionist cause, and in 1922 he was appointed to the Intellectual Cooperation arm of the League of Nations. When it became known in 1939 that German scientists were working on the fission process that would lead to the construction of an atomic bomb, he wrote his now famous letter to President Roosevelt. As a result of this, the Manhattan Project was set up, which resulted in the development of the atomic bomb by the Americans before the Germans. He was deeply involved throughout the war in organizations providing relief for refugees from war-torn Europe. He died at Princeton, New Jersey in 1955.

Perhaps the best epitaph for him is the German proverb he was fond of quoting to express his own convictions about the world: 'God is subtle, but he is not malicious'.

A solar prominance: these huge flares show the immense forces released in the Sun and other stars by the conversion of matter into energy, symbolized by Einstein's famous equation: $E = mc^2$.

EPICURUS (341-271 BC)

Epicurus was a Greek philosopher who became the first great thinker of the 'materialist' school (those who seek no further explanation of the universe outside the observable material order of things).

He was a citizen of Athens, and began his teaching career in 311 BC. Hostility to his ideas on the part of traditionalists who regarded them as atheistic forced him to move twice before settling in Athens in 306 BC, where he bought a house and garden in which to establish his school of philosophy, the first, incidentally, to admit women. He ran it less as an institution and more as a community of faithful friends and disciples, where his doctrines were not only learned but put into practice, aiming at moral perfection through spiritual peace and freedom from pain. He died in Athens, and his followers spread his teachings far beyond Greece. Indeed, it is to a later Roman poet, Lucretius (94–55 BC), that we owe most of our knowledge of his theories.

Ancient philosophy knew no limits, and its speculations on the nature of the universe ran freely into areas which we would normally classify as scientific. In his youth, Epicurus was influenced by the theories of the atomists, like Democritus (460–357 BC), who denied the older theory that there was one basic substance (infinite and divine) from which all things had their origin. The atomists believed that things had their origin in the actions of atoms, countless particles so small that they could not be divided any further. (The Greek word 'atom' actually means 'indivisible'.) This was the theory on which Epicurus based his scientific thought. Collisions between atoms of various size, weight and shape explain the origin of all things. There is no 'creation'; on the contrary, there had always been and would always be two natures: matter, made up of atoms, and space, through which atoms move. Because of their weight, Epicurus believed, all atoms must move in a downward direction, although at an equal velocity. In order to explain how they ever come into contact with each other, since they all move in the same direction, he invented a theory of deflection or swerve in their travel, for which he has been criticized ever since, because there is no scientific justification of this deflection theory.

There was no limit to the possible number of worlds, according to Epicurus, because the number of atoms was infinite. All that is required for the creation of a world is an atomic storm, out of which a world will evolve. As worlds evolve, so they will also disintegrate in time.

Here again, his real purpose was to show that there is no arbitrary divine purpose in the universe. Everything in it is mortal, because everything is material. He stressed this when he came to consider astronomical and meteorological phenomena, so full of myth and superstition for the ancients. He was prepared to allow that there might be several explanations of the origins of heavenly bodies and their movements; the point was that these explanations could not be anything other than scientific and natural.

The name of Epicurus, however, is chiefly remembered today for his doctrine that happiness and pleasure, together with freedom from fear and from pain, constitute the highest good to which man can aspire. But today's image of the 'epicurean' as one who indulges a cultivated taste for 'the good life' (material comforts) is a gross distortion of the teaching of Epicurus. Although he was a materialist, self control and moderation were central to his philosophy:

'Plain tastes bring us as great a pleasure as the most luxurious diet,' he wrote. Besides excess, the great enemy was fear. In particular, men had to be free not from death but from the fear of death and from the fear of the imagined anger and punishment of the gods, if they were ever to be happy. (In psychological terms, it may be fear of death which makes men indulge in excess.)

The theories of Epicurus taught that the gods lived their own lives and had nothing whatever to do with this world at all: hence it was useless to pray to them or to expect reward or punishment from them. Similarly, although man had a soul, it was a bodily atomic compound with nothing immortal about it; it dispersed when the body died, so that man had nothing to fear from threats of what might await him in an afterlife.

The theories of Epicurus were an anathema in the Christian Middle Ages, and the noble account which he gave of man and the elevated way of life were forgotten amid charges of atheism and hedonism. Only in the seventeenth century at the dawn of the new 'scientific' age was there a revival of interest, particularly in England, in his atomic theories and in his philosophy as a whole among 'mechanistic' philosophers, who were interested in the problem of motion and the explanation of natural phenomena. After an eclipse in the eighteenth century, he was to enjoy new admiration in the nineteenth among materialist thinkers. John Stuart Mill found support for his utilitarian ideas in Epicurus, while Karl Marx wrote his doctoral thesis on Epicurus in 1841.

An ancient bust of Epicurus, the Greek philosopher whose materialist theories, and belief that matter is made up of atoms, are not out of place today.

FARADAY, Michael (1791-1867)

Michael Faraday is best known for a brilliant series of experiments on the nature of electricity which resulted in the invention of the dynamo and the formation of his laws of electrolysis (the breakdown of solutions by electricity).

Faraday was born in Newington Butts, Surrey, on 22 November 1791, and was the son of a blacksmith. He became interested in science when he attended some lectures given in 1812 by Sir Humphry Davy (q.v.). After serving an apprenticeship in bookbinding, he sent his lecture notes to Davy, along with a request for a job. In 1813 he began work as Davy's assistant at the Royal Institution; later that year he accompanied Davy on a European tour, which was good experience for the modestly educated young scientist. Persistent conflict with Lady Davy, however, made the journey an ordeal.

After his return to the Royal Institution, Faraday had to work hard, since he was the main source of income for the Institution, which was then having financial difficulties. During this period Faraday worked on glass and steel, performed many chemical analyses and investigated the chlorides of carbon for Davy. His work resulted in the discovery of benzene in 1825.

Davy had by then left the Institution, but Faraday had been much influenced by him and performed many experiments for him. When Faraday discovered, in 1823, that gases could be liquefied by pressure, Davy took the credit. Later the two were in conflict when Davy opposed the election of Faraday as a Fellow of the Royal Society; Davy was apparently jealous of the younger man.

In 1821, the year he married, Faraday was asked by a scientific journal to write an article about the new electrical phenomena. There were many isolated discoveries at that time which defied explanation. For example, Oersted (q.v.) had noticed that a wire carrying current affects a compass needle. Faraday realized that a magnet would push a wire to one side, and devised an experiment to demonstrate it. He suspended a wire carrying current over a magnet, and found that it moved in circles around the magnet. This experiment made him famous throughout Europe, but led to some false charges of plagiarism.

By 1831 the Royal Institution was in better financial condition, and Faraday was able to concentrate on research. In that year he performed his famous ring experiment demonstrating electromagnetic induction. It followed from his idea of what caused the wire to move in a magnetic field, and he had been trying to demonstrate the effect since 1821. When a current flowing through a coil of wire on one side of an iron ring was switched on or off, it induced a current in a coil on the other side. He reasoned that a 'magnetic wave' was produced by the first coil and passed through the second, causing an electric current to flow. A way of sustaining the wave was to rotate the conductor (a copper disc) in a magnetic field; in doing so, Faraday had constructed the first dynamo.

In the next few years, by passing currents through solutions, Faraday showed that all kinds of electricity, however generated, were the same. In this way he developed his laws of electrolysis, which relate the amount of decomposition in solution to the amount of current passed through it.

In 1839 Faraday suffered a mental breakdown; his convalescence, in England and abroad, took four years. His breakdown left him with a poor memory, which grew worse with time. He returned to his work, this time investigating

Michael Faraday lecturing at the Royal Institution before the Prince Consort in 1855; his subjects included the chemistry of carbon and properties of gases.

The original ring Faraday used in his 1831 experiment demonstrating electromagnetic induction. Two wire coils are wound on the same iron ring; a voltage applied to one induces a voltage in the other.

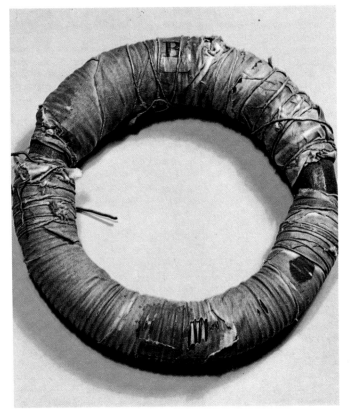

the effect of a magnetic field on non-metallic substances. These are weakly attracted or repelled, and Faraday introduced the names *paramagnetic* and *diamagnetic* for them. His scientific work began to suffer at the expense of his dabbling in other, less demanding activities. In 1853 Faraday investigated 'table-turning', in which supernatural forces were supposed to be at work. Two years later he wrote a letter to *The Times* about water pollution in the Thames. In the late 1850s he began to find lecturing more difficult. Lecturing was a love of Faraday's; he had carefully observed Davy as a young man and took much care with his own lectures. Ironically, it was during this period that he delivered his most famous lectures, including *The Chemical History of the Candle*.

In 1861 Faraday, then 70, retired from the Royal Institution and moved to a house in Hampton Court that Queen Victoria had offered him. By now his condition was so bad that he required permanent assistance. On 25 August 1867, he died, and was given a private funeral at Highgate Cemetery.

Faraday was able to blend theory and experiment in his researches to an extent few men have been able to match. He had little money to spend on apparatus and knew no mathematics. Many of his discoveries were not put to use until decades after his death. Perhaps his most important accomplishment was his research into electromagnetics, which was to be the seed of one of the major achievements of nineteenth century science: the development of field theory by James Maxwell (*q.v.*).

FERMI, Enrico (1901-1954)

'The Italian navigator has landed in the New World', was the cryptic message that went out on the afternoon of 2 December 1942, to announce the successful operation of the world's first nuclear reaction. Enrico Fermi, the Christopher Columbus of atomic energy, had simply smiled in satisfaction and said to his colleagues: 'The chain reaction has begun.'

Fermi's brilliance in physics was early apparent. Before he was 21 he had been awarded his physics PhD by the University of Pisa. Fermi was born in Rome but in 1944 became an American citizen. He grew up in a turbulent time for physics, when relativity and the quantum theory were sweeping aside classical ideas.

Fermi first made major advances in atomic study by using the so-called exclusion principle of Wolfgang Pauli to explain how the particles of a gas behave at low temperatures and high densities, where they no longer obey the classical gas laws. Such a *degenerate* gas (now also known as a Fermi gas) has the properties of a metal, and indeed the electrons in a metal behave like those in a Fermi gas. Particles that follow the law he formulated are termed *fermions*.

In 1933 Fermi gave the name *neutrino*, meaning 'little neutral one', to a particle he predicted must be produced when a neutron decays into a proton and an electron. In this process, known as *beta decay*, the electron seems to be emitted with too little energy. Fermi supposed that a neutrino was also formed during the decay and carried away some of this energy. These ghostlike particles, which lack both mass and electrical charge, were detected experimentally in 1955.

In 1934, Irene and Frederic Joliot-Curie announced that radioactivity could be induced in some atoms by bombarding them with protons. Fermi sent one of his assistants out with a bag to visit chemical suppliers in Rome, saying: 'Get all the elements in Mendeleev's table if you can.' (Mendeleev's periodic table is the complete list of chemical elements.) His team began to work their way through the periodic table, bombarding the atoms with neutrons, which Fermi reasoned would be easier for atomic nuclei to capture because they had no electric charge. Within two months, the Fermi team had produced several new radioactive isotopes.

During this work came the accidential discovery that a screen between the neutron source and the target actually increased the effect of the neutrons. This puzzling result was particularly marked when solid paraffin (wax) was used as a screen. Over lunch, Fermi had a flash of insight: perhaps the hydrogen nuclei in the paraffin were slowing the neutrons so that they became easier to capture. To test the theory, the group decided to see if water (which also contains hydrogen) would produce the same result. Passing their neutrons through a nearby goldfish pond, the team were able to confirm Fermi's hunch.

But the group remained puzzled by the results of bombarding uranium. Several decay products were formed, but they could not identify them. Though no one knew it at the time, this work contained the key that opened the door to the atomic reactor.

Fermi was awarded the physics Nobel prize in 1938 for his work in producing new radioactive substances and discovering the importance of slow neutrons. He never returned to Italy after collecting the prize in Stockholm. Fermi did not agree with the Fascist government at home, and racial laws threatened his Jewish wife. So they sailed on to the United States, where Fermi obtained a post at Columbia University in 1939.

Meanwhile, Otto Hahn and Fritz Strassmann in Berlin were proving that Fermi was in fact splitting the uranium atom into two much lighter atoms by his neutron bombardment: this was atomic fission. Fermi was quick to realize the implication of this new interpretation. Each time the atom split, more neutrons were released. Perhaps fission could continue in a self-supporting chain, thereby releasing energy all the time from inside the atomic nucleus.

A group of Fermi's colleagues persuaded Albert Einstein (*q.v.*) to write to President Roosevelt, drawing his attention to the fact that 'extremely powerful bombs of a new type' might be made in this way—and hinted that the Germans might already be engaged in their development.

The result was an immediate influx of money to develop nuclear power. Fermi's team began serious work on a nuclear reactor, using large graphite blocks to slow the neutrons because it was found that water absorbed too many neutrons.

The reactor effort progressed under great secrecy. There were problems of obtaining sufficiently pure graphite and uranium. A series of experimental piles—an apt description of the reactor's brick-like construction—were built before success was finally achieved.

Fermi's earlier work had shown that cadmium was particularly good at absorbing slow neutrons. Therefore cadmium rods were built into the pile to control the chain reaction rate. It was as these were withdrawn on 2 December 1942 that the first controlled chain reaction began—and Fermi had ushered in the atomic age.

After this first success of what was called the Manhattan Project, Fermi went to Los Alamos, New Mexico, to work on the atomic bomb. After World War II he joined the faculty at the University of Chicago, where the Institute for Nuclear Studies was eventually named after him. He wrote textbooks on various aspects of physics and was regarded as a gifted teacher as well as a research scientist. He collected a great many distinctions besides the Nobel prize, and was at the peak of his powers when he died, barely 53 years old.

Enrico Fermi operating a 100 MeV particle accelerator at the University of Chicago in May 1950.

FLEMING, Sir John (1849-1945)

One of the great pioneers of electricity and its practical usage was the Englishman, Ambrose Fleming. Generations of students have been brought up on his textbooks on telegraphy and telephony, and he was famous for his public lectures that showed the wonders of the electronic era.

Fleming's interest in electricity was apparent from his youth. While still at school he made battery cells and used them to produce electromagnets. Among his home-made playthings was an electrostatic machine with which he gave shocks to those who doubted his electrical abilities.

In 1870 he graduated from University College, London, and then taught for a while. In 1877 he moved to Cambridge, where the celebrated James Clerk Maxwell (*q.v.*) had just been made head of the newly formed Cavendish Laboratory. Fleming had no difficulty in catching Maxwell's eye, for often he was the only one attending the great man's lectures. Maxwell was a difficult teacher to follow because, as Fleming wrote, 'he saw so much deeper into scientific problems than ordinary persons that his utterances often appeared obscure'.

Fleming joined Maxwell's research staff, and was asked to calibrate several standard 1-ohm coils that were thought to be inaccurate. To do this Fleming designed a version of the Wheatstone bridge that Maxwell christened 'Fleming's banjo'. It remained useful in the Cavendish for many years.

Fleming became scientific adviser to the London branches of Edison's telephone and electric light companies, where he was responsible for much of the development of electrical distribution in Britain.

In 1885 Fleming became the first professor of electrical engineering at London's University College. When he arrived, his sole equipment was a piece of chalk and a blackboard. But it was here that he made his greatest researches.

To measure the light output of electric lamps he designed a photometer and then built a standard light source to compare them with, thus originating important photometric standards for the electrical industry. Another famous invention of his was the potentiometer, for comparing voltages.

Fleming and Sir James Dewar (*q.v.*) tried to measure the electrical resistance of metals at very low temperatures. They used liquid air as a refrigerant, but were bothered because it kept boiling away. Dewar sketched out a design for an insulating flask, which Fleming arranged to have constructed. This held the liquid air admirably for long periods, and is now known as a Dewar (or thermos) flask. Fleming dipped loops of wire into the liquid air, and found that they became better conductors at these low temperatures. The work was the foundation for the later discovery of superconductivity.

But Fleming's major advance, for which he is world famous and for which, in 1929, he was knighted, is the radio valve [vacuum tube]. Fleming had been intrigued by the strange effect that Edison (*q.v.*) noted when he put a metal plate next to the glowing filament of an electric light bulb: current flowed from the plate when it was connected to a positive terminal, but not when it was connected to a negative terminal. Fleming confirmed this electrical 'one-way street', and he also found that the incandescent filament was giving off particles which he said 'carried a charge of negative electricity'. Without realizing it, he was observing electrons.

Sir John Ambrose Fleming: his most important contribution to science was the thermionic valve or vacuum tube, used in radios and amplifiers until the invention of the transistor. His original type, the diode, is still in use for rectifying alternating current. He also designed the potentiometer, a widely used measuring device.

Fleming later designed equipment for Marconi (*q.v.*), for his transatlantic signalling experiments and for later projects. A persistent problem was to turn the high-frequency alternating currents generated in the receiving aerial into direct current to work the receiver devices. Acting on inspiration, Fleming took one of his old bulbs out of a cupboard and tested it to see if it would have the desired effect. 'The experiment was at once a great success,' he said. Although the alternating current on the plate terminal shifted from positive to negative, the plate conducted electricity only while the charge remained positive. The bulb was rectifying AC current into DC.

This device was patented in 1904. Fleming called it a valve, which, he said, was 'plain English', unlike the term 'diode' that became common. In 1906, the American Lee De Forest (1873–1961) added a grid to make an amplifying *triode*. De Forest was called the 'father of radio'; when he broadcast Caruso's voice in 1910, musicians decided that this was 'De Forest's prime evil'. But it was Fleming's invention which first made possible long-range wireless transmission.

FORD, Henry (1863-1947)

Henry Ford, the pioneer carmaker whose assembly line methods have largely been responsible for the tremendous outpouring of consumer goods in this century, was born on his father's farm, near Dearborn, Michigan. He never liked farm work; when he was twelve years old, he saw a steam tractor moving down the road under its own power, and realized that the drudgery of life on the farm could be relieved by machinery.

Ford left school at the age of 15 and went to work as an apprentice in a machine shop, working at night repairing watches. He then spent two years investigating the possibility of a steam tractor, powerful enough to do farm work yet small and light enough so that any farmer could afford to buy one. He was forced to abandon steam as impractical for his purposes, and built a four stroke, one cylinder internal combustion engine. It was based on the model of the Otto engine, which he had worked on as an apprentice, when nobody else knew anything about them. He discovered that a one cylinder engine was impractical for a road vehicle because of the weight of the flywheel necessary to balance it.

In 1893 Ford built his first car, which had two opposed cylinders, one delivering power while the other was in its exhaust stroke. It resembled the Benz car, which Ford had travelled to New York to see, but was lighter. It had a planetary (epicyclic) gearbox and belt drive; shifting the belt gave two forward speeds and a neutral position. There was no reverse gear. One of the things Ford discovered while building the car was the necessity for what he called a 'compensating gear' (differential) to allow equal power to be distributed to each drive wheel while the car turned corners. It was the only car in Detroit; Ford drove it about 1000 miles before selling it, later buying it back.

In the meantime, he had been working for the local electric power company, which offered him a promotion if he would give up tinkering with his 'gas buggies'. Instead he quit his job and went into the car business. In 1903 he built two cars which had four cylinder engines developing 40 hp, and hired Barney Oldfield to race them. The resulting publicity brought him enough backing to form the Ford Motor Company.

Over the next few years, Ford experimented with manufacturing methods and building different models, gathering enough experience to build the kind of car he had in mind: cheap and reliable enough so that anybody could drive one. He proved that the lower the price of the car the more people would buy it. He discovered vanadium steel, which has twice the tensile strength of ordinary steel, and thus could be used to reduce the weight of the car. He was able to buy enough stock in the company to have a controlling interest, and in 1908 he began to build the famous 'Tin Lizzie': the Model T. In June of that year the factory built 100 cars in one day for the first time.

The Model T had only four sub-assemblies: the power plant, the frame, the front axle and the rear axle. It was available with four different bodies, and the cheapest model sold for $825. During the first year, 10,607 cars were built.

More than 15,000,000 Model T cars were sold by 1927, when the last one was made. The Ford Motor Company, having begun with $100,000 worth of capital in 1903, had in 1927 $700,000,000 of reserve balance alone.

Henry Ford was a man of great practical ability and strong opinions. He believed that the purpose of manufacturing industries should be to offer the public the best quality product at the lowest possible price, and that profits would take care of themselves. He attributed the fantastic success of the Model T to the fact that it was simple and reliable (the slogan was that anyone could drive a Ford) and to the fact that it never went out of date, because the only changes made in the car were towards higher quality at a lower price, and never made obsolete the cars which had already been sold.

Ford perfected the assembly line method of manufacturing, reducing the duty of each employee to one simple operation which required no thought or skill. He managed to reduce the price of the car while the costs of labour and materials were rising. He foiled every attempt to take over his company, saying that bankers should stick to banking, and the money to operate a manufacturing concern should come out of the sales of the product. In 1914, he instituted a profit-sharing plan and offered the highest wages in the industry; the crush of people wanting to work for him was so great that the police had to be called out to handle the crowd.

Henry Ford and his wife in the earliest Ford car, built in 1893. It had belt drive and no reverse gear, but it was the only car in Detroit. Though he sold it, he later bought it back and it is now in a museum.

Below: early Model T assembly line. As complete chassis came off the ground floor line, the body, with seats in place, slid down the ramp and was fixed on. There was a choice of four body styles, but one colour: black.

He never lost his interest in farming, and began to build tractors during World War I. The first models were used in England, where farm women learned to drive them while the men were away at war.

Ford's social and political opinions were sometimes naive and regrettable. He tried to insist that his employees be non-smokers and regular churchgoers. Late in life he began to indulge in anti-semitic activities. His greatest accomplishment was to put the nation on wheels and get the farmers out of their rural isolation; having created an enormous demand for cars, he lost touch with the public, who wanted fancier, more comfortable cars. By the time his factories retooled in 1927 to build a more modern car, he had lost his number one position in the car industry, and never regained it.

FOUCAULT, Leon (1819-1868)

Although Léon Foucault was to become one of the most famous experimental scientists of his age, covering the fields of optics, electromagnetism and photography among many others, he was an unmanageable child at school, paying little attention to his lessons. His father, a well-known and fairly wealthy Paris publisher, died when Léon was 10, and he grew up in his mother's care.

A frail child, he missed much of his schooling through illness, and in any case preferred building his own scientific toys, including a steam engine, to the classical studies that were then regarded as a necessary education. His mother was not discouraged by her son's apparent idleness, and decided that his dexterity and scientific keenness could turn him into a good surgeon. When he was 13, his mother placed him under a private tutor with this in mind.

Foucault turned out to be repelled by the sight of blood and suffering people. But at the medical school he met a specialist in microscopic anatomy, Dr Donné, and became fascinated by light and optics. His skill and craftsmanship enabled him to make all his own apparatus, and he turned to constructing a wide variety of devices.

His best-known experiment, published in 1850, demonstrated the rotation of the Earth by using a long, freely-suspended pendulum that was able to sustain its vibrations unaided for some hours. Initially released to swing along a line marked on the floor beneath, it maintained its vibrations in the same plane while the Earth's rotation slowly turned the reference line and the spectators, with the result that the pendulum's line of swing appeared to change.

Foucault's Pendulum, as it is called, is on display in many museums. In the northern hemisphere, the apparent rotation is in a clockwise direction; at the equator, since the Earth's plane of rotation is in the same plane as that of the wire, no rotation occurs. Foucault published a law relating the rotation of the plane of the pendulum to the angular velocity of the Earth and the latitude of the site.

In 1852, Foucault announced details of the gyroscope, a

Left: the original Foucault pendulum in Paris. There is nothing special about such a pendulum except that it is very long, has a heavy weight and can move freely in any direction. It will then change its angle of swing relative to the Earth as the Earth turns under it.

Below: Léon Foucault was a small, unimpressive looking man with one long and one shortsighted eye, giving him a slight squint; his workshop was full of the most famous scientists.

device using a rapidly-spinning wheel which, through an effect known as gyroscopic inertia, strongly resists any attempt at changing the direction of its axis. Like his pendulum, therefore, the gyroscope tends to maintain the same angle in relation to the stars while the Earth turns. The first gyrocompass, which used this device instead of a magnetic pointer to indicate north or south, was installed in a German warship in 1910; they are now widely used in both terrestrial and space navigation.

Foucault's other great research was into the velocity of light, which had not previously been accurately measured, although many attempts had been made. He shone an image on a rapidly rotating mirror, which reflected it to another mirror across a distance of 66 feet (20 m). By the time the light had arrived back, the first mirror had rotated slightly. This produced a second image, whose displacement from the first depended on the speed of light.

Between 1850 and 1862, Foucault derived a value of 185,000 miles per second (298,000 km/s) for the velocity of light through air, within 1% of the present accepted value. By putting a tube of water between the two mirrors, he discovered that the velocity dropped by about 25%—showing that the speed of light depends on the medium through which it travels.

The Foucault test for a concave mirror, which uses a knife edge placed at the exact focus of the mirror, makes it possible to detect deformities a few millionths of an inch in the shape of the surface. Before the introduction of the Foucault test, mirrors for astronomical telescopes were ground largely by trial and error.

Foucault carried out much of his work as a physicist at the Paris Observatory His dream of having enough money to set up his own private laboratory, with costly apparatus, made him turn to industry, and at the Exposition of 1867 he was constantly in attendance at his demonstrations of regulators for woodworking and weaving machines. His efforts brought him the money, but left him weakened physically. In 1867 he began to notice the first signs of paralysis, and on 11 February 1868 he died.

FRANKLIN, Benjamin (1706-1790)

Benjamin Franklin, born of an English family which had emigrated to America, became one of the most colourful and popular characters of the eighteenth century. He became a publisher, inventor and statesman and lived life to the full, serving his fellow men more fully and in more ways than anyone else in American history. He wrote copiously, founded service organizations of various kinds as well as one of the first libraries in America, and represented the Colonies in London. After his warning that the stamp tax was not a good way to raise money from the American colonists was not heeded, he went home and served on a committee for the drafting of the Declaration of Independence. Later he was American ambassador to France. His autobiography is still required reading in many American schools.

Franklin learned to love books at an early age, and served a printing apprenticeship with his brother James, who published a newspaper in their home town of Boston. Ambition and independence asserted themselves when he went to Philadelphia to seek his fortune at the age of seventeen. There, he produced the famous *Poor Richard's*

Almanack, full of collected aphorisms such as 'God helps those who help themselves'. He proved that hard work and self education can reap their own reward when he had made enough money to retire from publishing in 1748.

In the field of science, Franklin was a man of imagination, foreseeing many things that he would not live to see for himself. He wondered if the ability of men to get along with one another would develop as fast as their knowledge of science. One of his earliest inventions, about 1740, was the so-called Pennsylvania fireplace, or Franklin stove, which improved on existing fireplaces by using the heat from the fire to warm air that circulated through the back of the stove. Franklin said that this early convector heater made his common room 'twice as warm with a quarter the wood'.

It is Franklin's work on electricity that is most remembered by science, and his published collection of the latest theories on the subject made him world famous. In 1746 he saw a demonstration of static electricity by a Dr Spencer from Edinburgh. He bought Spencer's equipment and experimented with it during the winter of 1746–47. He formu-

Left: Benjamin Franklin wearing bifocals, which he invented.

Below: Franklin's famous lightning experiment, from a French book, 'Les Marveilles de la Science', c. 1870 – just one of innumerable pictures of the event.

lated the idea of positive and negative electricity by watching how static electricity jumped from one of his colleagues to another. He said that a person who had more electricity than another was positively charged, and when a spark jumped from that person to another, it was because that person was negatively charged. He described how a 'battery' of glass panes could be charged with electricity (the forerunner of the multi-plate capacitor). Franklin also invented the lightning rod, which was first used in experiments in Paris in 1752. Franklin's electrical terminology survives; although it is now known that electricity is a flow of negative electrons, electricians still say that it flows from 'positive' to 'negative' terminals.

Franklin's most famous experiment was designed to prove that lightning was an electrical phenomenon. In 1752 he flew a kite in a thunderstorm, making the kite out of a large silk handkerchief and two crossed sticks. At the end of the twine was a silk ribbon, with a key where they joined. When the twine was wet enough from the thunderstorm, said Franklin, the 'electric fire' would 'stream out plentifully from the key on the approach of your knuckle'. Franklin was lucky; other people who tried the experiment were killed.

Franklin did pioneer work in meteorology and oceanography. He found how storm systems arise from ascending warm air in the tropics and then move away northwards. He learned about the Gulf Stream from mariners, and on his trips across the North Atlantic he made temperature measurements of what he described as his 'river' in the sea that could speed the passage of eastbound ships.

In 1784, during one of his postings as ambassador to France, he invented bifocal lenses. By that time he had to wear spectacles continually, but was annoyed at having to change powers between close reading and distances, so he had half of each lens mounted in the same frame. This enabled him, at dinner, both to see what he was eating and to observe the features of those who were speaking to him: especially, one suspects, the features of the pretty women. 'I understand French better by the help of my spectacles', he wrote.

Franklin never patented any of his inventions. He believed in the free exchange of thought and knowledge because, he wrote, 'As we enjoy great advantages from the inventions of others, we should be glad of an opportunity to serve others by an invention of ours'.

FULTON, Robert (1765-1815)

Robert Fulton, the American pioneer in the development of the steamboat, was born in Little Britain (now Fulton), Pennsylvania, in 1765, the same year James Watt (*q.v.*) took out a patent on the separate condenser, which greatly increased the efficiency of the steam engine.

At the age of 14, Fulton built a manually operated paddle-wheel boat which he used for fishing on the Conestoga Creek. But his first professional success was as a painter of miniature portraits; he made enough money as a young man to buy a small farm for his mother. In 1787, he went to England to study with Benjamin West, another American painter. He received commissions and exhibited at the Royal Academy.

Giving up painting for engineering, he studied the problems of canal construction in hilly countryside, where locks were unsatisfactory. In 1796 he published a *Treatise on the Improvement of Canal Navigation*, in which he advocated the use of inclined planes instead of locks, and the construction of small interconnecting canals. His patented design for the inclined planes called for two boats suspended in wheeled cradles which ran on rails, with the ascending boat counterbalancing the descending one.

In 1791 Fulton moved to France, where he worked on exploding gunpowder underwater. He designed and constructed a torpedo-carrying submarine called the *Nautilus*, and tested it successfully in the Seine, staying 25 feet (7.5 m) underwater for four hours, using compressed air for respiration. He also attached a torpedo made of gunpowder to the underside of an old vessel and blew it up. Napoleon showed

Right: Fulton's paddle steamer Clermont, *which began operating with commercial success in 1807.*

Below: plans for the Demologus, *the first steam powered warship. The gun deck was 140 feet long.*

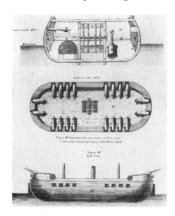

Robert Fulton, inventor of the steamboat, became a rich man through his partner's monopoly of steam navigation on New York's Hudson River.

interest in these experiments, but the French government finally rejected Fulton's suggestion that they develop and operate these weapons against the British.

Next Fulton began studying the problem of commercially successful navigation by means of steam power. Familiarizing himself with the earlier development of the steam engine, he discovered that earlier steam boat designs had failed because the propelling machinery was too heavy, displacing so much water that there was no room left in the boat for passengers or cargo. Fulton's steamboat experiments were financed by the American Minister to France, Robert Livingston (1746–1815). Livingston was himself an amateur engineer, whose experiments with steamboats were unsuccessful. Livingston had, however, managed to get a law passed in New York state giving himself the exclusive right to navigate steam or fire-propelled boats on all state waterways for twenty years. He and Fulton became partners in 1802.

Fulton experimented with various kinds of oars, paddles and screw propellers, finally deciding on 'wheel-oars' (paddle wheels) as the most efficient way to use steam on the water. On 9 August 1803, he demonstrated a successful boat on the Seine, using a wood-fired, low-pressure boiler designed by his American friend, Joel Barlow.

Returning to England in 1804, Fulton tried to sell his torpedo and submarine idea to the British Admiralty to use against the French, but had no success. He observed the trials of the steam tug *Charlotte Dundas* on the Forth and Clyde canal (the *Charlotte Dundas* was never put into commercial production). Fulton and Livingston commissioned the firm of Boulton and Watt to build a steam cylinder 24 inches (61 cm) in diameter with a four foot (1.2 m) stroke, and returned to the United States in 1806, where they installed the engine in the *Clermont*, a boat built by Charles Browne of New York.

The *Clermont* was 133 feet long, 13 feet wide, 7 feet deep and had a two foot draught ($40 \times 4 \times 2 \times 0.6$ m). The 20 horsepower engine drove two 15 foot (4.23 m) paddlewheels, one on each side of the boat. The bell cranks, spur gearing and flywheel were designed and built by Fulton.

Four years to the day of the Seine trial of her prototype, the *Clermont* started her maiden voyage up the Hudson River from New York to Albany. The journey of 150 miles (240 km) took 32 hours. On 4 September 1807, she made her first commercial voyage; refitted the following winter, she ran as a 'packet' for seven years. By 1813, Fulton and Livingston had three boats carrying passengers up and down the river, enjoying a profitable monopoly until their deaths.

Fulton's last achievement was the construction of the world's first steam warship, the *Demologus*. Originally called *Fulton the First*, it was designed for coastal defence and to break the British blockade of the United States during the Napoleonic Wars, which had resulted in what is known in America as the War of 1812, with Britain. The boat was built and tested the year before Fulton's death, but the war ended before the boat saw action.

GALILEO (1564-1642)

Galileo played an important part in the development of physics and of astronomy in the early seventeenth century. Although he is perhaps best known from the story that he dropped two different-sized balls from the Leaning Tower of Pisa, to show that heavy objects drop no faster than light ones, this was not his main work and there is no evidence that it ever even happened. Nevertheless he was one of the first people to use the results of specially conducted experiments as evidence for a scientific theory.

Galileo, who was born in Pisa and lived all his life in Italy, was trained in medicine but soon turned to physics. He later said that he had first become interested in the motion of pendulums when as a child he watched a lamp swinging in the cathedral at Pisa. He had used his pulse to time the swings, and found that each of them took the same time. What we know of Galileo's early scientific work, however, seems to indicate that at first he completely accepted the conventional ideas of his time. It is possible that his later emphasis on experiment was partly due to the influence of his father, Vincenzio Galilei, a distinguished theorist of music, who conducted experiments on the notes produced by strings made of various materials. Not all the experiments Galileo describes would in fact give the results he claims, and there is some dispute over how many of them he actually performed.

The work for which Galileo is chiefly remembered was done late in his life. He was, by the standards of the time, well into middle age when he published the discoveries he had made with the newly-invented telescope. The work which described the discoveries. *The Messenger from the Stars*, was published in Venice in March 1610. Galileo, who by then was teaching at the University of Padua, tells how he had heard of an instrument with which distant objects could be seen distinctly as if they were near. There is no doubt that Galileo did not actually invent the telescope, which is another popular legend, but the design of telescope which he used is still called the Galilean telescope.

He outlines the theory of the telescope and then goes on to

describe what he saw when he turned his telescope towards the Moon in January 1610. He supplies drawings of what he saw, and explains why he concluded (quite correctly) that there were mountains and plains on the surface of the Moon. His estimates of the heights of the mountains are, however, far too large. The *Messenger* also describes how Galileo saw many stars invisible to the naked eye, how he saw that the Milky Way was made up of stars, and how he discovered four satellites which moved round Jupiter.

Later Galileo observed that there were dark spots on the Sun, and that they changed with time. In fact, sunspots can be seen without a telescope: Chinese astronomers had seen them in about 90 BC, by looking at the Sun through a filter of white jade. In seventeenth century Europe, however, it was usual to accept Aristotle's belief that heavenly bodies were incorruptible and unchanging. Galileo was denounced from the pulpit in 1614, though the 'incorruptibility of the heavens' was a point of Aristotelian rather than of Catholic dogma. Many years previously, in a letter to Kepler (*q.v.*), Galileo had said that he believed in the theory of Copernicus (*q.v.*) that the planets moved round the Sun rather than round the Earth, but it was not until 1613, in his book on sunspots, that he declared this belief publicly.

Early in the sixteenth century the Copernican belief that the Earth moved had been attacked by Protestant theologians as contrary to scripture. In the early seventeenth century the Catholic church, engaged in the Counter-Reformation and eager to be seen to be placing greater emphasis than before upon the Bible, began to condemn Copernicanism. In 1616 Copernicus' *On the Revolutions* and several other works were 'suspended pending correction', but it seems that no action was taken against Galileo.

In 1632, however, after he had published his *Dialogue concerning the two Chief World Systems*, which ostensibly merely presented arguments for and against Earth-centred and Sun-centred planetary systems, Galileo was summoned before the Inquisition. He had already made many enemies by attacks on Aristotle, and the Pope saw some parts of the *Dialogue* as an attack upon himself. As a result of the trial the *Dialogue* was placed on the Index of forbidden books and Galileo was condemned to house arrest for life.

Early in 1634 he was moved to his villa at Arcetri, in the hills above Florence, where despite his failing sight he continued to work. He was completely blind by the time his last work, *Two New Sciences*, was published, in Holland, in 1638. *Two New Sciences* concerns the science of the strength of materials and the mathematical science of the study of motion. It points forward to modern experimental science.

Galileo is reputed to have been sharp-tongued, becoming very involved in arguments. His sarcasm and short temper made him many enemies, from the Pope downwards. He never married, though in his earlier years he had a mistress, who bore him several illegitimate children.

Above right: crayon sketch by Ottavio Leoni of Galileo Galilei at the age of 60, in 1624.

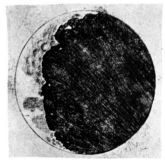

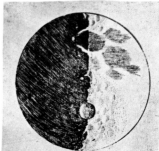

Right: some of Galileo's drawings of the Moon. He was not the first to draw the Moon as seen through a telescope (it was an Englishman, Thomas Harriott, in 1609) but he was the first to publicize it. In particular he realized that the bright spots just on the dark side were mountain peaks catching the rays of the Sun.

GAUSS, Carl Friedrich (1777-1855)

Carl Friedrich Gauss, mathematician, astronomer and physicist, was born in Brunswick, Germany, of uneducated working class parents. He was a child of precocious abilities, and fortunately his father recognized his genius sufficiently to allow him to continue his education. From 1792 to 1807 a grant from the Duke of Brunswick enabled him to study first at the Brunswick Collegium Carolinium and later at Göttingen University. In 1807 he became director of the new Observatory at Göttingen, a position he retained until his death.

His earliest enthusiasm was for mathematics, and he contributed significantly to most branches of that subject. In 1799, he gave the first rigorous proof of the fundamental theorum of algebra: that an nth degree algebraic equation with real coefficients has n roots. His *Inquiries into Arithmetic* of 1801 won him universal recognition; it used methods and concepts basic to the subsequent development of number theory as well as algebra.

In the early years of the nineteenth century his interest in astronomy deepened. In 1801 the minor planet Ceres was observed for the first time—and lost again when it went behind the sun, but with the available observations and his own improvements in orbit theory, Gauss was able to calculate the minor planet's path. Using his predictions it was found again. This was just one of many investigations into theoretical astronomy, and Gauss's accumulated work on celestial mechanics was published in 1809 in his *Theory of the Motion of the Celestial Bodies*. In 1807 the directorship of the new Göttingen Observatory, not fully built and equipped until 1821, brought with it new responsibilities.

In 1817 Gauss became preoccupied with geodesy—surveying large areas of the Earth's surface. His interest was aroused by a need to find accurately the geographical position of the Observatory, and by a plan conceived to triangulate Hanover. This latter survey, completed in 1847, did not produce a very accurate map of the area, but nevertheless resulted in a number of important advances, both in the mathematics of curved surfaces, and in surveying techniques. In particular Gauss invented the heliotrope, an instrument in which light from the sun is reflected by a mirror to a distant observer to make accurate angle measurements possible.

In 1828, on one of his rare expeditions from home, Gauss met the young Wilhelm Weber, who was to become famous for his work on electricity, at an international conference in Berlin. Partly as a result of this meeting Gauss's interest in terrestrial magnetism grew, and a deterioration in his health also encouraged him to turn from geodesic observations to less strenuous branches of experimental physics. In 1831, the year that Faraday (*q.v.*) discovered electromagnetic induction, Weber came to Göttingen and began work with Gauss. Their investigations of electromagnetism, and their use of the deflection of a magnetic needle for current measurement, led them in 1833 to construct an electric telegraph.

Movements of a large coil over a magnet constituted the signal, and caused an electric current to be set up, which was carried by long wires to a second coil where it produced deflections of a magnetic needle, which thus acted as a receiver. Gauss and Weber set up a telegraphic line across Göttingen from the Observatory to the Physics Laboratory. The telegraph was later developed independently by Morse (*q.v.*) and others.

From 1840 onwards the intensity of Gauss's scientific activity began to decline, and he suffered increasingly from the fits of depression which had dogged him since 1809 when his first wife died, and by bouts of ill health, real and imagined. Although he remarried, he remained throughout his life an isolated character, both intellectually and socially, never really happy except perhaps during the brief period of his first marriage.

Above right: Carl Friedrich Gauss, in professor's cap.

Right: the first telegraph key, built by Gauss and Weber in 1833 after Faraday discovered electromagnetic induction. A moving coil produced a signal.

GODDARD, Robert (1882-1945)

Robert Goddard was a pioneer in the field of rocketry whose ideas and experiments paved the way for manned flights to the moon, but did not live long enough to see his work result in anything more useful than warfare.

He was born in Worcester, Massachusetts, obtained a PhD from Clark University there in 1911, and began teaching at Clark in 1914. By that time he had already worked out a theory of multistage rockets to escape the gravitational pull of the Earth, and had a detailed mathematical theory of rocket propulsion. Experimenting with solid-fuelled rockets, he proved that they would not only work in a vacuum but that they would work better that way. These experiments were financed mostly out of his own pocket, and were necessary because there was confusion between rocket theory and jet theory, which needs an atmosphere for the jet engine to push against.

During World War I Goddard developed military rockets of 1.5 to 7 lb (0.7 to 3.2 kg) to be fired from hand-held launchers; these were being successfully tested when the war was over, and were the forerunners of the bazooka of World War II. In 1919, the Smithsonian Institution published Goddard's paper, *A Method of Reaching Extreme Altitudes*, which disguised rockets as a device for meteorological research, but on the last page proposed a rocket to be fired at the moon, with flashpowder payload so that astronomers would be able to see if the shot were successful. The Institution also provided funds for research.

In the early 1920s, Goddard gave up solid fuels in favour of liquid fuels, realizing that the rate of consumption of a liquid fuel could be controlled. He began to build high pressure steel motors with tapered nozzles for greater thrust, and fired his first liquid fuelled rocket on 16 March 1926, near Auburn, Massachusetts. It went 41 feet (12.5 m) high, landed 184 feet (28 m) away and averaged sixty mph (96.5 kph).

In 1930 Charles Lindbergh, the first man to fly the Atlantic solo, helped Goddard to get a grant from the Guggenheim foundation, and he was able to move to the desert in New Mexico to perform his experiments. Before World War II he had flown a rocket faster than the speed of sound and developed and tested a system of gyroscopic stabilization. He had received dozens of patents on the multistage idea, on pumps for propellents, regenerative cooling for engines, variable thrust engines, retrorockets for braking purposes, and many more. It is sometimes lamented that he did not receive more funds for research, but as it was pointed out after his death, he was probably happier conducting his experiments than he would have been overseeing others and defending his research to Congressional committees. Throughout World War II he worked on rocket motors and Jato (jet assisted take-off), and he died in 1945.

During the war the Nazis infringed his patents to build the V–2 rockets. In 1960 the United States government paid a million dollars for use of the patents in its own programme; in 1962 the National Aeronautics and Space Administration (NASA) dedicated the Goddard Space Flight Centre at Greenbelt, Maryland.

Below: Dr Robert Goddard (front) and assistants at work on a liquid fuelled rocket in 1940. From this small beginning came the huge Saturn rockets (overleaf).

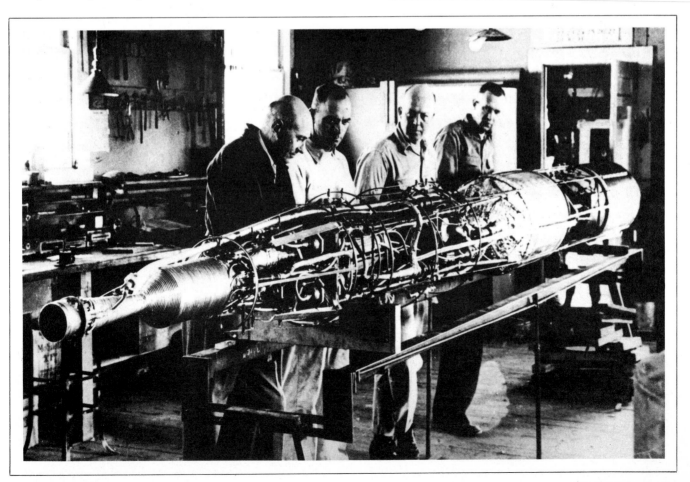

GOLDMARK, Dr Peter Carl (1906-1977)

Peter Goldmark was born in Budapest. He became president of CBS Laboratories in New York, a division of the Columbia Broadcasting System. His career is an example of a twentieth-century phenomenon, the corporate inventor: part executive, part scientist. He eventually held more than 160 patents; he was most famous for his introduction of the modern long-playing gramophone record, in 1948.

Goldmark's great-uncle Joseph was a chemist who discovered red phosphorus, a substance used in the manufacture of matches. Another great-uncle, Karl ,was one of Hungary's greatest composers. Peter Goldmark himself was a talented amateur musician, and remained an enthusiastic player of chamber music all his life.

He attended the Berlin Technical High School, studying engineering, and obtained a degree in physics from the University of Vienna. While still a student, he discovered an error in one of the papers of Rutherford (q.v.) then England's greatest physicist. Also while still a student, he became fascinated with electronics, and with television in particular.

The Scot John Logie Baird (q.v.) had invented an electro-mechanical method of broadcasting pictures in the form of radio waves, and in 1926 persuaded the BBC to transmit experimental pictures. Goldmark built the first television receiver in Vienna. The picture flickered, and it had a red cast because he had used a red neon tube in its construction, but it received the signal from London. Goldmark later remembered it as one of the most exciting moments of his life.

Upon receiving his degree, Goldmark went to Cambridge, England, and found work with Pye Radio; there he built a television set and helped to set up a television engineering department. After two years he sailed to New York and to RCA (Radio Corporation of America), where Vladimir Zworykin (q.v.) was developing his iconoscope, a variety of cathode ray tube which became the basis of black-and-white television. Those were Depression years, and RCA had no job for a young unknown engineer; but CBS wanted to set up its own television department, and someone there had read one of Goldmark's papers. Soon he was directing the construction of a television transmitter atop New York's Chrysler Building, and before long he was president of CBS labs.

When Goldmark happened to see his first colour film (*Gone With The Wind*), he immediately began thinking about colour television. Three months after he made a proposal to the CBS management, he had designed and built his own system, a mechanical system owing much to Baird. It employed three colour filters at the transmitter, one each for red, blue and green. At the receiving end the filters were built into a disc which was turned by an electric motor: impulses were flashed to represent each filter, and when the transmitter 'saw' red, the receiver 'saw' it too. The device depended upon persistence of vision to make sense of the picture 'streaked' on the screen. It was demonstrated for the press in September of 1940, and it worked perfectly.

Television was still experimental; in fact, the trade press regarded it as a new kind of radio. Goldmark thought that when commercial television began, it should start right out with colour; his system was not compatible with existing black-and-white technology. RCA were working on a colour system using several valves [vacuum tubes] which would have allowed colour sets to receive monochrome transmissions. At this point World War II intervened, and during the war Goldmark worked at Harvard and in England on devices for jamming German radar.

After the war he built a colour system which used the undeveloped ultra-high frequency (UHF) part of the spectrum. When it was demonstrated, the Federal Communications Commission (FCC) ruled that it used too much of the spectrum.

In the meantime, between VE day and VJ day in 1945, Goldmark and his wife were visiting one evening in the home of friends, who played for them a new recording of the Brahms Second Piano Concerto, with Horowitz playing piano and Toscanini conducting. Brahms was Goldmark's favourite composer. The friends listened to the set of records several times, and Goldmark, who did not own a record player, became increasingly irritated with the clicking and thumping of the record changer and the interruptions in the music caused by the short playing time of the 78 rpm records. Immediately his mind began considering the laboratory aspects of the problem.

Records which revolved at slower speeds were nothing new; they had been used to accompany films in the 1920s, and RCA had marketed $33\frac{1}{3}$ rpm records in the mid-1930s, made of a rough plastic called Victrolac. They failed because of high surface noise. It is a fact that the higher the speed the better the sound, all other things being equal.

Goldmark realized that for an appreciable extension of playing time, a new record would have smaller grooves closer together, as well as revolving more slowly. This would require a whole new technology for cutting the master disc and playing it back. The new record would have to be made of a smooth plastic instead of the gritty compounds then in use; the new plastic would also be softer, which meant that playback tracking pressure would have to be much lower. Another problem would be 'rumble', or low-frequency noise from the turntable motor. But the biggest problem would be keeping the playback stylus in the groove at the lower pressure.

CBS Labs went to work. In order to keep the project secret, they had to grind their own cutting and playback stylii and build their own motor. Philco was contracted to build the new record player, and they also had to work in secrecy. Security also had to be maintained at the record pressing plant in Bridgeport, Connecticut. The whole project was one of the best-kept industrial secrets of the post-war years; when the editor of a trade publication rang up to find out what was going on, CBS quickly announced plans to press 78s out of plastic, with as much publicity as possible.

There were a great many bugs along the way. At one point the researchers were plagued with an annoying crackle coming from the grooves of their experimental discs; they discovered that a supervisor in the pressing plant was ordering frequent sweepings of the floor, and the resulting dust raised was being pressed into the records.

When the new record was ready, the marketing of it was a gamble, and this was typical of Goldmark, who was once described as having a 'genii complex'. CBS had no way of knowing whether anyone wanted the new record; there was not a single privately-owned record player in the country capable of playing it, and to make matters worse, Philco's production of the new machines was behind schedule. Gold-

The long-playing records Goldmark holds in his arms have the same playing time as the stack of 78s on the left.

mark himself thought that the new system would appeal only to lovers of symphonic music, and had no idea that he was about to revolutionize the record business.

RCA introduced a 45 rpm record at the same time. They too had designed a new record player; the new record had a centre hole $1\frac{1}{2}$ inches (3.81 cm) in diameter, and a large spindle contained all the mechanism for supporting and changing a stack of records. The changing was quick, positive and quiet, but the record was limited in size to 7 inches (17.78 cm), which severely limited its playing time. A 'battle of the speeds' ensued, which lasted for some years; when it subsided, the 45 disc was the medium for popular singles and the 78 was gone forever.

Goldmark's new record was called the 'Lp' by Columbia Records, the American CBS record division. It not only represented far better value, giving more playing time for the customer's money, but took up less space for a given playing time, encouraging larger record collections and larger inventories in shops. It was also shatterproof, which meant that shops could put records on display. Soon Lps began to appear in supermarkets and drugstores. Record sales quadrupled in twenty years, more than three-quarters of the sales being accounted for by Goldmark's invention. After a few years, a computer was hooked up to the master disc cutting lathe to 'listen' to the master tape, so that the grooves in the quiet portions of the music could be cut even closer together; this resulted in Beethoven's Ninth Symphony being squeezed onto one record for the first time.

In the meantime, Goldmark's colour TV system was not so lucky. He had successfully found a way to squeeze his system into the lower part of the broadcasting spectrum, and a new FCC demonstration was ordered in 1949. Time was of the essence, for the Goldmark system was not compatible with existing monochrome sets, whose number had already increased from 7000 in 1945 to seven million. Goldmark's device worked perfectly, while RCA's did not. (There were stories after the demonstration of RCA's green monkeys eating blue bananas.) The FCC found in favour of CBS, but RCA went to court, and mounted a crash programme to perfect their system, spending $130,000,000. The US Supreme Court found in favour of CBS, but by then there were so many monochrome sets in use that the FCC reversed itself and the RCA system is the one we have today. CBS had the last laugh, however: RCA's system used the shadow-mask tube, which CBS had quietly been inventing and patenting. RCA had to pay royalties to CBS.

Goldmark's device is still used in close-circuit systems, for example in medical education, because it has the advantage of working well with a limited amount of light. For the same reason, it was chosen in 1969 to broadcast colour from the moon. When a NASA official called it a 'technological breakthrough', Goldmark said, 'It may be the first technological breakthrough that is 28 years old.' In the event, the camera worked for only 44 minutes on the moon; it was probably damaged by the heat of the Sun.

Goldmark had also built a scanning camera which sent back the first high-resolution pictures of the moon's surface from a lunar orbiter, and a tiny television camera which takes pictures inside the human body. Not all his inventions were successful, however: his cassette tape system was beaten in the marketplace by the Phillips system in use today, and his compatible stereo record was passed over by the industry in favour of a record which could be played only by a stereo cartridge. He built an ingenious electronic video recording (EVR) system for the playing of films on existing television sets, but it had the disadvantage that users could not make their own films, and has been superceded by video tape.

After 35 years of cracking the whip over his team in the CBS Labs, Goldmark retired to start his own business in 1972. His Goldmark Communications Corporation convinced the Federal government to fund a New Rural Society experiment. The idea was to solve the problems of the cities and of energy consumption by encouraging people to move back to the rural areas; he thought electronics would make it unnecessary for businessmen to go to the office every day.

Like many idealistic innovators, Goldmark often left human nature out of his calculations. The New Rural Society project was cancelled: there is no substitute for the stimulation of the city itself. Goldmark thought that children would be encouraged to read by using the EVR device to show pages of books on the TV screen; he thought that door-to-door salesmen would be welcomed by housewives if they carried their sales pitch on EVR machines. His faith in technology was touching.

Music lovers, however, will always be in his debt for the invention of the modern long-playing gramophone record. For many years the record companies sent him complimentary copies of each new release, and the Soviet Union sent a copy of the first long-playing record made in that country.

Dr Peter Carl Goldmark was killed in a car crash in New Jersey on 7 December 1977.

GUERICKE, Otto von (1602-1686)

Otto von Guericke, German physicist and engineer, is best known for his invention of the air pump, and for his experiments on the vacuum; but science for Guericke was always a leisuretime activity. Destined from the start to be a politician, his education, at the Universities of Leipzig, Helmstedt and Jena, was mainly in law. He continued these studies at Leiden, but there he also attended lectures of mathematics and engineering.

After his studies, Guericke returned to his native town of Magdeburg and became an alderman of the city in 1626. Guericke played an increasingly important role in civic affairs, but he was forced to leave the town after its nearly complete destruction in May 1631, during the Thirty Years' War. He then successively became the official engineer in Brunswick, in Erfurt, and for the electorate of Saxony.

Guericke later returned to Magdeburg and again became absorbed in local politics. During the period 1646–76, he served as mayor of Magdeburg. In 1666, in recognition of his services to the community, he was raised to the ranks of the nobility, and he was given the title 'von' Guericke.

Guericke began his scientific experiments only in 1646, but current arguments about the nature of space and the possibility of obtaining a vacuum had been preoccupying him for some time. There were two theories in vogue: the first, based largely on metaphysical arguments, and held strongly by the seventeenth century French philosopher Descartes, asserted that a vacuum is totally impossible and that space is perpetually filled with matter; the second, based on a growing understanding of atmospheric pressure and on experiments carried out by Torricelli (q.v.) and others, claimed that a vacuum could exist.

Guericke attempted to resolve the dispute experimentally. First he tried to pump water from a well-caulked beer barrel using a suction pump, but he found that air leaked in. He then attempted to pump air directly from a hollow copper sphere, with the result that the sphere caved in and collapsed, thus supporting the idea of the impossibility of forming a vacuum. Not yet satisfied, Guericke devised his own air pump and repeated the experiment, this time succeeding in producing at least a partial vacuum. It was this pump which was improved by Boyle (*q.v.*) and used in his famous experiments. In 1657 Guericke first performed the well-known Magdeburg experiment, where two large copper hemispheres were fitted together, and the air between them pumped out. Two teams of horses, one attached to each hemisphere, could not pull them apart. This, and other public demonstrations, were made at Magdeburg, Berlin and Regensburg.

Although famous for his experiments on the vacuum, Guericke was interested in a total explanation of the physical universe and its phenomena. In particular he felt that magnetic force might in some way explain the motions of the planets. In an attempt to simulate, on a small scale, the planet Earth and its magnetic properties, he made a sphere of sulphur and by rubbing it produced static electricity and noticed its attractive power. He did not, however, clearly distinguish between electrical and magnetic effects.

In 1681 Guericke left Magdeburg, this time to escape the plague. He retired to Hamburg, where he spent the remaining five years of his life.

Right: Otto von Guericke: engraving from his own 'Experimenta Nova', 1672.

Below: the famous Magdeburg hemisphere experiment; the horses failed to pull the evacuated hemispheres apart.

GUTENBERG, Johann (c1394-c1468)

Johann Gutenberg was the inventor of printing using movable type, that is, type whose characters are individually cast in metal. He was born probably between 1394 and 1398 in Mainz, at the junction of the Rhine and the Main in Germany. His family belonged to the patrician class, and his father had an interest in the local mint belonging to the Archbishop of Mainz.

Nothing is known of Gutenberg's early life, but he evidently learned the skills of the many local goldsmiths. In 1428 he had to leave the town after a series of struggles in which the local craftsmen's guilds forced many of the patrician families to leave, and settled in Strasbourg, further down the Rhine. Here he relied for his living on allowances from Mainz, and probably also exercised his skill as a goldsmith. Two years later he returned to Mainz, and in 1436 was accused of breach of promise in an offer of marriage. He lost his case (though he never married) and his hot-headed behaviour at his trial helps to explain the series of lawsuits he was involved in throughout his life.

Until Gutenberg's invention, printing was done by using single blocks of wood or brass cut with the design for the whole page. This was a slow and expensive method. The exact circumstances of Gutenberg's first experiments with the principle of modern printing are not clear; however the introduction of movable type was an important step forward in the development of printing. For the first time type became reusable, simple and cheap to manufacture. Of necessity type sizes began to be standardized. In Strasbourg, Gutenberg went into partnership with Andreas Dritzehn and Andreas Heilmann, undertaking to teach them firstly a new method of making mirrors, and secondly a secret new process. Dritzehn died in 1438 and Gutenberg became involved in a legal battle with Dritzehn's brothers, who wanted to be admitted to the partnership. Gutenberg won the case and though the nature of the secret experiments was not admitted at the trial, they were probably trying to cast type with a mould capable of casting individual letters of varying widths.

In 1444 Gutenberg left Strasbourg, unable to find further money for his experiments, and in 1448 entered into partnership with a Mainz lawyer, Johann Fust. During the following years he perfected his new techniques with the help of a calligrapher, Peter Schoeffer, and printed the first books.

Gutenberg agreed with Fust that he would concentrate on printing a Bible, but he also printed popular things for his own profit, including indulgences and school grammars. Angry at this break in their agreement, Fust took Gutenberg to court in November 1455 and, winning the case, obtained possession of Gutenberg's printing materials.

As a result the two men separated, but the first, and possibly the finest, important book was already printed. The Gutenberg 42 line Bible (so called from the number of lines on each page) took three years, and was probably finished late in 1455.

After parting from Fust, Gutenberg went on printing at Mainz and printed several small popular books. In 1458–9 he printed a second Bible (the 36 line Bible) at Bamberg, using slightly larger type, and then returned to Mainz to work until he retired in January 1465. He died in 1467 or 1468. Among Gutenberg's remarkable accomplishments, apart from the fact that he invented the first modern printing process, is the beautiful quality of all his work.

Top: copy of the oldest known print of Johann Gutenberg; the original was accidentally burnt in 1870.

Above: a page from his 42 line Bible.

Overleaf: Gutenberg's movable metal type has evolved into this one-piece plastic letterpress plate.

HARGRAVES, James (c1720-1778)

Below: improved version of James Hargreaves' jenny.

Bottom: 1769 patent specification of the water frame.

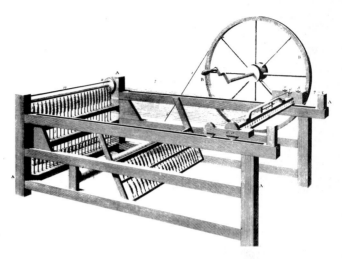

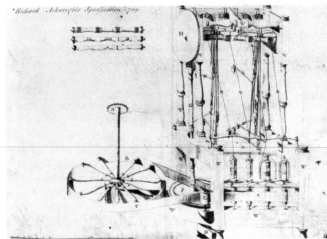

The parish register of Stanhill church near Bolton in Lancashire records the marriage in 1740 of James Hargraves, inventor of the spinning-jenny, to one Elizabeth Grimshaw. The name is very definitely Hargraves and not Hargreaves, as is so often quoted, and while we know the date of his marriage the precise date of his birth is a mystery.

As a young man it is very likely that James Hargraves was well versed in the art of weaving cloth using a hand loom. Hargraves lived on a farm and it was very common for farmworkers to weave at home in their spare time in order to supplement their agricultural wages which were very low. Hargraves is supposed to have been a good carpenter as well.

About 1760 James Hargraves was asked by Robert Peel to make a carding engine. Robert Peel, the grandfather of Britain's first prime minister, was a neighbour of Hargraves and interested in textile weaving and printing designs on calico, a rough and cheaply made cotton fabric. A carding engine was required in order to mechanize the process by which the tangled fibres of cotton in its natural form are straightened and re-arranged prior to spinning the cotton into long, thin threads. Hargraves' carding engine was the first of a series of improvements made in the eighteenth century to the carding process.

In 1733 John Kay had invented a device called the fly-shuttle. The fly-shuttle was used on weaving looms to pass the threads of wool or cotton more rapidly from side to side of the width of cloth being made. The fly-shuttle carries a thread called the weft which is passed back and forth between a set of threads called the warp threads.

John Kay's fly-shuttle made it possible for textile weavers to work very much faster and to produce much more cloth. An important consequence was that spinning became a serious bottleneck in the textile industry. The old fashioned method of making threads by hand-spinning carded wool or cotton simply could not produce enough thread to keep the weavers supplied.

The need to mechanize spinning became critical and in London in 1761 the Society of Arts decided to offer a prize, worth £50, to anyone who could invent a spinning machine capable of making six threads at once with only one man to work it. James Hargraves and Robert Peel may or may not have known of the competition but at any rate Hargraves invented a spinning machine in about 1764, which he patented in 1770. How he arrived at a suitable design is not known but there is a story that he got the basic idea when an old-fashioned spinning wheel was knocked over and as the machine revolved on the floor Hargraves saw how to make a device capable of spinning lots of threads all at once.

Hargraves' spinning machine was basically quite simple; it was made of wood and hand operated. It was called a spinning jenny, which is probably not a reference to a person's name but rather a local way of saying spinning engine.

As a spinning machine Hargraves' jenny was such a success that many people who earned a living using spinning wheels in their homes became fearful for their jobs. Hargraves' home and his store of machines were attacked and many things were broken. Probably about 50 years old at the time and, so we are told, 'a stout, broadset man of five feet ten inches high, or rather more', James Hargraves left Stanhill and went to Nottingham in order to escape further persecution. In Nottingham Hargraves manufactured spinning-jennies and, together with a man called Thomas James, set up a mill to spin cotton mechanically.

Another man was spinning cotton mechanically in Nottingham. Richard Arkwright, a native of Preston, had also been impressed by the need to mechanize the spinning process and in 1769 he patented his so-called water-frame. This name was used because Arkwright's spinning machine could be driven by water-power, so allowing a much bigger spinning machine handling many more threads to be operated. Moreover Arkwright's machine worked on a somewhat different principle to Hargraves'; each man's machine had its good and bad features. It was logical, therefore, that the next development in spinning machines should feature an amalgamation of the two types. The result was the famous spinning mule of Samuel Crompton of 1779; apparently the name derives from the fact that Crompton's machine was a hybrid of those of Arkwright and Hargraves.

In the eighteenth century textile production in Britain changed from being a small scale domestic affair to a mechanized factory-based industry. Men like Richard Arkwright and James Hargraves were influential in bringing about these changes. But whereas Richard Arkwright became wealthy and famous—he was knighted in 1786—James Hargraves died in obscurity in 1778 at the age of about 60.

HERO of Alexandra 1st century AD

Hero of Alexandria is such a mysterious figure that until recently there was considerable disagreement about when he lived. It is now known, however, that he must have been alive in the first century AD because a lunar eclipse which Hero describes has been shown by modern calculation to have occurred in 62 AD. Otherwise we know nothing of Hero's dates of birth and death, his life, or even what he looked like.

In Hero's time the city of Alexandria was the intellectual capital of the ancient world. Named after Alexander the Great, Alexandria retained its Greek traditions and institutions even under Roman rule. It is probable that Hero was connected with the University of Alexandria and it was there that he wrote, in Greek, his various studies of mechanics and mechanical technology.

The Ancient Greeks' interest in mechanical technology ranged from automatic toys and gadgets to heavier but simple machinery for doing useful work. Unfortunately, very few of the original Greek descriptions of these machines have survived. Of the handful which are known, Hero's descriptions are the most important because his considerable writings are mostly in the original Greek. The works of other authors only exist in fragments and these bits and pieces are mainly in the form of later translations into Latin and Arabic.

One of Hero's works, probably the most famous, is called *Pneumatics*. It contains details of nearly 80 gadgets and devices utilizing not only pneumatic principles but mechanical and hydraulic ones as well. Compressed air is a feature of a lot of the items described. The hydraulic siphon is often used to move water from one place to another and in a few instances geared drives are illustrated for the first time. Occasionally Hero depicts applications of steam pressure.

In the *Pneumatics* and another work called *Automatic Theatres* Hero emphasizes toys, novelties and devices intended primarily to entertain. The themes of his other writings are more practical and useful. *Dioptra* is about surveying and contains a description of the construction and use of an instrument designed by Hero himself. A dioptra was an instrument combining the functions of a theodolite and a level. In the least well-known of Hero's works, *Belopoiica*, he discusses catapults for throwing missiles in warfare.

The last of Hero's works, *Mechanics*, is only known in an Arabic version prepared long after Hero's time. In many ways this is the most interesting work of all because it deals with the basic machinery of lifting and haulage: the windlass, lever, pulley, wedge and screw. Many applications are analyzed, notably the use of the screw press to crush grapes and olives.

For many centuries after his death, Hero's works remained unknown. About 500 years ago they began to be studied with increasing interest in Western Europe and they became established as basic sources of information about technology. This phase passed rapidly, however, as European mechanical engineering progressed and improved. Nowadays, Hero of Alexandria is important mainly as our principal source of information on the scope and character of Greek mechanical technology, the principles which were understood, the ways they were used and the tasks to which they were applied.

Left: Hero's whirling aeolipile, the first ever reaction turbine, the first use of steam power to turn a wheel, and an ancestor of the rocket. Water boiled in the urn at the base, sending steam up the two tubes, which also acted as pivots for the sphere. The jets of steam, blowing in opposite directions, drove it round.

Below: like Hero's own aeolipile, as well as the gyroscope, the helicopter and many other examples, many quite advanced mechanisms have first been used in toys or other useless gadgets. This is Hero's automatic door opening mechanism for temples. When a fire was lit on the altar, water in a concealed tank boiled, forcing water down the pipe at the right into the sphere, which was in the basement. Water in the sphere was forced by steam pressure into the bucket, which slowly gained in weight and descended, turning the rope-wound spindles, which were connected to the doorposts.

HERSCHEL, F W (1738-1822)

If William Herschel were not famous for his discovery of the planet Uranus, he would be well known as the discoverer of infra-red radiation, or equally as the 'father of stellar astronomy'. His son John was a brilliant scientist in his own right, a pioneer in many branches of physics and chemistry as well as astronomy. Yet William Herschel started his career as a muscian in the Hanoverian Guard, and until he was 35 showed no signs of becoming anything more than a successful, if rather obscure, musician.

William Herschel was the son of an oboeist in the Guards band of the state of Hanover, in Germany. After an elementary education at the garrison school, William also became an oboeist in the band, which followed the regiment on a number of encounters. Eventually, the situation in Europe became sufficiently warlike for the band to be forgotten, and William was able to leave the regiment without any trouble. He made his way to England, where life was quieter, to make his career as a musician.

In this he was quite successful. He had a fine musical talent, and held a number of posts in Durham, Leeds, Newcastle and other northern cities. At the age of 28, he was offered the post of organist at a private chapel being opened at Bath, then the centre of the fashionable world.

The next few years were hectic with composing, playing and giving music lessons. When he was 35, William also became deeply interested in astronomy, which had long

Right: Sir William Herschel at 81. He was known for his benign personality and tolerance of constant visitors.

Below: a reflecting telescope he made, which still works.

Left: photograph of Sir John Herschel at 75 by Julia Margaret Cameron, who was a family friend. She insisted on tousling his hair for dramatic effect.

Right: Sir William Herschel's great 1.2m aperture, 12m long reflecting telescope, which was used until 1839, when it became unsafe and was dismantled.

fascinated him. Finding that hiring telescopes was costly, he set about making his own, and began a complete review of the sky, searching for double stars.

He found plenty of these, but in March 1781 he found one very unusual object which his telescope showed as a small disc. It moved from night to night, and Herschel reported it as a new comet. It was soon realized that this was no comet but a new planet, orbiting the Sun beyond Saturn. The discovery was unexpected because Uranus was the first planet to be actually discovered: all the others had been known since earliest times.

The discovery, which was largely due to the ability of his telescope to show the tiny disc, brought Herschel fame. The King, George III, awarded Herschel an annual grant, enabling him to give up his musical life and move near Windsor. Making telescopes became a profitable sideline.

At last William was able to devote all his time to astronomy, observing every hour when stars were visible and making telescopes by day. He built what was for many years the largest telescope in the world, the 'Forty Feet', of 48 inches (1.2 m) aperture, though this was rather cumbersome and was not used regularly.

As a result of his sky surveys and other work, Herschel deduced that the Milky Way, the band of faint stars which stretches round the sky, is actually a flat lens-shaped structure with the Sun not at the centre but some way towards one edge. He showed that double stars are not chance alignments but are binary systems, with the stars orbiting each other, and also found that the Sun has its own motion through space in a particular direction.

While trying to find a filter that would block out the heat from the Sun, but not the light, Herschel discovered that the region beyond the red end of a prism's spectrum (the infrared) has a strong heating effect, and realized that this invisible radiation obeys the same laws of refraction as visible light.

Throughout his observing, Herschel was aided by his devoted sister Caroline, who patiently recorded all his observations so that he would not have to look away from the eyepiece. Caroline was an observer in her own right, and was later awarded many scientific honours for her work. Observing was done outside, rather than in a dome—on some occasions, Herschel found that his feet were frozen to the ground and even the ink was solid.

In 1788, when he was 50, William married a local widow, Mary Pitt, whose husband's private library he had often visited. They had one son, John.

John Herschel eventually graduated as Senior Wrangler at Cambridge, the top mathematical honour, once held by Isaac Newton (*q.v.*). His famous name played little part in his success: his less successful colleagues included Charles Babbage (*q.v.*), the pioneer of the calculating machine, who remained a lifelong friend.

In addition to his mathematical work, John Herschel also became interested in chemistry. One of his discoveries was that sodium thiosulphate ('hypo') will dissolve silver salts—to become useful later on.

John chose to help his father, who had been knighted in 1816. When Sir William Herschel died at the age of 83, John was continuing his reviews of the sky, later extending these to the southern hemisphere by moving to the Cape of Good Hope with his telescopes.

When in 1839 he heard of the recent photographic discoveries of Daguerre(*q.v.*), Herschel applied his knowledge of chemistry to the subject. Within days he had successfully used a process of his own, involving a glass plate coated with silver halide, to photograph the old Forty Feet telescope, which was shortly to be pulled down. Remembering his earlier discovery, he used hypo to 'fix' the plate, producing what he called a 'negative'. The 'positive' was made in a similar way on paper. Although his first results were inferior to Daguerre's, this is basically the process used today.

When he was in his early thirties, John Herschel's scholarly career was beginning to wear him down. Friends realized that marriage would help, and introduced him to a family which had two eligible daughters. The plan worked, and Herschel became devoted to his clever young wife and the family which soon arrived. They eventually had three sons and nine daughters. and the family happiness of the Herschels was well known.

Although Sir John Herschel's work cannot be tied down to many specific discoveries, he played a major role in the development of science in the nineteenth century, being regarded as one of the most distinguished scientists of the period. Like Newton, be became Master of the Mint, and he was buried near Newton in Westminster Abbey.

HONNECOURT, Villard (c1180-c1250)

Little is known about the life of Villard de Honnecourt, a Cistercian monk and architect born at Honnecourt, a small village on the River Scheldt near Cambrai, in about 1180 AD. As an architect he might have passed almost unnoticed, although he was responsible for the design of Cambrai cathederal, had he not left a remarkable notebook which luckily has survived, although a few pages are known to be missing. This book contained personal jottings and sketches on matters concerning his work. It is of interest primarily because of descriptions of mechanical devices which were in use in the thirteenth century and of which we would otherwise be totally ignorant.

The larger part of Villard's notebook is taken up with architectural studies. Other sections deal with the construction of automata, such as a model of an angel which could be made to rotate or of an eagle which could be made to turn its head. Devices of this kind were quite a common feature of ecclesiastic buildings of this period. An interest in them may be seen as an extension of the architect's function, although by then they already had a long history rooted in the works of the Greek scientists at Alexandria in the first century AD. Villard's sketch of the pivot for the angel, however, shows that he had come very close to solving the problem of designing an escapement for a mechanical clock.

Two sketches in the notebook deal with equipment for handling building materials, one being a screw jack, the other a hydraulic saw. The first is described by Villard quite simply as being useful for lifting heavy burdens. It is depicted as little more than a nut and screw operated by a cross-handle and contained within a stout wooden frame. It was evidently designed for lifting heavy pieces of wood or stone during building operations. No similar screw jack is known until about 1480, when jacks came into common use for training cannon and lifting wagons.

The hydraulic saw described by Villard has two functional elements. The saw blade is suspended vertically between a sapling branch at the top, which acted as a spring, and a hinged bar at the bottom. This bar could be forced downwards by a series of cams projecting from the main shaft of a water-wheel. After each such downward movement the saw blade was returned by the sapling spring. A wheel with projecting spikes was attached to the main shaft in such a way that it forced the log being sawn against the blade. Similar saws are unknown until the Renaissance, when one finds them described by such engineers as da Vinci (*q.v.*).

A further device sketched by Villard is a system of gimbal rings designed for carrying a small fire-basket. It shows six concentric rings with the fire-basket in the centre, while the carrying handle would have been attached to the outer ring. The rings are pivoted so that, no matter at what angle the handle is held, the fire-basket would have remained upright. Probably Villard had in mind the carrying of censers, then greatly used in churches, when he drew this design. However, gimbals were not in general use until the Renaissance, when they were applied to magnetic compasses to keep them steady at sea.

While Villard's primary interest lay in ecclesiastical building, he was equally obliged to consider questions of military defence, since no distinction was then made between architects and engineers. In his note book there is a series of sketches of a stone-throwing machine or trebuchet.

In his day Villard's notebook was certainly not unique, for other architects are known to have kept their own records, but these have since been lost or destroyed. Furthermore, Villard's book does not suggest that he was a great innovator, but rather that he was in the habit of making notes of things he had seen and which he felt might prove useful. The book thus assumes an importance far beyond that intended by its author. For the historian of technology it serves as a reminder that our understanding of the Middle Ages is less than perfect, and that some machines which we might otherwise believe to be inventions of the Renaissance were in fact known and used at least two centuries earlier.

Villard de Honnecourt's drawings of a water driven power saw (below) and the first ever screw jack (right).

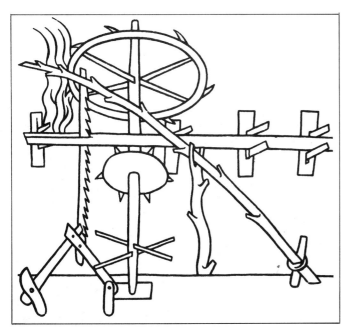

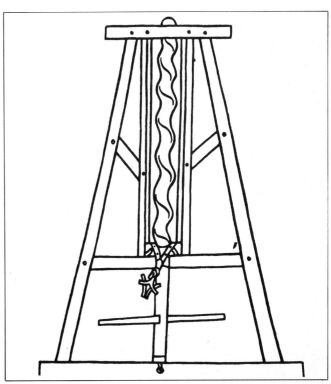

HOOKE, Robert (1635-1703)

Robert Hooke was one of the most versatile scientists of his time; he is best remembered for his work in physics, mechanics and microscopy.

Born on the Isle of Wight, the son of a minister, he was apprenticed to a painter before entering Westminster School. Later, at Oxford, he met a group of scientists, becoming assistant to Robert Boyle (*q.v.*). Here he made an improved air pump and began work on designing watches regulated by springs instead of pendulums, an important step towards the chronometer, a rugged but accurate clock for finding a ships' longitude at sea. Hooke had a great capacity for making instruments and apparatus and conducting successful experiments.

After some of his Oxford friends had joined in forming the Royal Society of London, Hooke was appointed Curator of Experiments in 1662. His duties were to provide several experiments for each of the weekly meetings. In 1665 he became Professor of Geometry at Gresham College in London, and here he spent the remainder of his life.

His most successful publication was the *Micrographia* of 1665, a book of microscopical observations, famous for its magnificent illustrations. Here Hooke's contemporaries could, for the first time, see the detailed structure of a bluebottle or a flea, or observe the compound eye of a fly. Many were intrigued by this sight of a new and unknown world; many more thought Hooke was absurd in studying such trivia—especially fleas and lice.

His interests ranged from astronomy to geology and included theories of light and combustion. The fundamental law of elasticity still bears his name. He made an important contribution towards explaining the motion of planets by saying that their orbits resulted from combining an inertial motion in a straight line with the attractive force of the Sun, and that this attractive force varied inversely as the distance squared. Though Hooke could not demonstrate mathematically that this was the case, he passed his insight on to the far superior mathematician Sir Isaac Newton (*q.v.*), and later complained when Newton would not acknowledge his contribution.

Hooke's abilities were not confined to what we could call science. After the Great Fire of London in 1666, the City appointed him as surveyor and he worked for many years under his friend Sir Christopher Wren. Not only did he survey sites and foundations, but as an architect in his own right, he designed a number of important buildings.

Hooke was hardly a very happy man. He was touchy, especially when he thought someome was stealing his ideas. He was often ill, and continually subjected to indigestion, headaches and insomnia. There is no surviving portrait, but he was certainly ugly—thin and crooked, with a sharp chin and large eyes and forehead. His hair was long and untidy. But appearances were indeed deceptive. Beneath this forbidding exterior was a man of humanity and great scientific intuition. The perceptive Samuel Pepys wrote after their first meeting that Hooke 'is the most, and promises the least, of any man in the world that ever I saw'.

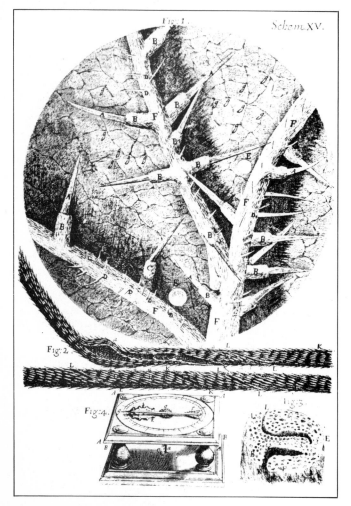

Left: from Robert Hooke's 'Micrographia', a book of microscopical observations. Fig. 1 is the underside of a stinging nettle leaf; Figs. 2 and 3 are side and cross sectional views of the beard of a wild oat, showing why it expands when damp. Hooke put this effect to use in his hygrometer, Fig. 4, for measuring air humidity.

Below: the Hooke universal joint, now used on car driveshafts, was in fact invented by him as part of the adjustment system of a microscope.

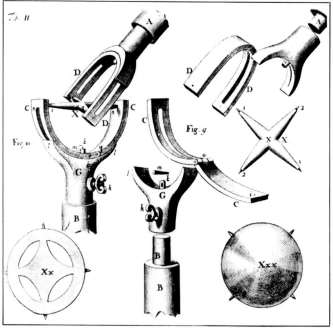

HUYGENS, Christiaan (1629-1695)

Christiaan Huygens was born in The Hague on 14 April 1629. His grandfather, his father, and later his older brother were in the service of the House of Orange, and Christiaan grew up in a very cultured environment. His father, Constantijn Huygens, an accomplished man of science and letters and a brilliant poet, carefully planned Christiaan's private education in languages, literature, mathematics and music. The French philosopher René Descartes was a frequent visitor to the Huygens household and the precocious Christiaan was heavily influenced by Descartes' 'mechanistic' philosophy of nature, according to which the universe is entirely filled with 'vortices' of particles of various sizes, and all natural phenomena had to be explained in terms of particles pushing or hitting other particles. Huygens remained a 'Cartesian' until his death.

After two years at the University of Leiden and two years at the College of Orange in Breda, Huygens returned to his father's house where, supported by his father, he devoted himself to the study of nature. Except for several trips abroad, he stayed in The Hague until 1666, and during this very fruitful period he made important contributions to mathematics, astronomy, optics, and mechanics, quickly establishing himself as one of Europe's foremost scientists, and when he accepted the prestigious appointment to the newly founded Académie Royale des Sciences of Paris in 1666, he was regarded as its most distinguished member. He lived in Paris, except for several trips home, until 1681, when for reasons of health and religion he returned to The Hague.

In 1656 Huygens was able to adapt the principle of the pendulum to the regulation of the clock, an idea which increased the accuracy of clocks enormously. His *Horologium* of 1658, in which he described the pendulum clock, however, was only a beginning. Huygens went on to investigate the pendulum, showing that only a pendulum bob describing a cycloidal arc was truly isochronous (having regular periodicity), and establishing the fundamental relationship between length and period of a pendulum. His *Horologium Oscillatorium*, published in 1673, presented these researches, as well as his calculation of centrifugal force and the value he had found for the acceleration of a falling body due to gravity ('g') by means of the pendulum.

Having taught himself how to grind lenses, Huygens set out to improve the telescope. By 1655 his telescopes were good enough to allow him to discover a satellite of Saturn (later called Titan). Shortly afterwards he also solved the problem posed by the strange appearance of the planet itself, and in his *Systema Saturnium* (1659) he published his results: Saturn is surrounded by an unattached ring. Among his other contributions to astronomy is the first determination of the rotation period of Mars. He continued his efforts to improve the telescope, and as telescopes became longer in order to minimize the optical problems posed by the primitive lenses, Huygens introduced the aerial telescope, in which the objective lens and the eyepiece (now over 100 feet apart) were no longer connected by a tube.

Theoretical investigations of optical systems and the nature of light were not neglected. In the early 1660s he invented a compound eyepiece which minimized the colour fringes caused by the non-achromatic lenses then in use; this 'Huygenian eyepiece' is still used in telescopes. In the late 1670s, in response to the theory of the compound nature

Left: reconstruction of Huygens' original pendulum excapement, the most important development in clocks till this century. He studied the physics of pendulums, telescopes and centrifugal force, and postulated a wave theory of light.

Below: Christaan Huygens, from a contemporary engraving.

of white light—a theory which supposed light to consist of particles travelling through a vacuum—Huygens developed his wave theory in defence of Cartesian philosophy. He postulated that light is an irregular series of shock waves travelling with a finite speed through the 'aether' made up of elastic Cartesian particles. Light then was not an actual transfer of particles, as it was according to Newton (*q.v.*), but rather a tendency towards motion, transmitted by the continuous but irregularly spaced particles. Each particle transmitted the pressure (or impact) to all particles touching it in the direction of the pressure, and therefore each particle can be considered as the originating point of a new hemispherical wavefront of this pressure. Only in the overall direction of the light's path is the cumulative effect of these individual wavefronts perceptible. He published this principle in his *Traité de la Lumière* (1690).

Although Huygens was certainly Europe's foremost scientist between 1655 and 1687 (the year of Newton's *Principia*) he fell into oblivion in the eighteenth century. His brilliantly elegant mathematical solutions, in the classical manner of the Greeks, were superseded by the calculus of Newton and Leibnitz, and his wave theory was forgotten with the general acceptance of Newtonian science and the corresponding decline of Cartesian science. Only in the nineteenth century was his wave theory of light resurrected through the work of Young (*q.v.*) and Fresnel (*q.v.*).

al-JAZARI, Ismaeel (c1150-c1220)

Ismaeel (Ibn al-Razzaz) al-Jazari was a craftsman and engineer who entered the service of the sultans of Amid, modern Diyarbakir, in northern Mesopotamia, in 1181. Little is known about his life but in 1206 he finished writing his *Book of Knowledge of Ingenious Mechanical Devices*, which he dedicated to his ruler. This book become so popular that it was later translated from the original Arabic into Persian and Turkish. Scholars today consider it to be the definitive work on mechanics in the mediaeval Islamic world. Although no other Arabic work shows such a wide grasp of mechanical principles, there are many omissions. For example, the book does not contain any mention of the making of astrolabes or balances, crafts in which Islamic scientists excelled. But al-Jazari chose to describe those machines which he felt would please his sultan. His descriptions have left a clear picture of the achievements and failures of mediaeval Arabic engineering.

Some of the machines described by al-Jazari are purely utilitarian. An example is a water-raising device in which a water-wheel, operating through cogs along its shaft, raises in sequence a series of water-scoops. Other devices included in the book are only for entertainment value. Among these are trick drinking vessels some of which appeared to contain water but could not be emptied, while others, seemingly empty, would allow water to be poured from them; both of these employed principles still to be found in practical joke devices. Most of al-Jazari's machines, however, fall between these two extremes: while being useful they are also amusing. His descriptions of fountains and water-clocks belong to this category.

The driving mechanism of al-Jazari's clocks was usually a weight attached to a cord that ran over a pulley-wheel on the same shaft as the dial or other time indicator. The rate at which the weight fell was controlled, for example, by a float which was fixed to the other end of the cord and which rode in a water tank from which the water was slowly discharging. In other cases an automatically tipping bucket gradually filled with water—when it tipped, the bucket struck a ratchet allowing a cog wheel to move forward one space, the vessel righting itself after emptying.

Most of the mechanical principles adopted by al-Jazari were very old. His machines incorporated cogs, gears, cams, ratchets, pulleys and levers. For the first time in the history of either Europe or Islam the crankshaft is used, and even if it was not invented by al-Jazari himself, it must have been quite novel in his day.

The majority of al-Jazari's machines involve the use of water and to this extent he was essentially a hydraulic engineer. In a country that was habitually short of water this is hardly surprising, although it is curious that, apart from his water-raising machines, so few of his devices had a practical purpose.

Environmental factors did not entirely influence the path that al-Jazari and his fellow engineers followed. The near obsession with amusing but not necessarily functional machines can be traced directly back to the writings of the ancient Greek engineers, such as those of Hero of Alexandria (*q.v.*), whose works had been translated into Arabic. The highly literate Islamic rulers had thus learned to expect their engineers to produce such devices, many of which are mentioned in Arabic literature such as the *Arabian Nights*.

Two of Ismaeel al-Jazari's devices, first a water clock with a float moving an indicator across the 'dial' of 12 circles, and below this, an ox-powered water raising device. The style makes the drawings hard to follow.

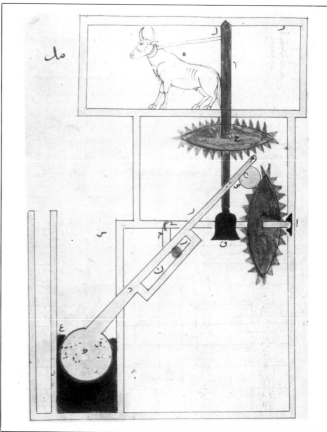

JENNER, Edward (1749-1823)

In Dr Jenner's time, smallpox was the most dread of diseases. Nearly everyone caught it, and in a bad epidemic as many as one out of three died of it. Those who survived it were usually pockmarked as a result, their skin pitted and scarred. An extreme case could make a face horrible to look at, and such disfigurement was feared more than death. The disease begins with a fever, and about two days later eruptions occur on the skin, which eventually scab over; when the scabs fall off, the scars remain.

Smallpox was one of the reasons for the relative ease with which the white men overcame the Indians in North America; because the traditional methods of treating the ill among the Indians were the very opposite of those required for a contagious disease, the Indians were continually weakened by it. For a long time the disease was confused with great pox (syphilis).

A mild case of smallpox was much better than none at all, because it conferred immunity on the victim from future outbreaks. For this reason, in Turkey and China there were attempts to catch the disease from people who had mild cases, and even attempts at inoculation with material from blisters on mild cases. This was very risky, for there was no guarantee that the new case would be a mild one. In the 18th century the idea of inoculation reached England from Turkey; it was not commonly practiced, but it excited medical interest.

Edward Jenner was the son of a clergyman at Berkeley, Gloucestershire, England. At the age of thirteen he was apprenticed to a surgeon, and received his medical degree in 1792. Like many medical men of his time, he was also interested in natural history, and competent enough in it to prepare and arrange specimens from Captain Cook's first voyage, and to be offered a post on the second.

Jenner preferred to practice medicine in Berkeley. In Gloucestershire and other counties of western England, there was a local tradition that people such as milkmaids who had caught cowpox were immune to smallpox. Cowpox, a relatively mild and localized illness, was not familiar to most medical men, but it is now thought that the viruses which cause several similar diseases are all derived from a common ancestor. At any rate, inoculation with one provides immunity to the others.

In 1796, Jenner inoculated a healthy boy with cowpox, using material from a blister on a milkmaid who had cowpox. The boy developed cowpox, but then was immune to smallpox. Further experimentation took time, because of the problem of finding people with active cases of cowpox,

Below: Gillray's caricature of the effects of vaccination, 1802. The inoculator is Pearson and the page holding the bucket is Woodville. Both these doctors were more famous in 1802 than Jenner.

The Cow-Pock _ or _ the Wonderful Effects of the New Inoculation! _ Vide the Publications of ye Anti Vaccine Society

but Jenner found ten people who had had cowpox and the associated immunity; he then discovered that cowpox is contagious among humans, and carries the immunity with it. In 1798 he published a summary of his findings with the title (here abbreviated) *An Inquiry into the Causes and Effects of . . . the Cow Pox.*

Jenner coined the word 'vaccination' to describe his process of inoculation, from the Latin words *vacca* (cow) and *vaccinia* (cowpox). His research was controversial, not least because nobody knew how inoculation worked until Pasteur (*q.v.*) explained it fifty years later. Jenner had purposely infected a child with cowpox and then smallpox; if the boy had become ill or died, Jenner would have been considered a criminal instead of a hero. But so great was the dread of smallpox that vaccination was quickly accepted; failures could easily be traced to poor technique. The British royal family was vaccinated; the first child to be inoculated in Russia was named Vaccinov; in 1807 Bavaria became the first country to make vaccination compulsory and other nations followed. Such was Jenner's fame and popularity that some British civilians being held prisoner by the French during the Napoleonic Wars were released because Jenner's name appeared on a petition.

Parliament awarded Jenner large sums of money, but the College of Physicians would not elect him a member in 1813 because he was unconcerned about the medical classics, such as the theories of Hippocrates. In the USA, Harvard medical school's Benjamin Waterhouse (1754–1846) took up the technique of vaccination, and in 1806 President Thomas Jefferson wrote to Jenner that 'Future generations will know . . . only that the loathsome smallpox existed and by you has been extirpated'.

This was over-optimistic. Although the incidence of smallpox has been dramatically reduced in developed countries, it is still very much alive. It is so rare in places like the USA that the occasional case of it is sometimes not diagnosed correctly until it has spread in the hospital. Epidemics still happen in under-developed countries; one of the factors in the incidence of smallpox seems to be the availability of mechanical refrigeration for storage of the vaccine.

Although it was a long time before any other diseases were brought under control, Jenner died knowing that he had relieved mankind of its terrible fear of smallpox. His qualities of optimism, personal courage and intelligent inquiry were perhaps typical of the best minds of the 18th century.

Opposite page: Edward Jenner, from 'The Gallery of Portraits', Vol VI, London 1833.

Below: a mass vaccination clinic in the East End of London. From 'The Graphic', London, 8 April 1871.

JOULE, James Prescott (1818-1889)

Manchester was a major centre of the industrial revolution. All the technologies associated with the industries were practiced in Manchester; and there was also an active scientific movement, centred on the Literary and Philosophical Society.

James Prescott Joule, born in 1818, was the second son of a brewer in nearby Salford. He studied for a while under John Dalton (*q.v.*), which helped to mould his practical scientific attitude as also did his Manchester environment, but Joule was mainly self-taught in science. When electricity became a fashionable science in the 1830s, nobody knew what, if any, were the limitations of the battery and the newly invented electric motor; it seemed possible that they could yield infinite power. Young Joule, inspired by this hope, applied his scientific genius to the perfection of the electric motor. But after three years he had to confess that, at best, his battery-driven motor was barely one fifth as efficient as the Cornish steam-engine, weight for weight of fuel used; zinc in the first case, coal in the second.

After this he went on to study the heat caused by an electric current. He found that it was proportional to the current squared multiplied by the resistance of the conductor. (Because of this law electrical energy is now transmitted at high voltage and low current so that heat losses are minimized; hence the high voltage grid distribution system used in most countries.)

The next step was the discovery that the more work the motor did, the less the heat generated in the circuit. Joule realized that heat and work were interchangeable, in fact that heat is a form of energy. The accepted idea then was that heat was a material substance, a 'subtle fluid' called 'caloric'. If heat and work are interchangeable, however, the exchange rate between them should always be the same. He therefore carried out many experiments to prove that, no matter how you turned mechanical energy into heat (for example by friction or compression), the work done was always in the same proportion to the heat produced. The *mechanical equivalent of heat* is an absolutely fixed exchange rate for all circumstances, materials, or processes.

It took years to convince the scientific world of his views. Joule was a diffident, retiring man. He gave few public lectures. From 1849 onwards, however, two years after his marriage, his views began to gain prevalence thanks to the help of Lord Kelvin (*q.v.*) (William Thomson), with whom he later collaborated. Thereafter his task was to measure the

mechanical equivalent of heat as accurately as possible. He used a set of brass paddles, driven by falling weights, to stir water in a brass calorimeter, and thermometers of great accuracy. In his last experiments (1878) he obtained a result very close to the modern one.

After the death of his wife in 1854 Joule became something of a scientific recluse, devoting his time to research and to the affairs of the Royal Society, of which he was a Fellow, and the Manchester Literary and Philosophical Society.

Joule was also one of the first to put the kinetic theory of gases on a firm basis. He contributed to many branches of physical science, but his main achievements were the establishment of the mechanical equivalence of heat and the axiom of the conservation of energy. The international unit of work is now known as the joule, and 4179 joules of work are produced for every kilocalorie of heat.

James Prescott Joule, depicted below in an unusual combined portrait and diagram, was the son of a wealthy brewer, and his private means allowed him to devote his time to scientific reserach. Here he is shown comparing the heating effects of two coils of insulated wire, submerged in water and insulated in a calorimeter to reduce heat losses.

Below left: schematic diagram of the experiment for which he is best known: finding the mechanical equivalent of heat. Falling weights turn a paddle wheel in water, heating it; the temperature rise is directly proportional to the distance they have fallen.

KELVIN, Lord (1824-1907)

Lord Kelvin, born William Thomson, was responsible for stimulating much of the scientific progress and practical industrial advance in the latter half of the nineteenth century. He is remembered by scientists for his contributions to electromagnetic theory, thermodynamics and geophysics, and by society for his profound influence in the growth of electrical engineering, practical mathematics and navigation.

William Thomson was born in Belfast of Scottish-Irish ancestors but he and his family moved to Glasgow in 1832 when his father, a self-educated mathematician, was elected to a chair at the University. His early education was received solely from his devoted father and he entered Glasgow University at the age of 10. Before he was 16 he produced a lasting work on the origin of the Earth's shape. In 1841 he entered Cambridge University and, characteristically, worked harder on research interests than on examinations.

After graduation Thomson worked with Regnault in Paris on the measurement of heat constants for use in the development of the steam engine. This early practical experience influenced his later formulating (almost simultaneously with Clausius) of the laws of thermodynamics and a unique proposal for an absolute system of temperature measurement, which is still called the Kelvin scale.

At 22, Thomson was elected to a chair at Glasgow University, to his father's great delight. Though repeatedly offered positions at Cambridge and Oxford, he remained at Glasgow for the rest of his life. Here he began research on magnetism, later perfecting sensitive current meters. He also set up one of the first laboratories for physics instruction, and co-authored a pioneering text on applied mathematics.

Thomson's continued work in thermodynamics launched him into many debates in later years on the age of the Earth. His work indicated that the Earth could not be much older than 100 million years—far too little a time to satisfy the time scales required by uniformitarian geologists and Darwinists. He remained always convinced of his work on the Earth, even as, close to the end of his life, radioactive heat sources in the Earth were discovered that allowed greatly increased measurements of its age.

By 1855, after publishing over 90 papers, several of which were very influential in the later discovery of radio waves by Hertz, Thomson became involved in the design and construction of the first successful trans-Atlantic submarine telegraph cables. He quickly saw through many design problems that required precise knowledge of physical principles of electrical conduction. In 1866, when two efficient cables were stretched across the Atlantic, Thomson was knighted by Queen Victoria for his participation in the revolutionary venture. In 1892 Thomson was again honoured by a peerage as Baron Kelvin of Largs. Thomson chose the name 'Kelvin' after a local river; the town of Largs was near his country residence, reportedly one of the first to be illuminated by electricity.

Thomson's life span carried him from the age of Victorian classical science into the beginnings of a new era where some of his most cherished concepts—those of the all-pervading ether and the vortex theory of the atom—began to be replaced. To the end, William Thomson was an untiring and prodigious worker, whose greatest aim, as one of the last great classical minds, was the unification of all physical reality into one exact and homogeneous scheme.

Lord Kelvin, left, is commemorated in the name of the Kelvin (absolute) temperature scale, but much of his work was on electricity. He invented the mirror galvanometer, shown below, as an aid to telegraphy; using a mirror reflecting a beam of light instead of a needle makes small deflections easier to see.

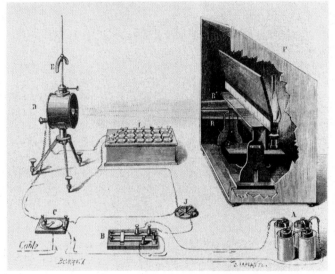

KEPLER, Johannes (1571-1630)

Kepler gave the first substantially correct description of the solar system in his *New Astronomy* (1609). His three laws of planetary motion were shown by Newton (*q.v.*) to be consequences of the law of Universal Gravitation. He also made significant contributions to mathematics and to optics, and the inverting refracting telescope he designed in 1611 was adopted so widely that it is generally known simply as the 'astronomical telescope'. Religion, however, seems to have been the driving force behind Kepler's scientific work.

Johannes Kepler was born into an unconventional family in Weil der Stadt, near Stuttgart. He was born with defective eyesight and, as a child, was in constant ill-health, contracting smallpox when he was four years old. He was left with permanent weakness in his hands, which later prevented him from constructing his own telescope. (On the few occasions when he later made astronomical observations he always arranged for other people to be present to confirm what he saw.) Kepler's precocious brilliance and the exceptional educational facilities ensured him of an education in which his parents had had little interest. His outspoken opinions, whether right or wrong, on religion and science made him unpopular at school, but his scientific genius and precision did not go unnoticed by his colleagues and patrons.

Kepler, a Protestant, had intended to enter the Church, on completion of his university studies, but was persuaded by his teachers to accept a post teaching mathematics at Graz. At the University of Tübingen, Kepler had been taught that the planets moved around the Sun rather than around the Earth, and in his first published work, *Mysterium Cosmographicum* (1597), he points out that the new system has the great advantage of explaining various facts not explained by the old one: for instance, the fact that Venus and Murcury are never seen far from the Sun. The new system also enables calculation of the relative sizes of the orbits of the planets, and Kepler found that these orbits could be constructed fairly accurately as spheres fitted between the five regular polyhedra, each polyhedron being inscribed in a planetary sphere and having the next sphere inscribed within it. (A regular polyhedron is a three-dimensional figure with sides all of the same shape and size; the commonest example is a cube.) The physical fact that there were six planetary spheres was thus explained by the geometrical fact that there were only five regular polyhedra. Kepler's theory is a geometrical formulation of the law now more familiar to astronomers as the algebraic Titius-Bode low of planetary distances. It is explicable in terms of statistical mechanics.

Proudly he sent copies of his book to several leading scholars including Galileo (*q.v.*) and Brahe (*q.v.*). But it was not until 1600, when religious persecution finally drove him and his Austrian wife from Graz, that he met the Dane Tycho Brahe in Prague where he was then established as Imperial Mathematician. Kepler became his assistant and was assigned to study the orbit of Mars, a notoriously difficult planet because of its closeness to the also rapidly moving Earth.

Tycho had set Kepler to work on the orbit of Mars, since predictions of the planet's position had proved to be seriously in error. Kepler later described his eight-year 'battle with Mars' in the *New Astronomy of the Planet Mars, reasoned from causes* (1609), in which he gives orbits for all the known planets and in which his first two laws are found: the orbit of each planet is an ellipse with the Sun in one of its foci, and a line drawn between the planet and the Sun will sweep out equal areas in equal times as the planet moves around the orbit. When Brahe died in 1601, Kepler succeeded him as Imperial Mathematician. After various legal battles with Tycho's heirs Kepler was allowed to continue to use Tycho's immense and treasured store of accurate observations of positions of stars and planets.

Upon the death of Rudolph II in 1612, Kepler moved to Linz and avoided the turmoil of civil war and epidemics in Prague. Matthias, Rudolph's successor, confirmed his title of Imperial Mathematician, which he retained until his death. In Linz, Kepler, who had been widowed before his return to Austria, married again against the advice of his friends—for Susanna Reutlinger had neither rank nor wealth. His second marriage seems to have been happier than his first, but these were difficult years for Kepler. Against the turbulent background of war, the death of his favourite daughter, religious rejection and his mother's witch trial, Kepler wrote what he considered to be his most important work, the *Harmony of the World* (1619). There seems to have been no irony intended. In the course of this work, Kepler states his third law: the squares of the times taken by the planets to complete their orbits are proportional to the cubes of the mean distances of the planets from the Sun. He also examines the relations between geometrical figures, musical intervals (expressed as ratios of lengths of

Johannes Kepler, shown below, believed that his geometrical construction, bottom, was the basic form of the Universe. It has some basis in fact.

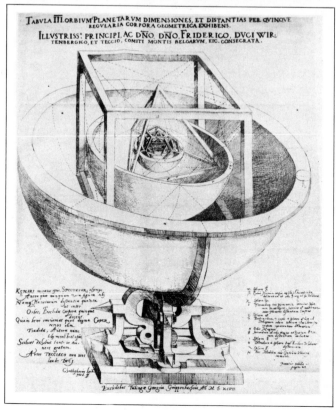

Frontispiece of Kepler's Rudolphine Tables, *naming ancient and recent astronomers; Kepler himself works by candlelight on the left side of the base.*

vibrating strings), astrological aspects, and the ratios of the velocities of planets at different points of their orbits. In the *Harmony of the World* he explains that laws of Nature show the ideas according to which God created the World, ideas which Man, being made in the image of God, is capable of grasping and should strive to grasp since they bring him closer to its Creator.

Kepler was driven from Linz by religious persecution, and spent the last years of his life in Silesia under the protection of Count Wallenstein, a Protestant military leader then at the height of his power. Kepler finally completed his work on the *Rudolphine Tables* nearly 30 years after Tycho's death. Chaotic conditions, printing difficulties and lack of finances were probably the most influential factors in delaying the publication of these long-awaited tables. Logarithms, then newly invented, were used by Kepler in calculating these tables, which give the positions of stars and planets, based on Tycho's observations and Kepler's laws.

The final trek Kepler made to try to collect some of the salary long owed to him was his last. A few days after his arrival in Regensburg (Ratisbon) he died of a fever. The cemetery where he was buried was destroyed during the Thirty Years War, but the epitaph which he wrote for himself is preserved—'I measured the skies, now the shadows I measure, skybound was the mind, earthbound the body rests'.

KEYNES, J M (1883-1946)

John Maynard Keynes, who revolutionised the thinking of twentieth century economists, was born in Cambridge into an upper-class and highly intellectual family environment. His father, John Neville Keynes, well known as the author of *The Scope of Political Economy*, was a fellow of Pembroke College. His mother was one of the earliest students of Newnham College. There was therefore an abundance of intellectual discussion in his childhood upbringing. Educated at Eton, and at Kings College, Cambridge, his talents had the fullest opportunity to flower. Like other influential economists before him he specialized first in mathematics; then he studied economics under Marshall (*q.v.*). After some time as a civil servant in the India Office he returned to teach economics at Cambridge. This he was to do for the rest of his life, along with advising the government at the Treasury.

In 1925 he married a famous Russian ballerina, Lydia Lopokova. The couple spent a considerable part of their time in the countryside in Sussex, and Keynes became a keen part-time farmer.

He first gained world-wide fame when in 1919 he published *The Economic Consequences of the Peace*, which argued quite correctly that for the victorious nations of the First World War to impose heavy sanctions on Germany had been a big mistake. Although this anti-establishment view did not endear him to the traditional economic authorities of the day, he was subsequently frequently asked to advise the government; in the Second World War he was particularly active in the Treasury, in organising the nation's financial resources and in negotiating the setting up of the International Monetary Fund with United States representatives.

Apart from economic theory and advice, there were many other sides to his life. To start with he was an astonishingly successful financier, converting a few thousand pounds into some half a million by dealing on the foreign exchange, commodity and stock markets; he also advised Kings College on how to run their finances and made for them extremely large sums of money. At the same time he took considerable interest in the arts, founding the Arts Theatre at Cambridge. In politics he devoted much time to the Liberal party. And earlier on in his career he published, in 1921, a *Treatise on Probability* which is still an important landmark for statisticians.

But it is as an economic theorist that Keynes will be known longest. For the early part of his career Keynes was simply a notable economist, developing the tradition that Marshall had established. In 1936, however, he published *The General Theory of Employment, Interest and Money*, a book which set out a new theory of the capitalist economy, based on the doubts that had accumulated in his mind over the applicability of the previous (neoclassical) theory. The chief advantage of his new theory was that it was able to explain the systematic and continued existence of unemployment in the modern Western economy. It explained why Adam Smith's 'invisible hand' of the market did not seem to be working for the Western world's economies which were in depression for long periods of time.

Keynes' argument rested on a rejection of Say's Law (after J B Say, 1767–1832) which had been adhered to by earlier economists. This law stated that supply would always create its own demand, and that a situation of over-

John Maynard Keynes, photographed in his study in Gordon Square, London, 1940.

production was therefore impossible, at least in the long run. Keynes argued that the aggregate supply of goods and services could indeed by suppressed even if there was spare capacity in the economy, if the aggregate demand was too low. Firms would not offer employment if there was no expectation of selling their products. Therefore what determined the total amount of employment offered and therefore the level of unemployment was the level of aggregate 'effective demand'. And the level of effective demand was in turn determined principally by its three main constituents: consumers' demand, businessmen's demand for more investment, and the government's expenditure.

One central part therefore of Keynes' theory was his theory of aggregate consumer's demand. He argued that this depended on the income they received, in such a way that, for every £100 increase in income, consumers' demand increases, but by less than £100 (for example £80). Thus, suppose income were to increase by £100 for some reason, that leads to a £80 increase in consumers' demand. But this latter increase leads to a further increase in income, since that increase is spent on consumer goods which people have to be employed to produce. Thus, where there was an original increase of £100 there is now an increase of £180 on income. And indeed, some portion of the extra £80 will also get spent which will again lead to more employment. This process, whereby an initial increase in income is multiplied, is called the 'multiplier'.

Keynes integrated the concept of the multiplier into a complete model of the economy, which could explain persistent unemployment. For, according to him, the amount that businessmen decide to invest is variable depending on the volatile mood of investors. Should their mood become depressed they would lower investment, which would lower income and employment. And then the multiplier process takes over in the downward direction, so that the economy diverges further and further away from the full employment position.

To complete the argument Keynes had to show that the economy could in theory rest in a position of unemployment. The previous economic orthodoxy would have argued that if investment fell then savings would also fall, consumption would rise, and all that would happen would be a switchover from machine industries to consumer goods industries—this is the essence of Say's Law; there would be no general downturn in the economic activity. But Keynes argued that investors are not the same people as savers, and that there existed no mechanism to ensure that savings fell when investment fell. In particular, the rate of interest was unable to perform this function.

Alternatively, the previous economic orthodoxy would (and did) argue that if there is unemployment then this means that wages are too high; therefore unemployment was caused by unions who refused to allow wages to fall. Keynes argued that wages were not too high anyway, since depressions were caused not by union wage policies but by fluctuations in the level of investment. Moreover, if wages were lowered this would lead to lower demand (because workers would have less money to spend) and lower prices, but would not solve the unemployment problem.

Thus the only way to break clear of the persistent unemployment equilibrium to which the economies of the Western World had sunk was to stimulate the level of effective demand deliberately by government policy. This meant the government increasing its own level of spending, or alternatively decreasing taxes, thereby leaving more spending money in the hands of the public. After the initial stimulus to demand, the multiplier would do its work, and the economy could be restored to full employment.

The theory thus produced a clear-cut policy for governments to adopt: increase government spending to avoid unemployment. (Also the converse is true: if aggregate demand was too high, decrease government spending to avoid inflation.) And in fact this produced a neat justification for what governments had by 1936 already begun to do.

Keynes' arguments are most distinctive when he is discussing an economy in depression. For an economy at full employment already, his discussion of monetary policies and expenditure policies are important, but are not fundamentally different from the orthodox arguments that existed before. Possibly for this reason the 1970s have seen a reassessment by governments and economists of the correctness of Keynes' arguments; whereas before then since World War II Keynesian policies had reigned supreme. There are frequent attempts to reinterpret the meaning of *The General Theory*. It seems clear that the system of that book is the economics of a depressed economy. Keynes produced there a fundamental theoretical explanation of why the 'invisible hand' of the market can break down.

Politically Keynes' theories lent themselves to a somewhat leftish interpretation, for they led to the advocacy of greater government expenditure. However the appearance is deceptive. For Keynes was a passionate advocate of individualism and of free enterprise; the role of the government should, he thought, be limited to enabling a healthy climate for these to flourish. In many quarters, then, he was regarded as the saviour of capitalism.

KIRCHHOFF, Gustav Robert (1824-1887)

Kirchhoff was an important figure in the development of physics in the 19th century, a time when a huge number of discoveries were made in all fields.

He was born in Königsberg in Prussia, the third son of a lawyer. As a child he was happy and talkative, small for his age and rather delicate-looking. Kirchhoff entered university at the age of 18, intending to read mathematics. He was impatient with the way physics and chemistry were taught, but greatly influenced by the physicist Franz Neumann. His first published paper was inspired by Neumann and won him a prize which lead to his election to the Berlin physicists' society. Kirchhoff was greatly surprised. He felt that the social life he had been leading might have given the impression of idleness. His paper on electronic conduction in straight and circular conductors also served as his thesis.

Kirchhoff's early work extended electrical conduction theory by an analogy to heat flow, discussing the character of conduction in three dimensions. Later, in 1857, he applied this work to the propagation of electric signals in a telegraph cable, eventually proposing, in 1880, the useful physical principle that thermal conductivity in a solid is proportional to electrical conductivity. In the same line of work, and using theoretical deductions by Weber, Kirchhoff showed that the velocity of an electrical impulse was equal to the velocity of

light—a most important discovery for the eventual work of James Clerk Maxwell (*q.v.*) in electromagnetic theory.

Kirchhoff was given a government grant to go to Paris, but decided to go to Berlin instead. In 1850 he succeeded in obtaining a professorship in experimental physics in Breslau. The next year Robert Bunsen (inventor of the bunsen burner) joined the university as professor of chemistry. A great friendship and an important scientific bond between the two was formed. In 1854 Kirchhoff moved to Heidelberg and joined his friend Bunsen. They worked more or less together, on projects that were to become Kirchhoff's greatest contributions to science—the formulation and elucidation of the basic laws of radiation. Kirchhoff and Bunsen were the pioneers of chemical spectroscopy.

While on holiday at Königsberg two years later, he met Clara, 14 years his junior, the daughter of his old teacher, Richelot, and married her the next year.

For years scientists had been puzzled by the fact that when light from the Sun and stars was observed through a spectroscope, patterns of dark lines were revealed that were similar to bright spectral line patterns produced by hot metallic vapours created by placing metallic salts in a flame. Early workers, such as the physicist Fraunhofer, might have realized the true significance of the coincidence had it not been for that fact that, in almost every vapour spectrum, two bright yellow lines, very close together, were always present —no matter what was used as the source of the vapour. By mid-century, workers began seriously to suspect that the persistence of these two lines, identical to those produced by sodium, in all observed spectra, were simply due to the presence of sodium in extremely small quantities as an impurity in all laboratory samples of metallic salts. Kirchhoff's refined and precise laboratory techniques helped to show that this was indeed the case. He then devised a very simple technique (which Foucault (*q.v.*) had anticipated but had not carried out fully) of superimposing sunlight and a sodium flame to show that bright lines in the flame spectrum of sodium could be changed into dark lines in the solar

spectrum (the 'D' lines designated by Fraunhofer in his studies of the Sun's spectrum) simply by making the sunlight intense enough as it passed through the flame.

These two steps gave Kirchhoff the key to the modern realm of astrophysics, for when he put them together, he realized that the spectra of the Sun and stars yielded their elemental composition and revealed intimate details of their physical structure. Since Kirchhoff's time, astronomers have extended and refined his work, but the concept remains.

Shortly afterwards, in 1862, Kirchhoff generalized his findings in spectrum analysis. He demonstrated that the absorptive and emissive powers of any radiating body are the same when that body is at the same temperature as its surroundings—the fundamental statement concerning the 'ideal radiator' or 'black body', which is basic to all later developments in quantum theory.

In 1869 Kirchhoff's wife died and his habitual cheerfulness was not restored until his marriage three years later with Luise Brömmel, who worked at an eye hospital. In 1874, after several refusals, Kirchhoff accepted the chair of mathematical physics at Berlin where he worked on problems in analytical dynamics and continued his work on electrical conduction. In 1881 he was elected German delegate to the Electrical Congress in Paris. Kirchhoff died in Berlin, leaving a legacy of disciplined instruction in mathematical physics.

KOROLYOV, Sergei (1906-1966)

Korolyov was one of the most important men in the Soviet space programme and occupied a key position from an early age right through to his death, by which time he had achieved within the scientific and technological profession in Russia a unique reputation. He nevertheless suffered the fate of many other Russian scientists by a total absence of public acknowledgement by the authorities of the major part he played.

Korolyov was born at Zhitomir in the Ukraine on 30 December 1906, the son of a Ukrainian schoolmaster, and in 1927 began work in the aircraft industry, although continuing his studies at the Moscow School of Aviation. In 1930 he graduated from the Aeromechanic Department of the Bauman Higher Technological School where his interest in rocketry had been stimulated by Konstantin Tsiolkovsky (*q.v.*). In the 1930s Korolyov worked on problems of jet and rocket propulsion, and in 1934 published *Rocket Flight in the Stratosphere*.

During World War II, Korolyov's activities were directed to developing a rocket-assisted take-off system, and the experience gained on the liquid fuel rocket accelerators for aircraft at that time helped him in his post-war work. This involved leading a group working on the design of an intercontinental ballistic missile, which became the design accepted by the authorities, and was later to be the basis of the Vostok launcher. Korolyov's activities, however, did not

Above left: Sergei Korolyov (right) with Yuri Gagarin, the first man in space, for whose single orbit he designed the Vostok spacecraft.

Left: the 4500kg Vostok, unlike American manned spacecraft, was designed to land on the ground instead of in water. The charred appearance is due to the heat of re-entry.

stop with the development of the carrier rocket; he was also instrumental in the construction of recoverable vehicles for man's flight into space and perhaps one of his most famous achievements was as chief designer of the satellite in which Yuri Gagarin made the first manned spaceflight in April 1961. He was also responsible for the design of the first rocket system to orbit the moon and take the Zond series of photographs of the other side. Korolyov's manned space-flight work extended to not only the original single-manned Vostok launcher, but the Voskhod multi-manned spacecraft and by this time he had become chief designer for the whole Russian space research programme.

After his early work on spacecraft used for orbiting the Earth and Moon the automatic spacecraft developed under his guidance included the first interplanetary automatic stations to Venus (February 1961) and to Mars (November 1962) as well as interplanetary space probes of the Zond series which began in 1962 for both lunar and Martian flights. Korolyov also participated in the development of the first Soviet communication satellite, Molniya, and he shared in designing automatic lunar stations which ensured soft landing of research instruments on the Moon.

Korolyov was elected a full member of the USSR Academy of Sciences in 1958, and for a number of years he was a member of its Presidium. In addition, he won the Lenin Prize and received many other Soviet decorations. It was not, therefore, lack of honours bestowed on him which was the irony of Korolyov's life, but rather the lack of identification as to exactly why and on what subject these honours had been earned. Soviets will remember him indeed as a pioneer of their major technological achievements and the world will remember him also for his contribution to the technical progress of mankind. He died in Moscow in 1966, and after his distinguished career was accorded one of the highest honours in the Soviet Union in that he was buried in the Kremlin Wall, an honour reserved for Russians of exceptional distinction. Among them is Yuri Gagarin, the first man into space, whom Korolyov helped on his successful mission.

LAVOISIER, Antoine (1743-1794)

Antoine Laurent Lavoisier, the founder of modern chemistry, was born into a wealthy Parisian family. He originally trained as a lawyer, following the family tradition, but also studied mathematics, astronomy and botany. His interest in science was aroused by the geologist J E Guettard and Lavoisier helped him to prepare a mineralogical map of France. He then studied chemistry with G F Rouelle, one of the most important French chemists of the day.

After early work on the contents of mineral springs, and a proposed scheme for lighting cities, he was elected, in 1768, to the Academy of Sciences, of which he later became director and then treasurer. He decided to abandon law and devote himself to science; to do this, though, in an age when no one could hope to make a living from science, he had to secure some other income. He thus joined the 'Tax Farm', which was a private organization responsible for collecting the French taxes. This later proved to be a fateful decision for Lavoisier, but meanwhile he achieved a comfortable income, and he was soon able to marry Marie Paulze, the daughter of one of his partners. She was only 14 when they

Below: Antoine and Marie Lavoisier, painted by David.

Bottom: apparatus designed by Cavendish and used by Lavoisier to show that water consists of hydrogen and oxygen. Water runs through a heated tube containing iron, which absorbs some oxygen; the residue is condensed and hydrogen collected in the jar on the right.

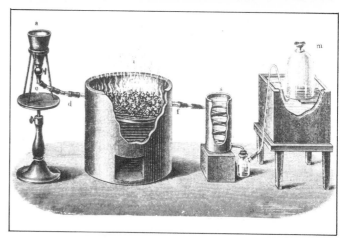

married in 1771, but she soon became an invaluable help: she learned English to keep him abreast of scientific developments, and she took notes and drawings of his experiments. Theirs was a very happy but childless marriage. Eleven years after Lavoisier's death, she married the American physicist Sir Benjamin Thompson (Count Rumford *q.v.*), but they later separated.

Lavoisier's most famous contribution to chemistry was his demonstration in 1775 of the nature of combustion, in which the burning substance combines with oxygen. In the same year, he was appointed Inspector of Gunpowder in the government and, until 1792, he and his wife lived at the arsenal. Chemistry in the eighteenth century had been freed from the wilder excesses of alchemy, but had no firm new aims to replace the discredited alchemical ones; chemists shared no agreed purpose, and achieved few advances. Lavoisier determined to reorganize chemistry completely. He set out on what he described in a notebook of 1773 as 'an immense series of experiments, destined to bring about a revolution in physics and chemistry'—and this was indeed what he achieved.

Lavoisier's new system was built on a new conception of chemical elements, which he defined as substances that had not so far been decomposed to simpler substances; this gave him 55 elements, as opposed to the four or less that had previously been accepted. Together with three collaborators, C L Berthollet, A F de Fourcroy, and L B Guyton de Morveau, he devised a new nomenclature to describe the different compounds of these many elements, which we still use today.

Once accepted, as it rapidly was, his new system gave chemists plenty to do: there were thousands of compounds to analyze qualitatively and quantitatively, expressing the results in Lavoisier's terms. The introduction of atomic theory some 20 years later by Dalton (*q.v.*) made the expression of these results even more exact, and chemistry has never looked back.

Lavoisier, a seemingly tireless experimenter, did not confine himself to chemistry, and among his scientific interests the process of respiration concerned him greatly. He did much to improve social and economic conditions and brought about scientific agricultural improvements.

His scientific work was brought to a premature end as a result of the French Revolution. Tax-collectors are seldom popular, and Lavoisier, together with the other partners in the Tax Farm including his father-in-law, was convicted on trumped-up charges and guillotined on 8 May 1794.

LILIENTHAL, Otto (1848-1896)

Otto Lilienthal was one of the leading figures in aviation pioneering, as well as being an engineer and inventor. During the course of his life he made many hundreds of heavier than air unpowered flights, and although accounts vary as to the distances he covered in his gliders it seems fairly well established that during the 1890s he achieved flights of at least 750 feet (229 m).

He was born in Anklam, Prussia on 23 May 1848 and trained in engineering at Potsdam Technical School, after which he studied at the Berlin Technical Academy from 1867 to 1870. As boys he and his brother Gustav used to study the flight of birds, in particular that of the stork, from which he established the fact than an arched surface wing was the most suitable design for heavier than air flight, and also the importance of rising air currents for soaring. In 1889 he published a book called *Der Vogel flug als Grundlage der Fliegekunst*, about bird flight, and this, together with his essays on flying machines in 1894, were acknowledged to be the basic works on aeronautics.

In 1880, after serving in the Franco-Prussian War, he founded his own engineering factory which produced marine signals, light steam motors, steel pulleys and sirens, many of

Reconstruction of one of Otto Lilienthal's gliders' showing how he supported himself on armrests, gripping a fixed crossbar which helped him control the craft.

which were his own inventions. During this time he carried on his aviation research and after much exhaustive experimentation with gliders and flying models with flapping wings he eventually built his first man carrying glider in 1891. This consisted of two curved, fabric covered wings to which he attached himself by his arms using his hanging body for balance. He launched himself from a running start and in fact even built an artificial hill 50 feet (15 m) high from which he was able to take off regardless of the direction of the wind. About this time he wrote 'The feat of launching by running down a slope into the wind until sufficient velocity is reached to lift the operator and his 40 pound wings requires practice. In the beginning the height should be moderate and the wings not too large or the wind will soon show that it is not to be trifled with. To those who from a modest beginning, and with gradually increased extent and elevation of flight, have gained full control of the apparatus, it is not in the least dangerous to cross deep and broad ravines.'

By 1893 the size of his glider had reached a 23 feet (7 m) span, with an overall plane surface of 16.7 sq yd (14 m²) and a weight of approximately 44 lb (20 kg). He continued his

In the legendary story of Icarus, wings made of feathers and wax were flown too near to the sun; the wax melted, and the man who would fly fell to his death. But in modern times men like Otto Lilienthal slowly and painstakingly collected data on the science of flight, culminating in the Wright brothers' first flight in 1903. Many of these pioneers, however, paid with their lives, like Icarus: Lilienthal was killed in a glider accident in 1897, a few weeks after this photograph was taken.

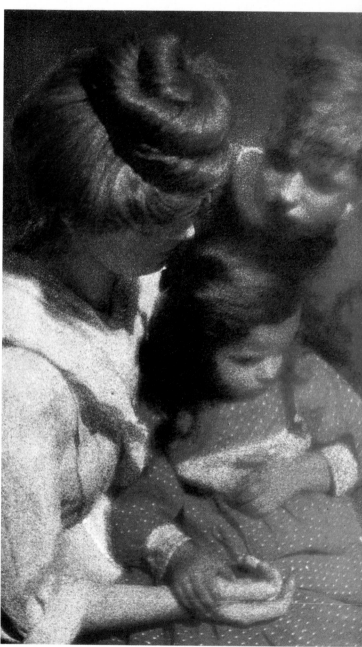

work on gliders until 1896 when he introduced a biplane powered by a small motor which flapped the wings. Before he could progress with this innovation, however, he was killed when his glider crashed in the hills near Rhinow on 9 August 1896.

His work, which directly inspired such other aviators as the Wright brothers (*q.v.*) and Octave Chanute, was continued after his death by his brother Gustav. Otto Lilienthal is commemorated by the Lilienthal Medal, one of the world's highest awards for soaring.

LUMIÈRE, Louis (1864-1948) and Auguste (1862-1954)

Louis and Auguste Lumière invented the cinema as we know it today. Though they were not the first to photograph movement, having been preceded by such pioneers as Marey, Muybridge and Edison (all *q.v.*), they were the first to project moving pictures on to a screen before a paying audience.

The Lumières' father, Antoine (1840–1906), was a French painter who turned to photography. When his sons were about twenty, they established a factory near their home town of Lyons to manufacture photographic materials, producing one of the early stripping films (films with a paper base which is stripped off before processing). In 1894, they saw in Paris Edison's Kinetoscope, patented three years earlier. The Kinetoscope's successful illusion of movement was achieved by viewing thirty pictures a second through a narrow slit, and this limited it to being a peep-show: not enough light reached the eye from each image to make projection possible.

The Lumière brothers (their very name is the French for 'light') perceived that any improvement on the Kinetoscope would require each picture to be held completely still for a split second. Louis, the mechanic (Auguste provided the

business brain), set to work developing a mechanism which would move film intermittently rather than continuously: the clue to solving the problem seems to have come from studying the movement of a sewing machine needle. Louis also realized that the peculiarity of the eye known as persistence of vision, the blending together by the brain of a series of still images into one continuous moving one, would work at a speed much slower than that used by Edison, and he settled on sixteen frames per second, which remained standard for cameras and projectors until the coming of sound to films over thirty years later.

On 13 February 1895, the Lumières patented a machine to photograph, develop and project moving pictures. The fact

Left: the 'cinématographe' could be used both as a projector, as here, with a separate carbon arc light, or closed up to form a light-tight camera.

Below left: Louis (wearing spectacles) and Auguste Lumière are shown here at work in their laboratory at Lyon, France.

that it did all three overcame problems of 'registering' (the positioning of images in precisely the same place on any piece of equipment) and ensured that its pictures were always steady. It was the vital breakthrough, and it is entirely proper that the name the Lumières gave to their portable, all-in-one box—the Cinématographe—should be that by which the industry which sprang from their invention would be known.

The first public performance of the Cinématographe was given in the 'India Room' of the Grand Café, Boulevard des Capucines, Paris, on 28 December 1895. On that date, cinema was born.

Though the Lumières had other achievements in the cinema, notably their 70 mm stereoscopic presentation at the 1900 Paris Exposition, their other greatest success took them back to still photographs. In 1904 they patented the Autochrome process. By covering photographic plates with tiny colour filters (actually, grains of potato starch dyed violet, orange and green), they made positive glass transparencies with very realistic and attractive colours, though the starch grains made them rather dark. The Autochrome, put on the market in 1907, was the first commercially successful photographic colour process.

MALTHUS, Thomas R (1766-1834)

Thomas Robert Malthus was one of the influential exponents of classical political economy. He was known in particular for his doctrine on population growth, which was throughout the nineteenth century a subject of debate, and which still influences discussions of population problems in less developed countries today.

His father was sufficiently wealthy to give him, one of eight children, a private education and to send him to Jesus College Cambridge, where he graduated in 1788. By then he was accomplished in English and French literature, in the classics, and in mathematics, as well as in political economy.

That same year he took Holy Orders. Then in 1793 he became a Fellow of Jesus College, but had to resign in 1804 when he married. After two years as a curate, he spent the rest of his life as Professor of Political Economy (the first such post to be held in Britain) at Haileybury College, which was owned by the East India Company. He had three children, two of whom survived him.

Malthus' ideas on population were first expounded in a pamphlet written in 1798, and five years later, after some travelling to investigate conditions in other countries, this was expanded into a book whose full title was *An Essay on the Principles of Population: A View of its Past and Present Effects on Human Happiness With an Enquiry Into Our Prospects Respecting The Future Removal or Mitigation Of the Evils Which It Occasions*. Malthus' view was that, while it was possible to go on expanding the production of food and the

basic means of subsistence, this would not keep up with the rate of population expansion. For food production could only be increased at the rate of increase of an arithmetic series of numbers (that is, 1—2—3—4—5 etc) but population would, if unchecked, expand at the rate of increase of a geometric series (that is, 1—2—4—8—16 and so on). That population does not in fact expand at this rate was due to the natural checks of poverty, war, sickness and famine, and to preventative checks such as 'moral restraint' or birth control. From this Malthus drew the conclusion that mankind was doomed to poverty, and that it was impossible for wages to rise for any length of time above a subsistence minimum. (Henceforth, political economy was known for several decades as the 'dismal science'.)

Moreover it followed that the natural checks to population growth should not be impeded by well-meaning governments. The Poor Law, which ensured that those who were destitute had at least some source of food to prevent starvation, should therefore, according to Malthus, be abolished.

There were problems in Malthus' argument. For he had provided that 'moral restraint' could allow workers to obtain wages above the subsistence level. Any critic who pointed to a society where workers were comparatively rich was countered with the view that those workers must be exercising 'moral restraint'. But while this left his doctrine impregnable to criticism, the force of it was diminished, for if 'moral restraint' were possible mankind was no longer condemned to poverty as Malthus claimed. Moreover, Malthus could provide no evidence—statistics being very hard to come by in those days—that the mechanisms he proposed actually operated.

However, Malthus' ideas soon became popular and widely accepted. This was partly because a census in 1801 seemed to indicate a sudden expansion of population (which was incorrectly taken as confirmation of his theories), and partly because of the extreme simplicity and reasonableness of the main proposition. But the main reason was that it provided a natural justification of the poverty in which most people lived, and therefore absolved the propertied classes from responsibility for it. Thus Malthus' writings were singled out for criticism by Marx (q.v.), who showed with his own theories that poverty was created by the economic system, and was not necessarily an inevitable fact of nature.

By the end of the nineteenth century, Malthus' doctrine had been completely discredited by the advance of technical progress in the newly industrialized countries; and so it died a gradual and natural death. However, the Malthusian spirit lingers on in the twentieth century, not only in discussions about developing countries which are said to suffer a new and more devastating population problem, but also in pessimistic modern discussions about the survival of mankind on limited energy and natural resources.

Malthus is also notable among economists for his 'theory of gluts', which he propounded in his second major publication, *Principles of Political Economy*, which was first published in 1820. In this he defended the importance to the economy of the 'unproductive consumer', one who consumes the products of productive labour without working productively himself. If there was insufficient 'effective demand' in the

economy there would be a tendency for it to stagnate, and to suffer from unemployment. This constituted a denial of Say's Law (after the French economist J B Say).

Say's Law was expounded most strongly by David Ricardo (1772–1823) who along with Malthus was one of the more influential economists of the early nineteenth century. This law was simply that supply would always create its own demand: that it was never possible to produce too much, and more pertinently that producers would never cut back production and employment for fear of lack of demand.

In the light of the new economics of the twentieth century, in particular that of J M Keynes, Malthus' denial of Say's Law was undoubtedly correct, even if his arguments did not carry the same force and simplicity as his population doctrine. However, his theory of gluts was not really an objective analysis of the economy; it was a defence of the land-owning classes to which he belonged. For, according to Malthus, the members of the capitalist class were by their nature not suited to consuming the profits from the workers' labour. Hence, the more these profits were dissipated in the form of rent to the owners of the land—who had the natural capacity to spend it—the more stable would be the economy. But in addition of course the landowners were thereby better off. Thus Malthus stood in a dual role, both as analyst of that newly emerged phenomenon, the capitalist economy, and as spokesman for a land-owning class with interests to defend against both the capitalist and working classes.

MARCONI, Guglielmo (1874-1937)

Guglielmo Marconi was an Italian, born in Bologna, but much of his pioneering work on wireless telegraphy, which led to his later development of radio communication and broadcasting, was done outside his home country, mainly in Britain, because the Italian government declined to give him financial support when he badly needed it.

Marconi was always more of a practical person than an academic and from an early age, to the displeasure of his father, he preferred tinkering with objects to studying. It was natural therefore that he should seize on the discovery by Heinrich Hertz, a German physicist, that energy could be transmitted from place to place in the form of electromagnetic radiation, just as James Clerk Maxwell (q.v.) had earlier predicted, for Marconi immediately saw the practical potential of 'Hertzian waves' as a means of communication.

Marconi was 20 when he first learnt of Hertz's work and he immediately embarked on a period of intense experimentation in two attic rooms of his family's country mansion outside Bologna. He filled these with equipment, including a coil and spark gap—for creating the electromagnetic waves —and a receiver for detecting them. Soon Marconi was able to show his mother (she was a source of constant encouragement, unlike his father) how a key which was pressed at one end of a room could cause a buzzer to sound 30 feet away.

Using his capacity for improving and inventing, Marconi gradually developed his apparatus so that he could transmit over greater and greater distances. And he soon discovered that a hill between transmitter and receiver was no obstacle. At that stage he emigrated to England in search of support, which he got, from both the Post Office and the War Office. By 1897, when he was 23, Marconi was sending wireless signals over a distance of nine miles.

Below: this 1896 photograph shows Guglielmo Marconi seated behind his first wireless telegraph.

Bottom: Marconi (centre) and assistants waiting for the first transatlantic radio signals in 1901. They were sent from Cornwall to St John's, Newfoundland.

The setting up of a company by Marconi and some British relatives, and the first transmission across the English Channel, followed in quick succession. In 1899 he visited the United States to demonstrate his technique—which by that time had to compete with those developed by other people and other companies—but the mission was not a great success because Marconi was reluctant to show off his then unpatented improvements to possible rival businesses. His aim by then, however, was to transmit across the Atlantic and this he attempted in spite of serious storm damage on both sides of the Atlantic to his original transmitters. The one at Poldhu in Cornwall was rebuilt and a temporary receiving aerial was flown on a kite in St John's, Newfoundland. Success came in late 1901 when he was 27, in the shape of the three dots that make up the letter 'S' in the morse code, which was the basis of all wireless communication in those days.

Marconi was closely involved in the commercial development of wireless and saw it installed in countless places including ships such as the *Titanic*, which sank in 1912, and the *Montrose* which carried the murderer Crippen to his arrest as the result of a ship-to-shore message in 1910. Marconi weathered a financial scandal surrounding his company (but not himself) in 1912 and after World War I devoted more of his time to his home country, both in a political and a technical sense. When he died in 1937 at the age of 63 the world paid the simplest and most impressive tribute—two minutes of radio silence.

MAREY, Etienne Jules (1830-1904)

Dr Etienne Marey combined a knowledge of medicine with a love of mechanics. This combination led him to invent a number of instruments for recording physiological change in animals and humans, and to realize that photography could arrest movements otherwise invisible to the eye. The result was a scientific measuring device which was in fact the first movie camera.

Marey was born in Beaune, in the French wine district of Burgundy. His father was a wine merchant, his mother a schoolteacher. He was sent to Paris to study medicine and, after taking his degree, began to develop measuring machines for use in diagnosing illnesses. His first such device, described in a scientific paper published in 1860, was the *sphygmograph*, which counted human pulse beats and recorded them on a revolving smoked glass disc. He went on to measure the wing movements of bees and pigeons, and the leg movements of horses and men. His machines were very ingenious: the horse, for instance, had a hollow rubber ball fitted inside each hoof, from which rubber tubes led, transmitting the variation in air pressure to a paper recorder in its rider's hands.

Marey, by now a Professor of Medicine, heard of the work of Eadweard Muybridge (*q.v.*) and was his host in Paris in 1881, arranging for him to give a demonstration to scientists there. From Muybridge's results, Marey perceived that photography was the answer to his problem of recording movement but, instead of Muybridge's many cameras, he used one. In 1882 his *fusil photographique* ('photographic gun') took twelve consecutive pictures per second. The images, the size of a postage stamp, were arranged round the edge of a revolving circular photographic glass plate, a development from the daguerreotype disc used nearly ten years earlier by the astronomer Pierre Jules Cesar Janssen (1824–1907) to capture the movement of the stars. Janssen's apparatus only made an exposure every seventy seconds and could hardly produce the illusion of movement. It was the advent of the dry photographic plate in 1880 which made possible Marey's shorter exposures and genuine analysis of motion.

The glass plate used in the photographic gun made it heavy and slow, and its pictures too small. But when George Eastman introduced gelatin-based film in 1885, Marey progressed to exposing sixty images per second, each 3.6 inches (9 cm) square. These were truly the first modern cinematograph films: lengths of film moving constantly, but stopping for a split second in front of a lens which was covered by a shutter while the film was moving. His experiments with cine techniques also involved time-lapse methods to speed up slow movements.

Marey was a scientist. He developed the inventions of Janssen and Muybridge, as he himself freely admitted, until they were capable of the split-second accuracy which he sought. He published his results freely. His pioneer work was continued by the famous Institut Marey, founded in Paris a year before he died. Had he been a businessman, he would probably now be acknowledged as the inventor of cinematography, instead of Louis and Auguste Lumière (*q.v.*), or any of the other claimants to that title.

Below: unacknowledged as the inventor of cinematography, Dr Etienne Marey nevertheless made the first continuous film record of movement.

Below left: Marey's 1882 'fusil photographique' (photographic gun) resembled a revolver loaded with film, giving 25 small pictures on a round plate.

Bottom: a further development, the 'chambre chronophotographique', presented his pictures of movement in this clearer form.

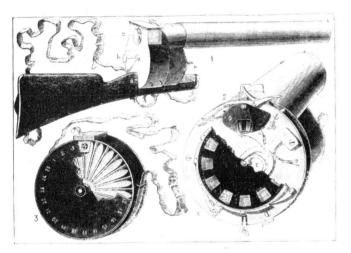

MARSHALL, Alfred (1842-1924)

Alfred Marshall was one of the greatest of the early 'neoclassical' economists, whose ideas have profoundly influenced the direction of economic thinking since the end of the last century.

Born into a typical middle-class Victorian family, his early education was at all times closely controlled by his father. As a result throughout his life he would never rashly publish his ideas, preferring to wait many years before setting them out in print. During that time he would try them out in his lectures to his students, so that by the time of publication everything was comprehensively checked by massive documentation.

Marshall's early training was in mathematics, philosophy and ethics, but his concern about poverty, which he considered the source of most social evils, led him to the study of economics. After marrying in 1877, he resigned his mathematics fellowship, and went briefly to Bristol—as Professor of Political Economy. But in 1883 he returned, after a year at Balliol College, Oxford, to the Chair of Political Economy at Cambridge where he held intellectual court until 1908 when he retired. In 1890 his major work was finally published: *Principles of Economics*. The Marshallian school of thought was, by the time of his retirement and for many years after, widely influential among Western economists.

Marshall described economics as 'the study of men in the ordinary business of life'. He was concerned that the subject should not stray too far from the real world, and so his theories were always decorated with many qualifications. Nonetheless it is his theoretical ideas that were most important. Marshall was an exponent of the 'marginalist' method of analysis. This applies both for the consumer and for the firm.

The consumer obtains utility from consuming the goods and services of industry. But what is analytically important, in determining the prices of goods, is the extra amount of utility which the consumer gains from a small increase in the amount consumed: this is called 'marginal utility'. For the firm, the production of goods involves costs. But what is analytically important, in determining the prices of goods, is the extra cost involved when there is a small increase in the amount produced: this is called 'marginal cost'.

While these ideas did not necessarily originate with him—as he was spending years allowing them to mature, other economists, such as Jevons (1835–1882), Menger (1840–1921) and Walras (1834–1910) were producing and publishing similar marginalist theories—Marshall's distinctive contributions were his systematic development of the ideas, and his method of combining them in a 'partial equilibrium' analysis.

'Partial equilibrium' meant that, as a first approximation, one should look at what is happening in one market only, without taking account of events in all other markets of the economy. The advantage of this was that if one tried to take into account the fact that all markets are related to each other it became so complicated that it was difficult to analyse the workings of the markets; but if one market was taken at a time, it was possible to predict the effects of changes—such as, for example, the effect on a price of a rise in consumer incomes, or a change in consumer tastes. This analysis was achieved through the Marshallian 'scissors' of supply and demand schedules in a particular market. The value of a good was determined jointly by supply conditions—which derived from the concept of marginal cost—and demand conditions—which derived from the concept of marginal utility.

In this way, Marshall gave the economics profession the tools with which to analyse rigorously the determination of prices under conditions of free enterprise. He thus made operational the concept of the 'invisible hand' of the market which Adam Smith (*q.v.*) had first produced over a century before.

MARX, Karl (1818-1883)

Karl Marx—economist, philosopher, political and sociological theorist, socialist and revolutionary—was born in Trier, Prussia. His father was a Jewish lawyer who had become a Protestant for social reasons in 1824. Intending at first to follow his father into law he studied at Bonn, but soon went to Berlin where he studied philosophy. There he came into the circle of 'young Hegelians', a group of liberals who had rebelled against the reactionary politics of the then dominant philosopher, Hegel. In 1841 Marx submitted a brilliant doctoral dissertation on the philosophy of Epicurus (*q.v.*), and intended thereafter to follow an academic career, but because of his association with the young Hegelians he was barred from getting a university post. Instead he accepted an invitation to work on a new radical paper, the *Reinische Zeitung*, of which he became chief editor in 1842. For some months Marx skilfully sidestepped the censorship that was imposed on all newspapers, and learned the art of journalism to which he was periodically to return throughout his life to alleviate his ever-threatening poverty. But in 1843 the paper was forced to close. However, through his experience on this paper, he came to realize that in order to understand the society in which he lived he needed to undertake an intensive study of political economy. This was to take up the major part of his life.

In 1843 he married Jenny von Westphalen, who came from a family of the Prussian nobility. Despite her upper-class background Marx received no dowry; they were to live their lives in poverty. They had three daughters, Eleanor, Laura and Jenny, who would later marry English and French socialists. Marx's poverty would have made it impossible for him to produce the major scientific works he did, if it were not for the generous support of Friedrich Engels (1820–1895), whom he met in Paris in 1844.

In 1845 Marx was expelled from France, and went to live in Brussels. With Engels, he wrote in 1845 and 1846 *The German Ideology*, in which he settled accounts with the young Hegelians from whom he had now broken. Here the philosophy of 'dialectical materialism' is set out. (This is the theory that political events are caused by social forces set in conflict by man's material needs.) In 1848 he and Engels wrote a historic document, *The Communist Manifesto*, hastily produced in time for the revolutionary upsurges all over Europe in that year. But Marx was soon expelled from Belgium and, unwelcome for long in either France or Germany, in 1849 he degan a life of political exile in London. There he lived with his family in poor circumstances until he died in 1883, two years after his wife.

He did not relinquish all political activities. In particular, he was the central figure in the foundation of the First Inter-

This painting, by K N Aksyonov, is a highly idealized version of Lenin's arrival at the Finland Station in what is now Leningrad, April 1917. The result of the scholarship of Karl Marx was the substitution of economics for metaphysics in the study of history. His followers, however, have interpreted his writings to suit their own ends: in reality, there were only a handful of people to meet Lenin at the station, and he did not make an 'inevitable' revolution, but only assumed power six months later, and then only because others had failed to bring order out of chaos.

The concept of the past as prologue is now well established. The French writer Michel Foucault takes a new view; that history is a series of radical discontinuities, or novel situations; the past is but a series of buried presents. If we are to make our own history, the task will require the intellectual honesty of Marx rather than that of his followers.

national in 1864—the 'International Working Men's Association'—whose object was to join together the various forms of socialist struggles throughout the world.

However, most of Marx's time was now spent as a scholar, usually in the British Museum, studying the theory of political economy. His diligence and the extent of his scholarship were extraordinary; before publishing anything he made it his business to read and know virtually everything that had been written on the subjects he was concerned with. Thus, for example, he studied many languages in order to be able to read his source materials in the original. He once attended night courses to learn how to operate machinery, feeling that he could not make assumptions about the working class without knowing how it felt to do the work. This alone sets Marx apart from many present-day 'Marxists'.

In 1859 he produced *A Contribution to the Critique of Political Economy*, which sets out for the first time his theory of value and surplus value; this was then fully developed in his most important work, *Capital*, in 1867. Only the first volume was published then. Two subsequent volumes were collected together and published by Engels after his death. Marx's work gave to socialism a scientific foundation which it previously lacked. Of the many aspects of his work, two major theoretical discoveries stand out as fundamental to

Marxism: the materialist conception of history and the elucidation of the relation between capital and labour.

The materialist conception of history explains the progress of history as resulting from continuous class struggle. Men in society are divided into classes defined by how they relate to the existing mode of production. The history of man is the history of conflict between these classes. The course which that conflict takes is determined partly by objective developments in methods and 'relations' of production, and partly by conscious political action. By the 'relations' of production are meant the relations that a man is forced to enter into in the course of his daily work.

Thus Marx gave priority to economic developments in the explanation of history—since, for him, the theory of production was the essence of economics. As a first approximation to understanding the world, all other aspects of life at any stage of history could be traced back to an explanation in terms of the existing relations of production. Thus he argues 'the mode of production in material life determines the general character of the social, political and spiritual processes of life'. While no single rigid formula is of course adequate for understanding the world, this materialist

Below: Karl Marx in his study, in London, 1852.

method formed the general guidelines along which he proceeded to analyse society.

Within this framework, Marx held that capitalist society would eventually give way to a new form of society based on communist principles, where there is only one class—which would emerge from the existing working class. In communist society, there would be no exploitation of one class by another, for there would be no class conflict. Instead 'the free development of each [would be] the condition for the free development of all'. This optimism reflected his fundamental humanity.

Using his materialist conception of history Marx characterised modern society as 'capitalist', because the principal relation of production was one where workers laboured in return for wages, paid to them by the owners of the means of production, the capitalists. The fundamental relation of modern society was thus the capital-labour relation. Marx developed a theory of value to elucidate the development of this relation, and therefore of the economy, which he adapted from the labour theory of value of the classical economists.

In feudal society—the mode of production which existed before capitalism—the peasant classes were openly exploited, in that the small minority of land-holders openly expropriated the produce of the working peasants. In capitalist society the relation between capital and labour appears on the surface to be an equal one, where a certain amount of labour time is exchanged for a certain amount of wages. But this is a delusion. For the value (expressed in labour time) that the worker adds to the material he works on is greater than the value of the goods he buys with his wages. The difference is called 'surplus value', and this is the source of profits. The capitalist is able to expropriate the surplus value. The worker is forced to accept the exchange in order to feed himself.

The net result is that the working man is left at the end of the day with nothing to show for it except himself for the following day. Moreover, he becomes progressively alienated from his productive activity because what he produces is not for himself, nor even for a member of his own class.

Thus the essential nature of capitalist society was the continued production of surplus value. Having elucidated this, it remained for Marx to develop the laws by which it is governed; this he does in *Capital*. There, for example, he shows how the production of surplus value is not always a smooth process, and is often subject to sudden crisis, wherein the possibility of production and realization of surplus value is for one reason or another suspended. This provided him with a fundamental explanation of economic and political crises.

The word 'Marxism' now is commonly associated with a political doctrine, or with a blueprint for a future society. Perhaps it is inevitable in view of historical developments since Marx's death, and the immense influence his political and economic teaching has had, that such conceptions as a 'Marxist society' will arise. However, such a concept never existed for Marx himself, who wrote very little about the nature of the future communist society. By far the greater part of his writing lay in the analysis of capitalist society. He was continually altering his views on the basis of new facts. Marx himself is reported to have said, 'I am not a Marxist'.

Marx provided the framework for much of twentieth century social, economic and historical enquiry.

MAUDSLAY, Henry (1771-1831)

Henry Maudslay was a pioneer of precision engineering, and one of the first to bring the standards of accuracy that previously had been limited to the making of clocks and scientific instruments to the manufacture of heavy machinery. He refined the screwcutting lathe so as to be able to produce screws not only of high accuracy, but also of sufficient uniformity to be interchangeable. On this principle modern mass production depends.

His father had served as a wheelwright in the Royal Engineers, but was wounded in action, and so given a post as a storekeeper, at Woolwich Arsenal where Henry Maudslay was born. At the age of 12 he began work there, filling cartridges. Soon he 'graduated' to the woodworking shop, and then on to the smithy. By the age of 18 he had acquired such a reputation for his skill as a metalworker that he was called in by Joseph Bramah to construct machines to manufacture his patent lock. There is some dispute as to how much Maudslay contributed to the design of the machines he executed for Bramah; he seems to have been always best at putting other people's ideas into workable practice, rather than an original thinker, and only with Bramah could Maudslay have been trained in the ways of complex machinery.

In 1791, he married his master's housemaid Sarah Tindale. Six years later, the father of three children, and recognized as Bramah's right-hand man, he asked for higher wages, and when this was refused set up on his own as a maker of precise metal work. While he was still with Bramah, the latter had patented a new type of lathe with a slide rest to hold the cutting tool so that its advance could be mechanically controlled; this would be particularly valuable when cutting a screw on a large metal bar or cylinder, where imperfect control would lead to irregular pitch. Maudslay may have built

Below: Henry Maudlsay's development of precision machine tools allowed the accurate construction of the steam engines and machinery of the Industrial Revolution.

this lathe; he certainly constructed a series of screw-cutting lathes of increasing accuracy not long after he left Bramah. Although the basic principles of slide rest and screw lathe were already known, Maudslay's (which still survive) were the most successful, and the techniques they embody were adopted, and adapted, by his successors.

A fine screw in his shop window led to a commission from Sir Marc Isambard Brunel (*q.v.*) to make models of a proposed series of machines for shaping blocks for the Navy. Maudslay then built the machinery itself between 1803–09. It applied the ideas of interchangeable parts and continuous flow treatment to the sequence of operations used in making these wooden blocks. On the profits of this, his greatest undertaking, Maudslay set up as a manufacturer of steam engines in Lambeth, in 1810. Marine engines became a speciality, but he also made sawmills, printing machines and machines for government mints. He was among the first to go over to belt transmission, and devised machinery to punch regular holes in the metal plates of boilers. But his main contribution was the introduction of surface plates to obtain a smooth plane surface and the improvement of screws by means of his lathes. The system of interchangeable bolts and nuts began in his workshop—formerly each screw would only fit its own nut. All this required measurement to new standards of accuracy, down to thousandths of an inch; Maudslay took over from the scientific instrument trade the micrometer, and turned it into an engine-maker's tool. He nicknamed his own micrometer 'Lord Chancellor', for from it there was no appeal.

Maudslay insisted that machines should be compact, firmly based and uncomplicated. Tidiness and order were his watchwords; he kept all his old models neatly arranged to guide him with future developments, and a collection of musical boxes to play while he was working. He had no great interest in ingenuity for its own sake, preferring to work out the simplest and shortest way to any particular mechanical objective. Many of the outstanding mechanical engineers of the next generation such as Clement, Roberts, Nasmyth (*q.v.*) and Whitworth (*q.v.*) worked under him. He patented little; but his genius made possible the British machine tool industry.

Below: a Maudslay lathe of 1810. Maudslay built the first lathes with automatic traverse of the carriage on precision made slideways and provision for thread cutting; note the feed screw for this at the bottom.

MAXIM, Sir Hiram (1840-1916)

Hiram Stevens Maxim was born on 5 February 1840 at Sangerville, Maine, in the USA where his father was a farmer. As a boy Hiram became acquainted with machinery when his father gave up farming to become a woodturner. Then at 14, young Hiram was apprenticed to a coachbuilder, but drifted into a wandering life trying his hand as a bartender, a machine tool operator and even a prizefighter.

At the age of 25 Maxim settled down with a company making gas machines and invented a new machine for making lighting gas. Other inventions followed, many of them for improvements to the steam engine, but again Maxim's career changed direction when at the age of 38 he became chief engineer to an electric lighting company. In 1881 he represented this company at the Paris Exhibition and while in Europe became interested in automatic guns. Maxim moved to London, where in 1884 he produced his most famous invention—a fully automatic machine gun appropriately named the Maxim gun. This brought him fame and fortune. He became a British subject in 1900 and the following year was knighted.

Not content with his success, Hiram Maxim turned his attention to the problems of flight and set out 'to build a flying machine that would lift itself from the ground'. This was only a half-way stage to true flight, however, for Maxim realized that controlling an aircraft in free flight was yet another problem. He was perhaps more interested in finding out about flight than actually flying himself. Maxim knew that the wings of an aircraft had to produce an upward force, or lift, greater than the aircraft's overall weight. The great difficulty was to find an engine which could develop enough power to overcome drag, or air resistance, and propel the aircraft at a suitable speed.

At the time Maxim was starting his experiments, the internal combustion engine was a new invention, unreliable and lacking power, so he turned to the well-tried steam engine. Unfortunately steam engines were large and heavy; consequently Maxim had to design a huge flying machine to lift the weight. The wing span was an incredible 104 ft

Below: Maxim's machine gun was a blow-back design, operated by gas pressure from the firing chamber.

(31.7 m) and the total weight was $3\frac{1}{2}$ tons (3560 kg). Maxim designed a lightweight steam engine which developed 180 hp, and fitted two of these to his machine, each driving a propeller almost 18 ft (5.50 m) in diameter.

In 1893 Maxim assembled his flying machine at Baldwyns Park in Kent. For a runway he built a railway track 1800 ft (550 m) long, but as he did not want to make free flight he built a second rail 2 ft (0.61 m) above the first to restrain the machine when it lifted off the main rails. The first trial was made in 1894 but the wheels did not leave the rails. The steam pressure to the engines was increased for the second trial to give more power, and the wheels just lifted. A third run at an even higher pressure was then prepared. On 31 July 1894, Maxim's flying machine reached 42 miles per hour (68 km/h) and lifted off the lower rails. Maxim had proved his point: the lift was greater than the weight, but it had been costly.

Maxim turned his attention to his other inventions which included mousetraps, fire extinguishers and even a merry-go-round. He once described himself as a 'chronic inventor'. But he returned to the problems of flight in 1908, when he wrote a book, *Natural and Artificial Flight*, and even designed an aircraft engine. He built an aircraft in 1910 but it never flew. Maxim died six years later at the age of 76. One of his steam engines and an internal combustion engine are preserved in the Science Museum, London.

Below: Sir Hiram Maxim with his most famous invention, the fully automatic Maxim machine gun.

Bottom: Maxim's captive, steam powered flying machine; the guide rails can be seen at the bottom of the picture.

MAXWELL, James Clerk (1831-1879)

James Clerk Maxwell was born in Edinburgh on 13 June 1831. He made many significant contributions as a scientist, perhaps the most celebrated of which was his prediction of the existence of electromagnetic radiation. He was the first to realize that light is electromagnetic and a form of wave motion.

Maxwell's scientific career started early, for at the age of 14, while still at school, he had a paper on geometry read at the Royal Society of Edinburgh. Two years later he started attending lectures at the University of Edinburgh and in his three years there he did research into polarized light and engineering problems such as bending of beams and twisting of cylinders. He then went to the University of Cambridge as an undergraduate but did little original research until his graduation in 1854. The next year his output of original work began to increase again, especially with work on colour vision.

In 1855 he published his first paper on electricity and magnetism, a discourse on the idea of 'lines of force' put forward by Michael Faraday (*q.v.*). Maxwell's picture was of 'tubes'

Below: this portrait of James Clerk Maxwell, the Scottish mathematical physicist, was painted on china from a photograph. It is to Maxwell that science owes the origination of the concept of electromagnetic radiation, as well as statistical mechanics.

of force containing an incompressible fluid which transmitted electrical force through space. His theory of electromagnetism was there in essence, although the extension of the fluid concept to that of waves was yet to come.

Three years as Professor of Natural Philosophy at Aberdeen (a post which he took to be nearer his father) were followed in 1860, when he was 29, by a most fruitful five years during which he was Professor of Physics at King's College, London. It was there that he did much of his great work on the theory of gases, which is thought to have been prompted by his earlier work on Saturn's rings, which he showed must consist of clouds of tiny particles. He was the founder of what is now called statistical mechanics, with his realization that all molecules in a gas do not travel at the same speed, but rather that the speeds are shared out among the molecules in a random manner according to probability theory. While at King's College he was able to keep in touch with Faraday, who worked at the Royal Institution in London, and during this period proposed that electromagnetic energy travelled in waves and that light was simply a particular kind of electromagnetic energy.

In 1865, upon the death of his father, Maxwell gave up his Chair to return to his small family estate in Scotland, because of ill health and because he enjoyed that kind of life and felt little compulsion to maintain a professional position. Six years later, at the age of 40, Maxwell was persuaded to come out of semi-retirement to become Cavendish Professor of Experimental Physics at Cambridge and to bring the idea of a physics laboratory there—the legendary Cavendish Laboratory—to fruition. It was opened in 1874 and his mark has been on it ever since. As Max Planck (*q.v.*) said, 'By his birth James Clerk Maxwell belongs to Edinburgh, by his personality he belongs to Cambridge, by his work he belongs to the whole world'.

Below: Maxwell was fascinated by the science of colour. This painting shows the stresses in unannealed glass as revealed by polarized light. He also made the first colour photograph, taken three times through different colour filters and projected to combine colours.

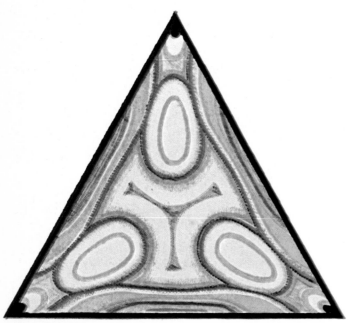

MENDEL, Gregor (1822-1884)

Johann Mendel's parents were peasants, and during his harsh childhood he tended fruit trees. He entered the Augustinian Order at Brünn, Bohemia (now Brno, Czechoslovakia) after having to leave university for lack of money, and was ordained a priest in 1847. He took the name of Gregor. For five years he studied theology, and then went to Vienna University to qualify as a teacher, since the Augustinian Order provided teachers in the Austrian Empire. In 1857 he became a science teacher, although he failed exams which would have allowed him higher qualification.

He then combined his love of mathematics with his knowledge of plants to make a hobby of botanical research. For eight years, beginning in 1857, he grew peas in the monastery garden, keeping a careful record of what he was doing, and laid the foundation of the science of genetics.

Mendel self-pollinated pea plants, wrapping them to make sure that they would not be cross-pollinated by insects, so that any inherited characteristics would come from only one parent. He saved the seeds from each plant and studied each generation. He discovered that if he planted seeds from dwarf pea plants, only dwarf plants sprouted, generation after generation, but of the tall plants, about a third of them 'bred true'. From the rest, however, some were tall and some dwarfed, in a ratio of 3:1.

Then he cross-bred dwarf plants with true-breeding tall plants and found that the dwarf characteristic disappeared; all the plants were tall. But when he self-pollinated the hybrid plants, the seeds developed into $\frac{1}{4}$ dwarf plants, $\frac{1}{4}$ tall plants, and $\frac{1}{2}$ non-true tall plants. Mendel also studied the plants for other characteristics, and kept mathematical records. He discovered the ratios which operate in genetics, and coined the terms 'dominant' and 'recessive' for the characteristics as they applied to the various plants.

But his most important discovery solved the remaining problem in the theory of evolution. The action of natural selection was slow, and if random mating resulted in a blend of intermediate characteristics, the whole theory was worthless. Mendel's research showed that the characteristics did not blend, but remained distinct, so that natural selection could work very slowly but still have its effect.

The library at the monastery had essential scientific books, and new books were acquired as they came out. Mendel started his work before the publication of the work of Darwin (*q.v.*), but he read *The Origin of Species* and even annotated it. Yet it is not clear whether he realized the importance of what he had discovered. He read two papers to the local natural science society in 1865, but they did not make much of an impression. He then corresponded with Germany's leading botanist, Karl Wilhelm von Nägeli (1817–1891), who was a professor at the University of Munich. But Nägeli was not interested in mathematics and did not see the importance of Mendel's work to the theory of evolution. Mendel himself had described his interest as simply plant hybridization.

Right: Gregor Mendel's immensely important genetic discoveries were largely ignored in his lifetime. One reason was that they were all about plants; though the same rules apply to animals, it might have been thought improper in those days for a monk to breed mice, for example.

Mendel was elected Abbot of his monastery, and administrative duties began to take up much of his time. In later life he retained his interests in beekeeping, meteorology, and agriculture, but avoided the subject of peas. He also became embroiled in a disagreement with the Austrian government on the subject of taxes paid by religious institutions. His work with the peas had been published in an obscure journal and was seen only by botanists with no mathematics, or mathematicians with no botany. He died

having no idea that he would become famous when his work was rediscovered. In 1900 three different botanists, independently of each other, duplicated Mendel's work and then discovered the original. None of them tried to claim the work as his own, and the laws of inheritance are still called Mendelian.

Below: this diagram shows how the mathematics of genetically acquired characteristics works.

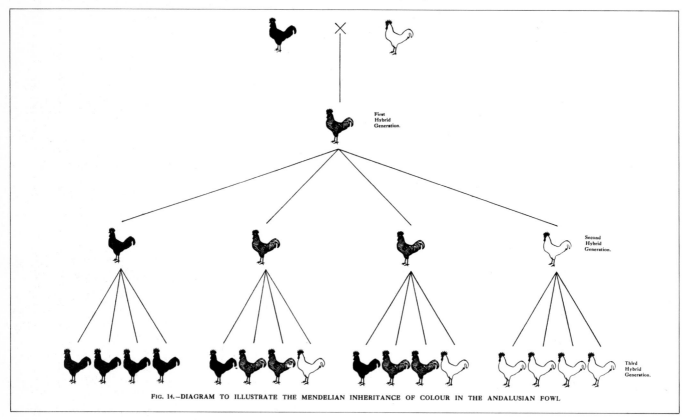

FIG. 14.—DIAGRAM TO ILLUSTRATE THE MENDELIAN INHERITANCE OF COLOUR IN THE ANDALUSIAN FOWL

MENDELEEV, Dmitri (1834-1907)

Dmitrii Ivanovich Mendeleev, the inventor of the modern periodic table of the chemical elements, was born on 8 February 1834, the seventeenth child of a schoolteacher in Tobolsk, Siberia.

Soon after Mendeleev's birth, his father was forced by blindness to retire on an inadequate pension, so his mother worked as manageress of a glass factory to support and educate her younger children. When Dmitrii was fourteen his father died, and his mother took him to St Petersburg (now Leningrad) to complete his schooling and to train as a teacher. She died very soon after their arrival, leaving Dmitrii alone and suffering from tuberculosis, but with the help of a scholarship he was able to complete his training.

After only one year of teaching chemistry in a school in Odessa (where his health recovered) he received a junior appointment at the University of St Petersburg in 1856, and after being sent by the Government to study in Germany for two years, he became Professor of Chemistry at the Technological Institute in 1861. Here he took a great interest in the new Russian petroleum industry. Throughout his life he worked to increase its efficiency, and it is for this, and for his work for Russian trade in general, that he is most honoured in Russia. Internationally, his reputation rests on his import-

ant textbook of chemistry, which went through many editions and translations, and his periodic table of the elements.

In the 1850s and 1860s several chemists in a number of countries put forward systems for classifying the elements which more or less resemble Mendeleev's; the most important of these were due to the English chemist William Odling (1865) and the German Lothar Meyer (1869). The idea of arranging the elements in increasing order of atomic weight, and determining how often properties recur, was a commonplace. So when Mendeleev put forward a new scheme in 1869, it was not thought remarkable or very useful.

What distinguished his system and ensured its ultimate adoption was his prediction in 1871 of new elements to fill the 'gaps' in the table; the discovery of gallium (1875), scandium (1879) and germanium (1886), whose physical and chemical properties had been predicted by Mendeleev, showed the power of his system: not only did it tie together an enormous amount of existing information about the nature of the chemical element, but it pointed the way to further discovery. Once the system was adopted as the foundation of inorganic chemistry, rapid progress could be made.

Mendeleev's personal life was always stormy. Following his early difficulties, his first marriage in 1863 ended in divorce thirteen years later. He then married an art student before the statutory period of seven years had elapsed after his divorce, but no action was taken against this illegal marriage and it was apparently a happy one. In 1890 he resigned his professorship at St Petersburg for political reasons, but three years later he was appointed to be director of the bureau of weights and measures, a post which he held until his death from pneumonia on 20 January 1907.

In 1955 a new and very radioactive chemical element having the atomic number 101 was synthesized at the University of California. It was named Mendelevium (Md) in honour of Mendeleev.

Below: portrait of Dmitrii Mendeleev by I J Repin.

Bottom: Mendeleev's first draft of his periodic table.

MORSE, Samuel F B (1791-1872)

Samuel Finley Breese Morse invented a telegraph apparatus, sent the first telegraph signal in the United States, and devised the Morse code, still used for certain kinds of cable transmission. Like Thomas Edison (*q.v.*), he had an intuitive mind rather than great scientific originality; like Robert Fulton (*q.v.*), he was a painter as well as an inventor.

Morse's father was a controversial clergyman who wrote some of the first American books on geography. After graduating from Yale in 1810, Morse received his parents' reluctant permission to pursue a career as an artist, and sailed for England to study painting. Encouraged by his success there, he returned to Boston to set up a studio, hoping to make a living painting historical scenes. The only kind of paintings Americans wanted to buy, however, were portraits, and there were not many commissions even for those. For some years Morse made a precarious living at portraiture.

Between 1825 and 1828, Morse's wife, his mother and his father died. Together with his difficulty making a living as an artist, this was the beginning of a difficult period in his life. In 1829 he sailed for Europe, where he was influenced by some of the stranger political currents of the time in France and Italy. On his return trip in 1832, one of his fellow passengers demonstrated some electrical apparatus, and Morse suddenly became consumed with the idea of transmitting intelligence instantaneously by means of electricity. He outlined in his notebook the three basic elements of a telegraph system: a sending apparatus to transmit by opening and closing a circuit; a receiving device operated by an electromagnet to record signals as dots and spaces on a strip of paper moved by clockwork; and a code. As he developed his idea, he realized that the code could be read by ear as well as recorded; he added dashes to the dots and spaces and his initial clumsy sending device became a simple sounding key. He did not consider his invention as a means of sending news and personal messages around the world, but as a means of transmitting important and secret government messages; accordingly he spent some time devising a secret code which required the use of a large de-coding book.

This was not Morse's first venture into technology. In 1817, with his brother, he had patented a flexible piston pump for fire engines; in 1822 he had built a marble cutting machine (he was also a sculptor) which unfortunately in-

Below left: daguerrotype of Samuel Morse, the portrait painter who invented the telegraph.

Below right: Morse's first telegraph apparatus of 1837. At the front is the sending key; behind it, on a wooden frame, the receiver.

fringed on an earlier patent. He also experimented with such substances as milk and beer in the grinding of his pigments. While he worked on the telegraph, he continued painting, and, like his father, also indulged in political and religious controversy. He ran for mayor of New York on a Nativist (anti-Catholic) ticket, receiving only 1500 votes.

In 1836 Morse showed his telegraph to his colleague Leonard Dunnell Gale. Morse's difficulty was that his knowledge of electromagnetics was several years out of date; he could not make his apparatus work more than 40 feet (12 m) from his battery. Morse and Gale experimented with wire wound round Gale's lecture room until they could send messages as far as ten miles (16 km). Morse then worked out a system of electromagnetic relays which would enable messages to be sent as far as desired. Similar developments were taking place elsewhere, notably in England, but a document filed in 1837 shows that the American research was original. In that year Morse reluctantly gave up painting and sailed for Europe again. He was honoured by scientists in France, but he could not obtain patents there or in England.

In 1843, a busy US Congress in a hurry to adjourn voted money for a telegraph experiment. A line was set up between Washington DC and nearby Baltimore; on 24 May 1844, Morse sent the famous message 'What hath God wrought' from the Supreme Court room; it was returned accurately and a short conversation followed. Morse wanted to sell the invention outright to the government and go back to painting, but the postmaster general at the time thought that the telegraph would never pay, so its development was left in private hands.

In 1854 Morse ran for Congress as a Democrat and was defeated. In 1857–58 he worked as an electrician for Cyrus W Field, who was laying transatlantic cables, but resigned because of company intrigue. He correctly predicted the failure of the second cable because of inadequate insulation.

After many years of struggle and relative poverty, Morse finally became a wealthy man because of his American patents. He was lucky in his choice of financial adviser, despite litigation with his enemies and his own capacity for being swindled. European governments showered him with honours, but continued to deny him patents. He was married twice and had eight children; his youngest son graduated from Yale more than sixty years after he did. When Morse died in 1872, the Congress paid tribute to his technical achievement but ignored his painting; since an exhibition of his painting in New York in 1932, he has been given credit for his influence on American art as well as his achievement in communications.

Below: receiver of Morse printing telegraph.

MUYBRIDGE, Eadweard (1830-1904)

Edward James Muggeridge, the son of a corn merchant, was born in Kingston-upon-Thames, Surrey, England, but emigrated to the United States as a young man of 22 and changed his name to Eadweard Muybridge to make it more Anglo-Saxon. He later became a professional photographer and worked with the famous topographical photographer Carleton A Watkins in San Francisco. Muybridge took hundreds of views of Yosemite and the Pacific coast and these were seen by millionaire Leland Stanford, a former Governor of California, which led to Muybridge becoming one of the first to make satisfactory photographic analyses of motion, and the first to show his results on some form of projector.

Etienne Marey's (*q.v.*) pictures of moving horses were known to Stanford and he wanted to prove for himself that a galloping horse's hooves all left the ground when its legs were bunched under its body, not when stretched out. Most authorities say that Stanford had a $5000 bet with fellow horse-owner Frederick MacCrellish, but there is no positive evidence for this. He asked Muybridge, now making a photographic survey of the Pacific coast for the US government, to photograph his favourite trotter, Occident, at full gallop (about 25 mph; 40 km/h) on the Sacramento race course. In May 1872, Muybridge got his first reasonably successful silhouette.

The experiments were interrupted by scandal (Muybridge was accused, but acquitted, of murdering his wife's lover) and he left the USA to take up photographic assignments elsewhere. He returned to California and Stanford's Palo Alto stud farm in 1877. He found that a white background made shorter exposures—perhaps only a thousandth of a second—and slightly clearer silhouettes possible. These at least proved that the horses did lift all four feet off the ground as predicted. Muybridge correctly deduced that this gait was common to all four-footed animals. But he and Stanford were not satisfied. More money was spent (over the years,

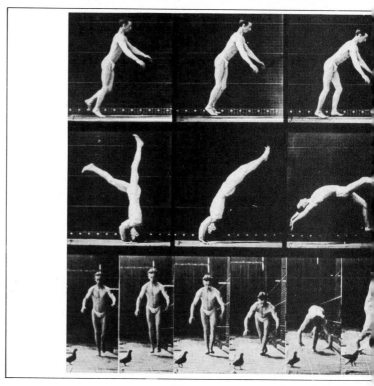

Stanford is said to have paid out $40,000) and a huge apparatus was constructed, with a rubber track to avoid dust being raised. Alongside ran a fence 50 feet (15 m) long, marked with vertical lines every 21 inches (53 cm). Opposite this was a row of 12 cameras, also at 21 inch (53 cm) intervals, set off by electromagnets. Later, Muybridge doubled the number of cameras, placing them one foot (30 cm) apart; they were actuated by trip threads under the horses' hooves.

Muybridge published and copyrighted his successful results in 1878 and went on to issue photographs of many animals. He toured America and Europe, addressing learned societies and demonstrating his invention, the *Zoopraxiscope*. In this, successive images were mounted around the edge of a revolving glass disc like that used by Marey. Until the *Kinetoscope*, invented by Edison (*q.v.*) twelve years later, this was the most successful machine for reconstituting the movement captured by the original photographs. At the University of Pennsylvania, which seemed ready to meet the vast bills for his experiments, Muybridge used the newly-introduced dry photographic plates to take many more pictures, including some of wild animals. His book *Animal Locomotion* (1887) included 20,000 of them. Three years before he died, Muybridge returned to Kingston, bequeathing to its public library his Zoopraxiscope, many photographs and lantern slides, and his press-cuttings books.

Left: Eadweard Muybridge, pioneer photographer of movement.

Below: front and side views of the same movement; the stills would have been mounted on a zoetrope (revolving disc) to give the illusion of continuous motion.

NASMYTH, James (1808-1890)

James Nasmyth, renowned in his own time as the inventor of the steam hammer which was crucial to the growth of railways and iron ships, did not patent his invention until he had already seen it realized by others. This was, however, only one of many innovations which he made in machine tool manufacture.

Nasmyth had a fortunate childhood; his father Alexander was a landscape painter in Edinburgh, whose house was frequented by scientists and artists. Among James's boyhood friends were the sons of an ironmaster and a colour manufacturer who let him learn chemistry and mechanics by watching the processes they employed. This stimulus served him far better than his formal schooling, which ended at the age of 12, although he continued to attend classes at the Edinburgh School of Arts and University. Meantime he had set up a little brass foundry—in his bedroom. There, and in his father's workshop, he made model steam engines which were good enough to pay for his studies, and to win him a post, when he was 21, as assistant in the Lambeth engine works to Henry Maudslay (*q.v.*). Even before his move south, he had designed a steam carriage and a mode of chain traction whereby steam could be used to haul canal barges.

In London James Nasmyth had not been with Maudslay long before he had designed a flexible wire shaft for a drill, and a circular mechanical file to produce hexagonal nuts of uniform size. Nasmyth learned much from his two years with Maudslay and, after his master's death in 1831, decided to set up in business on his own as an engine and machine tool maker, first near his native Edinburgh, next in Manchester, and then at Patricroft, where he established his Bridgewater Foundry in 1836, when not yet 28. Two years later he met Ann Hartop while on a visit to the Barnsley iron foundry where her father was manager. According to his account he fell in love and proposed within two days, although they were not married until 1840.

Nasmyth's move to Lancashire coincided with the railway boom, of which he was quick to take advantage. Now he added to the increasing repertoire of machine tools, devices for cutting key-ways and for centering rods before turning them on a lathe, and a shaper, nicknamed the 'steam arm' because the tool-holder was drawn to and fro by crank and connecting rod, rather like a horizontal steam engine. The shaper was intended for planing the smaller parts of locomotives, as he had contracted to build twenty of them for the Great Western Railway.

In 1839, their engineer asked for his advice on how to forge a paddle shaft for the *Great Britain*, because there was not a forge hammer which was powerful enough for such an undertaking. Nasmyth decided that the problem lay in having the hammer fall through an acute angle on the work (if the object to be forged was too large the hammer suffered still worse from 'want of compass, of range and fall') nor could it be made too heavy, or it would snap its helve. He conceived of a hammer held in guides directly above the work, rather like a piledriver or a guillotine, raised by steam. At first it was allowed to drop by gravity, but soon was modified so as to be double-acting. At first Nasmyth did no more than sketch out his ideas, and it was only after seeing one at Le Creusot two years later that he decided to patent it. It was an immediate success, forging all the heavy wrought iron members needed in marine engineering, such as shafts, plates

and anchors, and in locomotive building. When equipped with a die, the hammer could also be used to impart a given shape.

In 1845, Nasmyth adapted the same principle for a steam powered piledriver, and also based an inverted steam engine on similar geometry. Highly honoured and immensely successful, at the height of his career, Nasmyth resolved to retire at 48. He bought a cottage at Penshurst, Kent and spent the next 30 years as an astronomer, developing a number of fruitful theories on the surfaces of Sun and Moon, which he sought to demonstrate experimentally, becoming an authority on the Moon.

Nasmyth's autobiography suggests that he always had a yearning for the romantic and the antique; he produced drawings of his Gothic fantasies, and lamented that technical progress, to which he had contributed so much, was ruining beautiful old towns. But although a good businessman, his chief inventions were those of an artist interested in geometrical simplification—his joy in them seems almost aesthetic.

NEWCOMEN, Thomas (1663-1729)

The first practical steam engine was invented, not by James Watt (*q.v.*), but by an obscure ironmonger from Devon, Thomas Newcomen, who built his first steam engine over half a century before Watt's improved version. Despite research in recent years little is known about Newcomen: no portrait of him exists and even his date of birth is uncertain, but we do know he was christened in Dartmouth on 24 February 1663. His father was a merchant and the family were Nonconformists. Young Thomas probably served an apprenticeship in Exeter; then in about 1685 he set up as an ironmonger in Dartmouth with a partner called John Calley. When he was 42 Newcomen married his wife Hannah and their new house became a meeting place for local Baptists, including his partner Calley.

Very little information survives about Newcomen's early experiments or how much he knew of other people's experiments. In France during 1690 Papin (*q.v.*) had built a small model to show that steam could move a piston inside a cylinder—the basis of a steam engine. A few years later Captain Thomas Savery demonstrated a steam-powered pump to the Royal Society. This was partially successful, but it was not a true steam engine because it did not have a reciprocating piston. Savery's patent of 1698 which covered the atmospheric engine was, however, a great handicap to Newcomen's developments and in 1705 Newcomen and Calley entered into partnership with Savery.

The first steam engine was built in 1712. Newcomen had visited the tin mines of Devon and Cornwall in the course of business and realized that there was a need for a source of power to pump water out of the deep mines. They could not find a customer for their steam engine near Dartmouth but their Baptist friends with coal mines in the Midlands needed

pumps—and they had plenty of cheap coal with which to fire a boiler. The actual location of this first engine is a mystery but it was probably near Dudley Castle in Worcestershire. A drawing of the engine survives and, from the size of a man stoking the boiler, it was large and impressive.

Newcomen placed the large vertical cylinder above a domed boiler. Inside the cylinder, a piston moved up and down and this was connected by a chain to a see-saw beam mounted high in the engine house. At the other end of the see-saw, rods were attached and these descended to the water pump in the mine. The pump side of the see-saw was the heavier, and consequently it rested in the down position. A coal fire under the boiler heated the water and produced steam which was fed into the cylinder below the piston. The steam was condensed by a spray of cold water and this created a partial vacuum. The atmospheric pressure acting on the upper side of the piston forced it downwards. At the end of the stroke, the heavy pump rods which had been raised by the see-saw moved down again thus driving the water pump.

Newcomen's atmospheric steam engines, or fire engines as they were often called, became widely used not only in Britain, but also throughout Europe. Unfortunately because of the patent restrictions Newcomen did not gain full credit for his work nor did he become rich. He died while staying in London at the age of 66, almost unknown.

Below left and below: only one of Thomas Newcomen's engines survives in unaltered form and working order; originally at Griff, near Nuneaton, it is now in Dartmouth. These pictures show the chain and beam, and the 56cm diameter cylinder.

NEWTON, Sir Isaac (1642-1727)

On the early morning of Christmas Day 1642, in a Lincolnshire farmhouse, was born the greatest scientific genius the world has known. Isaac Newton was a premature and tiny baby, and the midwives who went off to get medicines for him doubted whether he would be alive on their return. Yet from these undistinguished origins arose the man whose mind laid the foundations of many branches of modern science.

Isaac's father, an illiterate yeoman farmer, had died three months previously. Although the cottage at Woolsthorpe is described as a manor house, and Isaac Newton became in effect lord of the manor, he was not heir to any fortune and he was expected to become a working farmer like his father.

His background did allow him to receive a good schooling in the local day schools and, later, in nearby Grantham. He was by no means an outstanding scholar—he was not very interested in the classical studies of the day, and spent much of his time making working models and studying the world around him. When prompted by his schoolmaster, by such tricks as placing him low in the class, he would make a successful effort to shine at his school work. All his pocket money, however, went on buying tools so that he could make better gadgets.

Newton's mother had married a local vicar and gone to live with him when Newton was only four, leaving him in the care of his grandmother: this may well have had a traumatic effect on him, affecting his later relationships with people.

When he was in his early teens, however, his stepfather having died, Isaac had to return to Woolsthorpe to help with the farm. He was of less use than his mother had hoped. When tending sheep, for example, he would get so engrossed with a book, some invention, or in watching the stream, that the sheep would very likely get into the corn. Once, when returning from Grantham, he dismounted for a hill, forgot to remount and plodded home leading the horse, deep in thought. Throughout his life, Newton had the reputation of being a true absent-minded professor.

His schoolmaster recognized the intellect that was within Newton, and persuaded his mother to let him return to school. When Isaac eventually went to university at Cambridge, the farm workers reckoned that was all he was good for, and would never make anything of himself.

Newton's degree was undistinguished, but at Cambridge he met Isaac Barrow, then Professor of Mathematics, who must have sparked off something within Newton for shortly afterwards the dreamy-eyed boy began to concentrate on his most original work. In his graduation year, 1665, when Newton was 23, bubonic plague broke out in England and he returned to Woolsthorpe to avoid it. It was here that all the influences on him had their effect: he looked back on those two years of seclusion at his mother's cottage as the most significant of his life.

Isaac Newton himself was the source of the famous story that while sitting in the orchard on a warm autumn afternoon, the fall of an apple to the ground set him wondering about the nature of gravity. Talking later, he said that he wondered why the apple always fell towards the centre of the Earth, and reasoned that all matter attracts the rest of matter to it.

At Woolsthorpe, too, he performed his experiments on the nature of light, passing white light through a prism to produce a *spectrum* (Newton's word) of colours. He realized that white light is no more than all the colours seen together, and made many more investigations into the nature of light and optics.

All this time, he was developing his ideas on mathematics, resulting in the discovery of the calculus or, as he called it, the 'Method of Fluxions'.

On Newton's return to Cambridge, Barrow stepped down in favour of him as Professor of Mathematics. One might imagine that Newton would publish the results of his work as soon as possible; actually he seems to have had little desire to publish, and when he did produce his results it was only at the insistence of others.

Newton's introduction into the full swing of academic life came with his election to the Royal Society in 1672 when he made the first working reflecting astronomical telescope. He gave a paper reporting his works on optics, and at once fell foul of Robert Hooke (*q.v.*), who upheld the wave theory of light as against Newton's corpuscular theory. Actually, each was right in his own way, according to modern quantum theory.

Hooke and Newton quarrelled many times over the years; there were also bitter debates as to whether Newton or the German mathematician Leibniz had invented the calculus.

Above right: Sir Isaac Newton at 60, in 1702, a copy of the Kneller portrait. Newton was grey before he was 40; here he wears a wig. By this time he had changed from being a withdrawn academic to a hardened administrator, used to dealing with the coin clippers and counterfeiters who were prosecuted by the Mint. His quarrel with Hooke had been ended by the latter's death, but his dispute with Leibniz was only just beginning. The duel was to be won by Newton's immense prestige, but Leibniz, too, was to be killed by the strain.

Right: reflecting telescope made by Newton for the Royal Society. This system, with its tranversely mounted eyepiece, is still known as the Newtonian design. The concave mirror is 3.4cm in diameter and the focal length 15cm.

The truth is that many of Newton's discoveries were in the air at the time, and would before long have been put forward by others; but Newton's skill and genius tied the loose ends together to produce the final results.

In the course of his pioneering experiments Newton formulated several of the fundamental laws of modern physics. A scientific 'law' is a general statement which can explain the results of a number of different experiments; this generalization can then be used to predict the outcome of other, similar, experiments. The basic principles of dynamics (the study of how forces act on objects) are summed up in Newton's three Laws of Motion first published in the *Principia* in 1684.

Newton's First Law says that *any moving body will continue to move in a straight line and at a constant speed unless it is acted upon by an outside force.* This is not immediately obvious, since on Earth we are used to moving objects eventually stopping. But this is because outside forces, such as friction and air resistance, act on the body to slow it down.

What happens when, as in most practical cases, an outside force does act on a moving body is covered by the Second Law: *if a force is applied to a body, its momentum will change in such a way that the rate of change of momentum is equal to the magnitude of the force.* The momentum is the mass of the body multiplied by its velocity (speed), and so another way of stating the second Law is that *the force on a body is equal to the mass of the body multiplied by the acceleration produced by the force:* Force = mass × acceleration. A consequence of this law is that if the same force is applied to two objects with different masses, the less massive body will accelerate more than the more massive one.

The Third Law states that *for every action there is an equal and opposite reaction.* The action and reaction refer to the forces on two different bodies; for example, the weight of a chair standing on a floor must be balanced by an upward 'reaction' force of the floor on the chair, or else (according to the second Law) the chair would be accelerated towards the centre of the Earth.

Anyone who tries to jump off a stationary toboggan notices an effect of the Third Law: the toboggan begins to move in the opposite direction even before the person's feet

Newton's work on gravitation was inspired by the fall of an apple (this is his own story). From this he reasoned that the force which attracted the apple towards the Earth's centre was the same as that which held the Moon in its orbit around the Earth.

leave it.

The action of a rocket demonstrates all the laws of motion. A rocket at rest on the ground, or coasting through space with the engine switched off, is obeying the First Law. When the engine is on, the force with which the propellant is ejected from the rocket must be balanced by a reaction force of the propellant on the rocket, and it is this reaction force which drives the rocket forward. These two forces must be equal, and act in opposite directions (Third Law). Since the mass of the rocket is much greater than that of the ejected propellant, the rocket is accelerated to a very much slower velocity than that of the propellant (Second Law).

Newton's Law of Gravitation describes how the gravitational force between any two objects varies with their masses and the distance between them. Each body experiences a force equal to the product of the masses of the two bodies multiplied by the universal Constant of Gravitation, G, and divided by the square of their separation. Newton was unable to explain the origin of gravitation, and Einstein's General Theory of Relativity proposed that the geometry of space near massive bodies is altered, so that the quickest

distance (the *geodesic*) between two points is not a straight line. By substituting the word 'geodesic' for 'straight line' in Newton's First Law, Einstein (*q.v.*) was able to incorporate gravity in the First Law of Motion. In spite of relativity, however, the Second and Third Laws are still, three hundred years after their formulation, fundamental to modern science.

Newton's investigations of the cooling of a hot body led to his law of cooling: *the rate of cooling is proportional to the difference in temperature between the object and its surroundings*. The rate of cooling is measured by the rate at which the temperature of a body falls; so a body at a high temperature relative to its surroundings will initially cool fast, and its temperature falls rapidly. As its temperature decreases, however, the cooling becomes slower, and so the temperature falls less rapidly. This type of behaviour is known as an *exponential decay*, and strictly speaking, although the temperature of the body becomes closer and closer to that of the surroundings, it will never become exactly the same.

Opticks was published in 1704. By this time Newton, seeking a more prominent situation than that of a mere academic, took on an important post at the Royal Mint, where he played a large part in revising the coinage system.

Newton never married, though there were romantic tales of a childhood sweetheart. He seems to have reserved his attentions for work only. He spent a vast amount of time studying theology, alchemy, and the chronology of ancient civilizations, but his work on these subjects is now practically forgotten. In his own day, as now, his work on physics and mathematics made him an internationally renowned figure. When he died in 1727, he was buried in Westminster Abbey, an honour previously reserved for monarchs, politicians, soldiers, and other such worthies.

Left: title page of Newton's Opticks, *which was not published until 1704, after his arch-enemy Hooke had died. Only then would Newton accept the presidency of the Royal Society, though he had been a leading member for over 30 years. In 1705 he became the first scientist to be knighted.*

NIÉPCE, Joseph Nicephore (1765-1833)

Seven years after the nineteenth century began, Joseph Niépce and his elder brother Claude patented a marine internal combustion engine. It worked well enough that the brothers confidently expected its instant purchase by manufacturers, but Claude spent most of the rest of his life unsuccessfully trying to exploit it in his native France and abroad. The credit for the other great Niépce discovery therefore belongs solely to Joseph, although Claude undoubtedly made some contribution. They christened the invention 'heliography'. We call it photography.

When Claude and Joseph served in the post-Revolutionary armed forces, the latter took an additional name, Nicéphore ('bringer of victory'), by which he is usually known. He caught typhoid in the south of France and, as the military hospital was full, he was nursed by a local family. He married their daughter and, when he was invalided out of the army, brought her to his home town, Chalon-sur-Saône, Burgundy. Later, Etienne Marey (*q.v.*) and Louis and Auguste Lumière (*q.v.*) also lived in Burgundy, so it is an important place in the history of photography.

Niépce interested himself in lithography and his attempts, begun in 1816, to copy engravings on to light-sensitive plates, were his first photographic experiments. They were similar to those of two Englishmen: Thomas Wedgwood, in the 1790s, and William Henry Fox Talbot, inventor of the negative-positive process on which modern photography is based.

At first, Niépce sensitized his plates with silver salts, which had been known for two hundred years to darken when exposed to sunlight. But his experiments failed in the same way as those of Wedgwood: without the right chemical to stop the darkening at the precise moment that the required image appeared, the process went on until the plate was black all over. Within three years, Sir John Herschel (*q.v.*) observed that sodium thiosulphate (it was called 'hypo-sulphite' at the time, thus 'hypo'), stopped the darkening, so 'fixing' the image. But it was too late for Niépce, who had already turned to bitumen of Judea, an asphalt-like substance which he must have known well from its common use in lithography, and which hardens and does not change colour. With it, he made successful copies of engravings in 1822. The process was a direct positive one, since the hardened bitumen, representing the highlights, was white against a darkened metal background.

Niépce conceived the same idea as Talbot did a decade later: if he could copy and fix engravings, why not do the same with life itself? He set to work to capture the images of the *camera obscura* by heliography. Over the next few years, he took a gradually improving series of views from his study window, finally getting a result he could call successful in 1826. It needed an exposure of about eight hours. These views, of which one still exists, were the world's first permanent photographs 'from nature' though, being made of bitumen of Judea on pewter, they in no way led to modern photographic technology.

But heliography did lead to the workable process developed by Louis Daguerre (*q.v.*), who had become Niépce's partner in 1829. Six years before daguerreotypes were revealed to the public, Niépce died. Had he lived until that exciting year of 1839, those beautiful and sharp pictures —which were to dominate photography for the next twenty years—might have been known by his name rather than by Daguerre's.

Above right: the earliest surviving picture taken by Niépce, dating from 1827; it shows the view over the rooftops from his window. The strange lighting is caused partly by the eight-hour exposure, during which the sun moved round, and partly by the photographic materials: white bitumen of Judea on dark grey pewter.

Right: contemporary mezzotint portrait of Niépce, made around 1800, when he was in his thirties. The mezzotint process, which gave intermediate shades of grey in a printed reproduction, would have been studied by Niépce, who was trying to do much the same himself in his early experiments with light sensitive materials.

NOBEL, Alfred Bernhard (1833-1896)

Alfred Nobel's name is perpetuated in the Nobel prizes for science, literature and peace, yet during the course of his life as a prolific inventor perhaps his most notable achievement was the development of dynamite, first patented in Britain in 1867 and in the USA in 1868.

He was born in Stockholm on 21 October 1833, the third son of Immanuel Nobel, a highly talented inventor and engineer who, although he went bankrupt in both his native Sweden and in Russia, contributed a great deal to both countries, especially in armaments. Alfred travelled widely, spending a year in the USA, and in spite of his lack of formal education became fluent in five languages.

His first patent, for a kind of gasholder, was granted in 1857, but he devoted most of his energies to the study of explosives, particularly nitroglycerine. Despite a disastrous explosion in 1864 which killed his younger brother and four other people, he developed a detonator using fulminate of mercury which made possible the commercial exploitation of explosives which did not explode with simple ignition.

He was determined to discover a method whereby the extremely potent but dangerous liquid nitroglycerine could be handled with reasonable safety. In 1866 he found that, by the addition of kieselguhr (diatomaceous earth), which acted as an absorbent, it was possible to produce a solid blasting substance which could be manufactured and used with relative safety, with the reduction in the explosive force of only 25%.

Following the immediate success of dynamite, Nobel continued his work on explosives and in 1875 introduced blasting gelatine, made by combining nitroglycerine with guncotton to produce an even more powerful explosive.

In 1871 he came to Britain and formed the Nobel Explosives Co Ltd, which opened a factory at Ardeer in the west of Scotland. He had a laboratory in Hamburg from 1865 to 1872, and he worked in Paris from 1873 to 1890, but the last years of his life were spent mostly in San Remo, Italy.

In 1887 he discovered *ballistite*, a military explosive that was one of the first smokeless powders and which greatly reduced the smoke cloud that had until then accompanied the firing of any piece of artillery. First used by the Italians, ballistite was a predecessor of cordite, and Nobel fought bitterly with the British government to prove that cordite infringed his ballistite patents, but he finally lost the case in 1895. Cordite is still used as a propellant.

The total number of patents granted to Nobel throughout the world was an impressive 355. He amassed a fortune through his inventions, and added to it with his investments in the Bofors munitions works in Sweden and in the Romanian oil fields at Baku which were run by his elder brothers Ludvig and Robert.

He was a lonely man who never married and who suffered from chronic illness most of his life. His cynicism and pessimism concealed his idealistic and benevolent nature, but perhaps also explain the apparent contradiction between his contributions to the armaments industry and the provision in his will for the vast bulk of his estate to be used for the establishment of the five world-renowned prizes named after him. These prizes, for physics, chemistry, physiology or medicine, literature and peace, were first awarded in 1901. The Nobel Foundation and the Bank of Sweden added a sixth prize, for economics, in 1969. Each award consists of a gold medal, a diploma and money. Alfred Nobel died in San Remo on 10 December 1896.

Left: 1897 photograph of the Nobel dynamite factory at Ardeer, Scotland. The explosive is being hand mixed; the floor is covered in sand to allow spilt explosive to be swept up. This would not be considered adequate in a modern factory.

Below: Alfred Nobel, by Ostermann.

OERSTED, Hans Christian (1777-1851)

A central theme of 19th century physics was the unification of previously separate branches of the science. In 1820 Hans Christian Oersted made one of the earliest and most significant discoveries in this respect when he found a connection between electricity and magnetism.

The son of a poor apothecary, Oersted grew up in the small, remote town of Rudkjöbing, which is on the Danish island of Langeland. There he and his younger brother conducted an extraordinary self-education programme which, with only slight tutorial assistance, took them all the way to entrance at the University of Copenhagen in 1794. Oersted's brother eventually gained great eminence in the Danish legal profession, while Oersted himself turned to science and became Denmark's leading physicist.

Oersted's physical research was profoundly influenced by philosophical ideas. Having learned German as a boy, Oersted absorbed German philosophy and completed his doctoral dissertation on Kant's philosophy in 1799. While visiting Germany in 1801, he met, among others, Friedrich Wilhelm Joseph Schelling. Schelling taught that all the apparently separate powers of nature (such as electricity and magnetism) were, in reality, unified. Oersted accepted Schelling's general view of nature but came to place more importance than did Schelling on the necessity of empirically demonstrating the connections between nature's powers.

Oersted's desire for empirical evidence stemmed naturally from his scientific interests. In 1800 he took charge of an apothecary's shop and delivered lectures on chemistry. In the same year the announcement of Alessandro Volta's (q.v.) invention of a battery caught Oersted's attention and led to his own electrical researches. In 1806, at the age of 29, he became Professor of Physics at the University of Copenhagen. During many years of scientific research, Oersted frequently expressed his belief in the unity of nature's powers and continued searching for a connection between electricity and magnetism. In 1820 he found it. While delivering a lecture, Oersted brought a magnetic needle close to a wire carrying an electric current. The needle was deflected. Unlike other forces in nature already known, the force between the electric wire and the magnetic needle turned out to be a non-central force. Whereas a falling rock, for example, is attracted towards the centre of the Earth, Oersted's magnetic

needle was not attracted towards the wire. No matter where it was placed in the vicinity of the wire, it pointed perpendicular to the wire. This indicated the presence of a force encircling the wire.

When Oersted sent word of his results throughout Europe a few months after his initial discovery, he caused a sensation and prompted a whole new line of scientific research. Attacking problems posed by Oersted's discovery, physicists found many other connections between electricity and magnetism and formulated far-reaching theories to explain them. Especially important were the researches of Ampère (q.v.) in France and Faraday (q.v.) in England.

Although primarily known for this one discovery, Oersted did research in other areas as well—most importantly on the compressibility of water. Also, his literary and political interests made him a figure of some note in the broader areas of Danish intellectual life.

Above right: engraving of Hans Christian Oersted. He seems to be holding a piece of aluminium, a recently discovered element of which he made the first pure sample in 1825. On the table is a compass needle, commemorating his famous experiment of 1819.

Right: the 1819 experiment. Current passing through the metal rod causes the compass needle to deflect at right angles to the current direction.

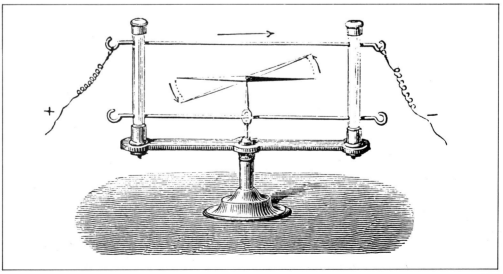

OHM, Georg Simon (1787-1854)

Although electricity had been known and studied for centuries, an electric current was not produced until 1800, by Volta (*q.v.*), when Georg Simon Ohm was 13 years old. It was in this new and exciting area of physics that Ohm discovered the fundamental law which bears his name.

Ohm, who was the son of a prosperous locksmith, grew up in Erlangen, Bavaria. His father had found his own knowledge of mathematics helpful and decided that Ohm and his brother should also study mathematics before joining the family business. Accordingly, when they finished elementary school, they entered the *Gymnasium* (secondary school) in Erlangen. Their mathematical successes there brought them to the attention of Karl Christian von Langsdorf, professor at the University of Erlangen. Langsdorf's proclamation of the brothers' genius launched them into scientific careers.

In 1805 Ohm entered the University of Erlangen. During the next few years he spent periods at the University of Erlangen and also held a series of teaching posts elsewhere. Finally, in 1817 at the age of thirty, he found a secure position teaching mathematics and physics at the Cologne Gymnasium. Now his interest began to turn more and more towards original research, and in 1827 he published his principal work, *The Galvanic Circuit, Mathematically Treated.*

Ohm's main finding concerned the relationship between the voltage, resistance, and current in an electric circuit. Now known as Ohm's law, the relationship can be written as $V = IR$, where I is the current in the circuit, V the voltage producing the current, and R the resistance of the circuit to the current. Hence, if the voltage is doubled, the current will be doubled; if the resistance is doubled, the current will be halved. The unit in which resistances are measured has been named the ohm. The inverse of the resistance is called the conductance (G), and the name of its unit is Ohm's name spelled backwards—the mho. This definition of conductance is expressed by the two equations: $G = I/R$ and $I = GV$.

Ohm's law is an example of a frequent occurrence in the history of science—the discovery of a very simple correlation of phenomena which previously appeared erratic and complicated. For various reasons, however, Ohm's results were not immediately accepted. One reason was the prevalence in early 19th century Germany of the view that experimentation and mathematics were irrelevant to a true understanding of nature. For supporters of this view, Ohm's results were simply beside the point. Others took Ohm's results more seriously but, with the experimental apparatus available, had great difficulty in verifying them. Recognition eventually came to Ohm in the early 1840s from British scientists. The Royal Society of London awarded him its Copley Medal in 1841, and in 1843 the great British electrician Charles Wheatstone praised Ohm's work as having guided his own.

This foreign acclaim reversed Ohm's fortunes in Germany. From a man somewhat embittered by neglect, he became a man of high reputation for the last decade of his life. He spent these last years developing a molecular theory to explain virtually all physical phenomena, but the theory was far from complete when he died. Einstein, Lord Kelvin (both *q.v.*) and others have tried to find a 'unified field theory' and failed, but the fascination with the concept remains. Nature seems full of obvious analogies.

Above: Georg Simon Ohm, wearing the Copley Medal.

Below: reconstruction of Ohm's current measuring device, supplied by heat powered thermocouples to avoid the voltage variations of primitive batteries.

PAPIN, Denis (1647-1712)

In the early history of the steam engine, Denis Papin, a French physicist, was first to propose that the condensation of steam in a cylinder would produce a vacuum into which a piston would be driven by the pressure of the air above. In this way he linked the experimental science of artificial vacuums with the needs of technology.

Denis Papin is always described as doctor of medicine, but cannot have practiced long, for at the age of 26 he was taken on by Christiaan Huygens (*q.v.*) as a research worker for the Académie Royale des Sciences in Paris, where he worked on Huygens' idea of evacuating a cylinder by the explosion of a charge of gunpowder, which was much more rapid than evacuation by means of a pump.

Two years later Papin decided to move to London, perhaps because as a Protestant he feared religious discrimination. Recommended by Huygens, he held a comparable position with Boyle (*q.v.*) and may have been responsible for improvements to Boyle's later air pumps. In 1681, he published his first major invention, the 'digester', a crude progenitor of the pressure cooker and the autoclave. As the boiling point of water is related to the pressure on it, water under great pressure will not boil until it reaches a proportionately high temperature. Water can thus be used to dissolve hard bones, and reduce them to an edible jelly. Members of the Royal Society were invited to a 'Philosophic Dinner' to taste the results. Papin then devised a scheme to use atmospheric pressure to drive an engine, but it came to nothing. Papin went to Venice for a while, returned to England in 1684, and in 1687 at last obtained a regular position as Professor of Mathematics at Marburg in Germany. He knew he was expected to show the mechanical applications of his knowledge. Within a year he had invented the earliest form of centrifugal pump, which was used in local drainage work; he applied the same principle to the ventilation of a coal mine. Neither version was widely adopted. Papin resumed the gunpowder experiments of his Paris days, but soon realized this was unsatisfactory. But, as he pointed out, 'since it is a property of water that a small quantity of it turned into vapour by heat has an elastic force like that of air, but on cold supervening is again resolved into water, so that no trace of the said elastic force remains' the expansion of steam would serve to raise the piston, and the subsequent condensation would provide the vacuum. This principle was duly tested and the results published in 1690. Papin hoped that he could use this to drive a ship, transmitting the motion of a row of pistons through racks and pinions to paddle wheels; there was a thought of land transport too, which may have reached the stage of a small model. But the centrifugal pump was the only invention which he developed so as to earn even a modest success. At Marburg he found few pupils and many trials, and in 1696 he moved to Cassel.

When Savery's steam engine was first presented before the Royal Society he was invited to give an opinion. But not until 1705 did he take up steam engine research again, abandoning his own idea for Savery's which he modified considerably. One prototype was built; it caused a stir locally, but was not exploited and was eventually dismantled. Papin then revived his notion of a steamboat, to be driven by his new engine, and he decided to return to London as there would be more call for such a ship in a great port. A small manually operated paddleboat had been tried out on the river Fulda,

Top: Denis Papin, engraving of 1689.

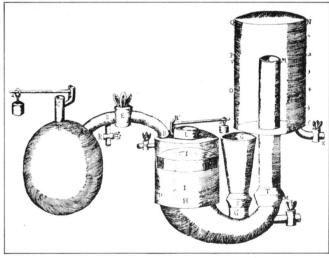

Above: Papin's improvements on the steam engine built by Thomas Savery (c 1650–1715). Papin recognized the superiority of Savery's machine, while Savery had abandoned development; but Papin died in poverty. The safety valves (with weights) are Papin's idea.

in Germany, but was smashed up by local bargemen, afraid of competition.

In London, Papin, now over 60, tried to persuade the Royal Society to sponsor his boat, asking for no more than £15 to cover the cost of the boiler; trials would show his version's superiority to the original Savery engine. But Savery now held the whiphand: Papin was turned down, and he died in London in poverty and obscurity. He had enjoyed the support of some of the greatest physicists in Europe, yet his life is a tale of wandering and frustration.

PARSONS, Charles (1854-1931)

Charles Algernon Parsons, who became famous for his invention of the steam turbine, was the son of the third Earl of Rosse, a distinguished engineer and astronomer. He was born in London, but spent most of his boyhood at the family home of Birr Castle in Ireland, where his father had built the world's largest telescope. Charles Parsons never went to school, but received private tuition from the eminent scientists who visited his father. He was a bright scholar, enjoyed outdoor sports—especially rowing—and spent many happy hours making things in his father's workshop. In 1866 Charles and his brothers constructed a 4 hp steam carriage which reputedly travelled at 10 mph.

At the age of 17 Charles Parsons entered Trinity College, Dublin, then two years later he moved to St John's College, Cambridge, where he obtained a degree in mathematics. At university his practical experiments included an unusual high-speed steam engine. This was an epicycloidal engine in which the cylinders actually rotated around the crankshaft, but at half its speed.

In 1877 Parsons joined W G Armstrong & Co at Elswick as an apprentice, and here he was allowed to build his engine. Kitson's of Leeds took over the manufacture of this engine and Charles Parsons joined them at the end of his four-year apprenticeship. He set up an experimental shop and turned his attention to torpedoes. In Leeds he met Katherine Bethell, and they were married in January 1883. Part of their honeymoon was spent watching torpedo trials at Roundhay Lake in Leeds. His wife unfortunately caught rheumatic fever, but recovered in the spring and their honeymoon was resumed with an extended visit to America.

When they returned, Parsons, now aged 29, joined Clarke, Chapman & Co at Gateshead and his most important work began. The firm wanted a high-speed steam engine to drive a dynamo and Parsons decided to forget the reciprocating engine and turned to the idea of a steam turbine. The principle of a turbine is rather like a windmill, but with steam turning tiny enclosed blades instead of the wind turning sails. There are no reciprocating parts, so the turbine is very smooth running, but extremely high speeds are necessary to achieve sufficient power. Parsons' first turbine was built in 1884; five years later over 350 had been supplied, including the first for a public power station. In 1889 Parsons set up his own company in Newcastle, which manufactured, besides steam turbines, dynamos [generators] and various electrical apparatus. Probably the most spectacular demonstration of the steam turbine was the unofficial appearance of his little vessel *Turbinia* at the 1897 naval review held at Spithead, in the south of England. The first vessel to be powered by turbine, she had a top speed of $34\frac{1}{2}$ knots and was much faster than any other ship afloat. The steam turbine replaced the old steam engines in many fields and even today most power stations are powered by steam turbines.

Parsons continued experimenting with gearing, optical instruments and attempts to crystallize carbon. He was knighted in 1911. He died 20 years later, while on a cruise in the West Indies.

Above right: Sir Charles Parsons in 1921.

Right: axial-flow turbo-blower designed and built in 1901 by Parson's own company in Newcastle.

PASCAL, Blaise (1623-1662)

Skill at mechanical engineering and experimental physics is not often combined in the same personality with intense religious feeling and a brilliant, nervous prose style: Blaise Pascal must be very rare in excelling at all four. The first to construct a workable calculating machine, he demonstrated atmospheric pressure, established theoretical principles for the hydraulic transmission of power, and contributed extensively to mathematics, from conic sections to probability theory.

His mother died when he was three and his father then devoted himself to the upbringing of the boy and his two sisters. Keenly interested in mathematics and in new ideas in science, as well as fervently devout, he passed these attitudes on to his son, who spent an enclosed and withdrawn childhood, suffering often from ill health. It is said his father would not teach him geometry for fear it would overtax his delicate system—so he worked out the basic theorems for himself, chalking on the tiles of his nursery floor.

When Pascal was 16 the family moved to Rouen, where his father was to be commissioner for upper Normandy. To help with the accounts, the boy developed an adding machine; a set of dials activated gears with ten teeth (or other numbers appropriate to non-decimal currency), which turned drums marked with the numerals. Each gear shaft bore a catch to move the next gear one tooth for each of its own revolutions. The figures to be added were dialled in turn, and the sum appeared in a window in the outer plate. The device could also be used for subtraction, but multiplication was a slow and awkward process. Over the years he did what he could to popularize his invention, and a few dozen models were built. But they were very expensive, so although their ingenuity was admired, few were bought.

In 1646, Pascal learned of the experiments by Torricelli (*q.v.*) on the artificial creation of a vacuum, and he began to re-create these experiments for himself, devising fresh apparatus, such as the 'vacuum within a vacuum', so as to observe what happens in the absence of any external force to keep the mercury column in its place. But what held the mercury in place in the single tube? Torricelli had suggested it was the weight of the air; Pascal argued this could best be proved by comparing mercury levels at the foot and the peak of a mountain. Tests were carried out on the Puy de Dôme, according to his instructions, in September 1648. His predictions were confirmed; he hoped this could now be used to measure the heights of mountains and changes in the weather, interpreted as changes in the weight of the atmosphere. Nevertheless he was involved in a long controversy about whether he really had created an artificial vacuum, for many then still held the belief in 'horror vacui'—a true vacuum is impossible in nature. The argument led him to treat air as a compressible fluid in his *Treatise of the Weight of the Mass of the Air*; he then proceeded to discuss the behaviour of the incompressible fluid, water, in his *Treatise of the Equilibrium of Fluids*. Here he demonstrated what became known as Pascal's Principle, that in a fluid at rest the pressure is transmitted equally in all directions. He was able to relate the state of equilibrium between two connected columns of water of different diameter to the law of the lever, and so link hydrostatics to general mechanics. He saw this principle could be used in machinery. Much later the hydraulic press and similar devices were derived from it.

Top: Blaise Pascal in a contemporary engraving.

Above: his adding machine worked like a car odometer.

All this research was done before Pascal was thirty—in 1654 he had an intense religious experience, and gave up science, mathematics and technology, except for some work on the solution of the cycloid (undertaken to distract his mind from toothache) and the promotion of a scheme for urban public transport. He was drawn into religious controversy; notes for a defence of Christianity were published as his *Pensées* (thoughts) after his death. More conscious than his contemporaries of the implications of the new physics for his religion, these thoughts were as incisive and original as his scientific work. But these last years of his life were dominated by illness and pain; he died before he was forty, having packed three careers into a short working life.

PASTEUR, Louis (1822-1895)

Pasteur was the son of a tanner, and received an excellent medical education. His doctorate had to do with crystallographic problems, and he became a pioneer in what is now called stereochemistry, but his name is a household word because he was the 'father of microbiology', developing the germ theory of fermentation and disease, as well as vaccines for anthrax and rabies.

In 1854 he became Professor of Chemistry and Dean of Sciences at the University of Lille, and felt an obligation to involve himself in the problems of local industries. The problem of why vinegar sometimes soured during its production from beet juice led to a study of fermentation which lasted twenty years, which in turn established the role of micro-organisms in these processes.

In 1857 he announced his germ theory of fermentation, which was immediately controversial. Pasteur was not only a painstakingly hard worker, but the quality of his scientific intuition was without parallel. At the time it was thought that fermentation was a chemical decomposition process which did not require any organisms. There was also a theory of the 'spontaneous generation' of micro-organisms. Although Pasteur had little experimental proof of his theories, his intuitive use of them made possible improvements in the economically important industries of wine, alcohol, vinegar and brewing. Finally he was able to use his experimental results to show that phenomena sometimes attributed to spontaneous generation could only be explained by the germ theory, which held that contamination was caused by the activity of 'organized corpuscles' already present.

Two other discoveries were made as a result of the work on fermentation. Pasteur noticed that air (the oxygen) inhibited the activity of bacteria which changed sugar solution into butyric acid. Recognizing the importance of this, he coined the word 'anaerobic' to differentiate these bacteria from the aerobic, which live in the presence of air. Also, a process of partial heat sterilization arose from his studies on wine, while he was looking for methods to improve its properties of storage. The process is used almost universally today in developed countries for making milk safe, and is named after its inventor: pasteurization.

In 1865 Pasteur was asked to investigate diseases which were attacking silkworms, and severely damaging the French silk industry. He was not able to isolate the organism causing the disease, but he taught the industry to separate the eggs with black spots which hatched diseased worms. Beginning in 1877, and for the rest of his life, he studied infectious diseases, beginning with animals.

Although he had known nothing about silkworms, for example, to start with, analogies were already to be made between fermentation and some infectious diseases, and smallpox vaccination had already been established by Edward Jenner (q.v.). It was known that recovery from an infectious disease gave immunity from further attacks.

Pasteur studied anthrax, chicken cholera, swine erysipelas and hydrophobia (rabies). The study was a two-pronged attack on each disease: the attempt to isolate the causative organism and grow it in a suitable medium, and the discovery of ways to treat the condition. In 1879 he observed that chickens infected with an old culture of chicken cholera failed to develop the disease. He then infected two groups of chickens with a fresh culture; the new chickens died, while those which had already been infected did not. From this arose the idea of attenuation: that the strength of an infecting organism could be reduced. Pasteur followed this experimentation until he was able to introduce a number of vaccines; the vaccine for rabies made him world famous.

Again, he was not able to isolate the organism now known to be a virus (and too small to be seen in a microscope) which causes rabies, but he discovered that he could grow it in living experimental animals. Attenuation was accomplished by storing in dry sterile air the infected spinal cords

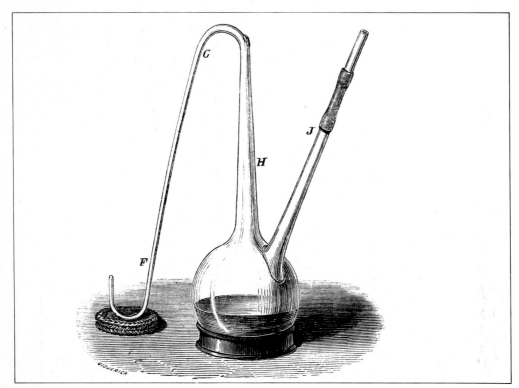

Left: flask used by Pasteur to show that fermentation and putrefaction are caused by air-borne germs and not spontaneous generation. The contents were sterilized and air-borne organisms stopped in the bend; there was no change until the flask was broken at H. From a French book of 1870.

Opposite page: photo of Louis Pasteur.

Overleaf: Pasteur at work in his laboratory with some of his early sterilizing equipment.

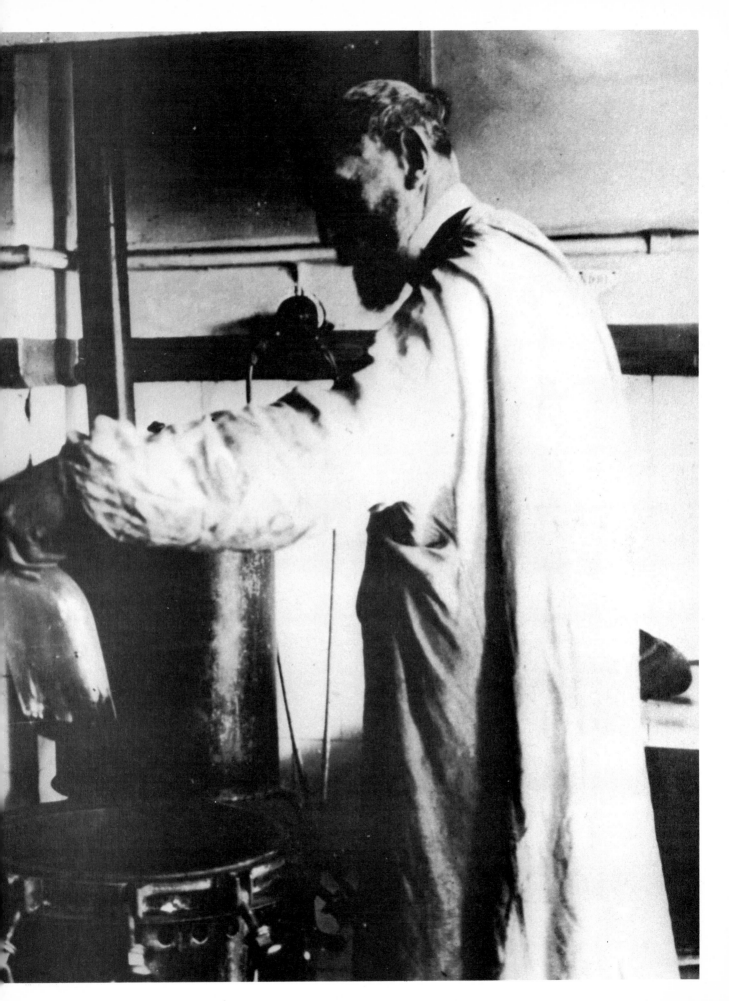

ARGUMENTUM AD HOMINEM.

"OH, JOSEPH! TEDDY'S JUST BEEN BITTEN BY A STRANGE DOG! DOCTOR SAYS WE'D BETTER TAKE HIM OVER TO PASTEUR *AT ONCE!*"

"BUT, MY LOVE, I'VE JUST WRITTEN AND PUBLISHED A VIOLENT ATTACK UPON M. PASTEUR, ON THE SCORE OF HIS CRUELTY TO RABBITS! AND AT *YOUR INSTIGATION,* TOO!"

"OH, HEAVENS! NEVER MIND THE RABBITS *NOW!* WHAT ARE ALL THE RABBITS IN THE WORLD COMPARED TO *OUR ONLY CHILD!*"

A George du Maurier cartoon from 'Punch', London, 20 July 1889. Many of the discoveries of the 19th century caused confusion in small minds.

from rabbits which had died of the disease. By repeatedly injecting dogs with progressively less attenuated virus, he was able to protect them from the most dangerous form of it, because of the formation of protective antibodies. Because of the time lag between infection and the onset of the dangerous development of the disease, the technique could be used to treat it as well as to prevent it.

The treatment of a badly bitten boy, followed by that of a shepherd, successfully established rabies vaccination, and ranks with Jenner's daring infection of a healthy boy with smallpox as one of the most famous moments in the history of medical science. Crowds of bitten patients flocked to Paris for treatment. Pasteur admitted his debt to Jenner in adopting Jenner's word 'vaccination' to describe his technique, although it had nothing to do with cowpox (*vaccinia*

in Latin).

Pasteur's greatest achievement was the founding of the science of microbiology, the importance of which cannot be overestimated. During the Franco-Prussian war, he persuaded doctors to sterilize their instruments and steam their bandages. Chemical sterilization was already known, but with the germ theory behind it, it became widely practiced (thanks to the Englishman Joseph Lister, 1827–1912). Pasteur was elected to the French Academy of Medicine in 1873; he did not have a medical degree, yet he was the greatest physician of all time. In modern biology only Darwin (*q.v.*) is in the same class; yet curiously, Pasteur could not accept a theory of evolution for the same reason he did not like 'spontaneous generation': these concepts offended his religious beliefs.

PLANCK, Max (1858-1947)

Max Planck is best known for his quantum theory of electro-magnetic radiation, which he first presented to a meeting of the German Physical Society in December 1900.

Born in Kiel in 1858, Max moved with his family to Munich where he attended school and university, later transferring to Berlin University to be taught by the great physicists of the day, Herman Von Helmholtz and Gustav Kirchhoff (*q.v.*). Throughout his long life Max Planck was interested in the study of heat, called thermodynamics. It was in this subject that he presented his doctoral thesis and published papers which led to his becoming a professor at Berlin University on Kirchhoff's death.

Unlike most scientists the breakthrough in scientific thought for which Planck is today remembered came rather late in life when he was 42. This was his discovery of the quantum theory of energy for which he was awarded the Nobel Prize in 1918. Planck was the first to realize that the energy of all electromagnetic waves (including light, heat and radio waves) can exist only in the form of discrete packages, or *quanta*, rather than being continuously distributed in a wave-like form. In this he returned to the 'corpuscular' theory of light which Newton (*q.v.*) had rejected.

Ironically Planck was both worried and frightened by the theory he proposed. A mild man descended from a long line of lawyers and civil servants, he was cautious in his speech and believed totally in the classical theories of electromagnetic radiation as explained by Maxwell (*q.v.*), which were shown by his theory to be inadequate at short wavelengths. Also he was not satisfied with the mathematical formulation of the quantum theory, as it gave the energy of a quantum of radiation as the product of the frequency of the radiation, and a small constant. Planck firmly believed that this constant could be removed. *Planck's constant, h*, as it is now called, is one of the fundamental constants of nature (like the velocity of light in a vacuum) and is vital to the understanding of the nature of atoms themselves and how they absorb and emit radiation.

Thus Planck was rather annoyed when his quantum theory was championed by an unknown Swiss clerk in a paper on the theory of relativity. The clerk's name was Albert Einstein (*q.v.*). After this bad start a firm friendship grew between the eager young Einstein and Planck, who was by now middle-aged. It was said that neighbours often heard them playing chamber music together, Einstein on his violin and Planck at the piano.

Perhaps it was partly this friendship as well as Planck's faith in God which enabled him to withstand the many trials in his life. He continued to teach physics in the decadent and crumbling Berlin and even to visit Hitler, in his capacity as secretary of the Prussian Academy of Sciences, until the age of seventy. Sadly for Planck and for German science, many of his colleagues, including Einstein, had to flee from the Nazis; and Planck's son, Erwin, was executed as an accomplice in the July 1944 plot against Hitler.

One of Max Planck's greatest sorrows was the rift in physics he felt he had caused. Until his death, at the age of almost ninety, he strove to reconcile the classical physics he believed in with the modern physics he had founded.

Right: Max Planck, and part of a letter he wrote to Arnold Sommerfeld in May 1916, dealing with the atom.

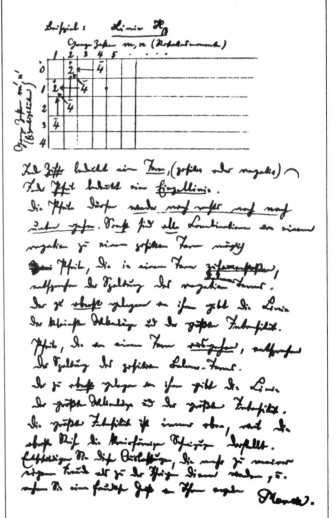

POULSEN, Valdemar (1869-1942)

Valdemar Poulsen was an engineer and inventor who helped the development of modern broadcasting and magnetic tape recording.

Poulsen was born in Copenhagen, where his father worked for the Danish Ministry of Justice. His early interests were strongly scientific, and he studied science but did not obtain a degree. In 1893 he joined the Copenhagen Telephone Company as an assistant engineer, and while he was still working there made his first important invention. This was the telegraphone, invented in 1898. It was a method of recording speech by magnetizing a steel piano wire so that the variation in the recorded magnetic field corresponded to the input signal. The machine would record for thirty minutes at a wire speed of 84 inches (213 cm) per second. Poulsen also described methods of magnetizing steel or paper tape coated with metallic powder, anticipating the development of modern tape recording. With these methods, the recording medium can be erased and re-used many times without loss of recording quality.

Poulsen applied in 1898 for a patent on his wire recorder; although a working model won the Grand Prix at the Paris Exposition of 1900, financial backing could not be found to produce the machine in Europe. With his associate P O Pederson, Poulsen formed the American Telegraphone Company to produce telephone recorders and dictating machines commercially, with the help of American financial backing. The machines were not well received by the public and there were differences between the stockholders which led to the failure of the company.

Next Poulsen turned his attention to radio communications. In 1903 he obtained a British patent for his adaptation of a singing arc generator. This had been invented in 1900 by an Englishman, W Duddell, who found that an arc lamp could be made to sing a musical note if placed in a direct current circuit containing inductance and capacitance. Poulsen's adaptation cooled the carbon anode and copper cathode and raised the power limit from 10 kHz to 100 kHz. When coupled to an antenna, the arc generated the first pure low-frequency continuous waves; in 1908, when it was first successfully tested, the arc had a transmitting range of 150 miles (more than 240 kms). His experimental radio station at Lyngby was a success, and long-wave stations with Poulsen generators which produced 1000 kW were in use by 1920. The United States Navy adopted Poulsen arc generators as standard equipment in 1912; in 1920 the Annapolis Naval Station (Maryland, USA) had two 350 kW Poulsen arc generators.

However, in 1913 a German Telefunken arc already had a range of 1550 miles (more than 2400 km), and with the invention of the thermionic valve [vacuum tube] by Lee De Forest and the introduction of valve transmitters in the 1920s, Poulsen's arc generator rapidly became obsolete. He continued his research into radio communications until his death in Copenhagen in July 1942.

Valdemar Poulsen's telegraphone, a wire recorder invented for recording telephone conversations. Poulsen's ideas anticipated all the magnetic recording of today, which is of enormous importance to communications and computer technology. His original steel wire has been succeeded by a plastic tape coated with ferric oxide, chromium dioxide or other magnetic materials, which is lighter, more flexible and allows the use of multiple tracks on the same tape; but wire recording is still used for flight recorders on aircraft, where robustness is the main requirement.

RÖNTGEN, Wilhelm Conrad (1845-1923)

Röntgen, the man who discovered X-rays, did not come from an academic family. He was the only child of a cloth merchant in the Rhineland, though the family moved to the elegant Dutch town of Apeldoorn when he was young. His early life was unremarkable, apart from an incident where his sense of fun got him expelled from his school when he was caught laughing at a caricature of a schoolmaster drawn by a friend.

Although no great scholar in his early years, he eventually managed to get a place at the Polytechnic Institute in Zürich, where he studied mechanical engineering. He spent much of his leisure time climbing the Swiss mountains, when not visiting a local inn called *Zum Grünen Glas*—'The Green Glass'. This was run by a former German revolutionary who had fled his native country, and who gave the students lessons, helped them with Latin translations and taught them fencing. After gaining his doctorate at the age of 24, Röntgen married one of the innkeeper's daughters, Bertha.

Meanwhile, his scientific reputation was growing and he was eventually made physics professor at Würzburg in Germany, where seven years later he made his greatest discovery.

In the winter of 1895, when he was 50, Röntgen was experimenting with a cathode ray discharge tube (or Crookes tube) completely enclosed in cardboard so that no light could escape. He observed that a sheet of paper coated with barium platino-cyanide some feet away from the discharge tube was glowing in the dark. This fluorescence had in fact been observed by several notable physicists, including J J Thomson (*q.v.*), over the previous decade, but ignored as being of no interest. Röntgen, however, realized the importance of this accidental discovery, and in the following six weeks he spent all his time investigating all the properties of these X-rays; he even ate and slept in his laboratory.

These new rays appeared to be emitted from the anode of the discharge tube, and unlike the cathode rays which were confined by the glass wall of the tube, penetrated the air outside the tube for a distance of some 6 ft (2 m). When Röntgen investigated the opacity of various substances to X-rays he found that in contrast they would only penetrate 1 mm of lead. As he was putting a small disc of lead into place in the beam, Röntgen noticed that apart from the black shadow of the lead, he could detect the outline of his finger and thumb. And because the opacities of flesh and bone are different, he could actually make out the slightly darker image of his bones within the fingers.

Röntgen correctly deduced that his newly-discovered rays must be a very short wavelength form of electromagnetic radiation like light waves, and not charged particles, since they are unaffected by a magnetic field.

The results of his six weeks of concentrated work were published in a series of classic papers. Röntgen himself named this new phenomenon X-rays, and was somewhat embarrassed when other physicists insisted on calling them Röntgen rays after their discoverer. He gave only one public lecture on his discovery, and declined many honours which were offered to him.

Unlike many scientific discoveries which need many years of painstaking research before they can be applied beneficially, Röntgen's X-rays were of immediate use; indeed some two months after their discovery they were used in a

Right: Wilhelm Röntgen, one of the greatest of German scientists; his work on X-rays was only a part of his achievement.

Below: the first X-ray picture was of his wife Bertha's right hand (the wedding ring is worn on the right hand in Germany). This is a positive print, taken from the original publication of the discovery.

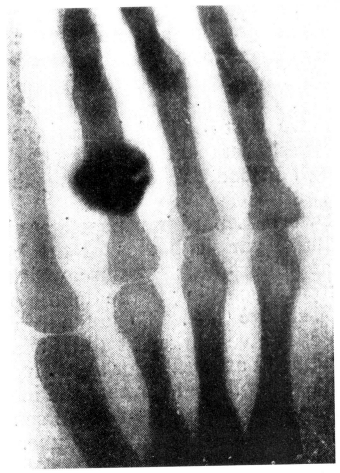

New Hampshire hospital in the diagnosis and treatment of a fracture, and it is in the field of medicine that they have gained almost universal usage. Their discovery led to important work by Becquerel (*q.v.*) in the field of phosphorescence and radioactivity. Such was their fame that in 1896 both *Punch* and *Life* published humorous poems in Röntgen's honour. In addition to his discovery and investigations into X-rays, Röntgen was an eminent physicist experimenting in magnetic effects of rotating dielectrics and electrical phenomena in crystals.

From Würzburg he moved to Munich at the turn of the century to take up a Chair in Physics, and died in that city at the age of 77, having spent the last three years of his life in retirement, revisiting his beloved mountain haunts of Switzerland.

ROYCE, Sir Henry (1863-1933)

For a man with the natural engineering ability of Frederick Henry Royce, he was born at the right time. At the turn of the century the motor car was still a novelty with tremendous scope for development, and in 1903 when Royce bought his first car, a second-hand Decauville, he already had a reputation for high quality workmanship and refinement of design detail. It was therefore not surprising that he soon began building his own cars.

Royce, the son of a miller, was born near Peterborough, in England, the youngest of five children. From an early age he showed a keen interest in how mechanical devices worked; at the age of three he fell into the mill race while examining the mill wheel and would have drowned had his father not managed to rescue him. When Royce was four his father's business failed and they came to London where he spent an impoverished childhood, his father dying when he was nine. He then sold newspapers until he was eleven, when he managed to attend school for a year. At 14 an aunt paid £20 for his apprenticeship to the Great Northern Railway, based at Peterborough. Here he acquired mechanical skills but no technical or commercial training and was forced to leave through lack of money at 17. In the meantime, however, he had taught himself electricity and algebra and, with electrical lighting gaining acceptance, managed to obtain a job with the London Electrical Light and Power Company

Above: Sir Henry Royce at the gate of his Sussex house.

Below: the most famous Rolls-Royce engine, the Merlin.

who sent him to Liverpool. Two years later he was once
more unemployed so, with a friend, set up a workshop in
Manchester. At first they made electric light filaments, later
electric bells, and business increased greatly when Royce
designed a reliable dynamo. Eventually they also made
electric cranes. But excellent though these products were,
they were not to make his name a household word.

After experimenting with the car he had bought, in 1904
Royce decided to build three experimental cars to his own
design. They were two-cylinder 10 hp models which included
overhead inlet valves (unusual for those days), ample water
cooling spaces to avoid overheating, additional leaves in the
springs for more comfort, and a gearbox with three forward
speeds and reverse. Royce designed his own coil and distri-
butor ignition system and his own carburettor, which had a
float spray feed and was fitted with an automatic valve. In
third gear the cars did 30 mph (48 kph) and each car weighed
about 1570 pounds.

The Hon Charles Stewart Rolls, who was looking for a
reliable British car to promote through his car firm, was
introduced to Royce, saw his cars, and in December, 1904
entered into an agreement with him. Royce was to produce
10 hp two-cylinder cars at a cost of £395 under the joint
name of Rolls-Royce. Such was their success that by 1908
they had opened a new factory at Derby. But by this time the
car they were manufacturing was the six-cylinder 40/50 hp
Silver Ghost.

In 1911 Royce's health failed and he was brought to
London, where doctors gave him only three months to live.
Years of working long hours, often without proper meals,
and deprivation in childhood had eventually caught up with
him. He recovered but was never to return to his factory at

Derby again; the rest of his life all his ideas would be
generated either at his villa in the south of France or his
home in Sussex. But his brain was active as ever, and so it
was arranged for a team of assistants to work on design
projects with Royce at his home. It is said that he could
design a component entirely in his head without taking a
single note, and then explain it in such detail that when
drawn by the draughtsman it was invariably correct.

At the outbreak of World War I any Rolls-Royce cars
that were around the factory were taken over for military
use, and the government asked them to produce aircraft
engines from both French and British designs. This was a
challenge to Royce, who decided to design his own. It was a
water-cooled 12-cylinder engine with two banks of six
cylinders in V formation; it weighed 900 lb and produced
200 hp. In 1915, after only six months' work, the first Eagle
engine was tested. This design was followed by the Hawk,
Falcon and Condor engines. Great ingenuity was shown in
Royce designs; the engines could often keep going after
some major parts had been shot away.

(Later, during World War II, the Rolls-Royce design
philosophy of modifying an existing design was shown to
good advantage in the Merlin aircraft engine. Originally
designed in 1934 for the Schneider Trophy seaplane races, it
had 790 hp; by the end of the war this had been increased to
over 2000, and the engine had powered the Spitfire, Hurri-
cane and Mustang fighter planes.)

Royce was knighted in 1930 and died in 1933. The work
he had begun was continued in his tradition of good workmanship. He was an extremely patient man who had never
accepted anything as being perfect, even his own designs.
A modest man, he claimed that he was 'just a mechanic'.

RUMFORD, Count (1753-1814)

Benjamin Thompson was born in Massachusetts. He worked as a shop assistant in Salem until he was badly injured in an accident involving fireworks, after which he moved to Boston, taking up a similar post. At the age of 19 he married a wealthy widow considerably older than he was, and they lived in a New Hampshire town called Rumford, which is now called Concord.

When the Revolutionary War broke out, Thompson's sympathies were with the King; indeed, there were more loyalists in those days than most Americans are aware of today. When the British troops left Boston, Thompson left with them, having spied for them on his countrymen. At the end of the war he considered himself to be in permanent exile. He was knighted by King George III.

In 1783 he went to the Continent, and eventually to work for Elector Karl Theodor of Bavaria, as a competent administrator. He established workhouses for beggars in Munich where army uniforms were made, and introduced the potato to the Continent. The Elector made him a Count in 1790, and for his title he took the name of the town where his wife had been born, though he had long left his wife and child behind in America.

In 1798 he made his most important contribution to science. While supervising the boring of cannon barrels, Thompson observed that they grew hot as the boring progressed, so that they had to be constantly cooled with water. Heat was still thought to be a mysterious fluid called caloric, and it was assumed that the boring allowed this fluid to pour out of the metal.

Thompson reasoned, however, that the heating continued as long as the boring did, and enough caloric was 'liberated' to melt the metal if it were put back in. He also noticed that the heating continued, and in fact speeded up, if the tool became dull so that less metal was being removed. He concluded that the motion of the machine was being converted somehow to heat, and that heat itself was a matter of motion. He also realized that the amount of heat could be measured by measuring the rise of temperature in the water, and was the first to try to calculate a mechanical equivalent of heat, although his figures were far too high and were corrected half a century later by Joule (*q.v.*).

Subsequently Thompson went back to England, where in 1799 he was admitted to the Royal Society, and performed an experiment with a quantity of water, which he weighed in both its liquid and frozen states. It weighed the same, proving that if caloric existed, it would have to be weightless. Also in 1799, he founded the Royal Institution, and invited such people as Davy and Young (both *q.v.*) to lecture. Davy, who became famous through his lecturing, agreed with Rumford's theory of heat, but most scientists still believed in the theory of caloric until Maxwell (*q.v.*) finally disproved it.

In 1804, despite the war between Britain and France, Thompson went to Paris, where he married the widow of

Count Rumford was an American of English parentage: he was knighted by King George III in 1784, and was made a count of the Holy Roman Empire for his service in Bavaria as Minister of War. He is best known for his work on the mechanical equivalent of heat, suggested to him by the heating up of cannon barrels during boring; he also founded the Royal Institution in London.

Lavoisier (*q.v.*), the famous chemist who had been a martyr to the French Revolution, and whose theory of heat Thompson had done his best to destroy. The marriage was not a happy one, and they separated after four years. In 1811 his daughter came from America to take care of him in his old age.

Thompson is said to have been an unpleasant man, and it would be easy to conclude that he had a flawed character. When he first came to England he apparently took bribes and he was suspected of selling military secrets to the French. He was finally unwelcome in Bavaria after the death of his patron, despite his accomplishments there. He married more than one rich widow, and reportedly said that Lavoisier was lucky to have got himself guillotined, because his wife was so hard to get along with. Moral attitudes in general were different then, however, and in any case Thompson had his idealistic side. Putting beggars to work making uniforms was a way of making them happy first so that they might become virtuous later, which was perhaps more practical than the opposite approach. He refused to patent any of his inventions, like Franklin (*q.v.*), and endowed a chair in applied science at Harvard.

RUTHERFORD, Ernest (1871-1937)

Rutherford's parents were first generation settlers in the South Island of New Zealand; his father had a flaxmill and sawmill near Nelson. There Ernest had such success, first at school and then at Canterbury College, Christchurch, NZ, that he was awarded a scholarship to study as a research student at Cambridge in England. He began with work on radio transmission, but soon after his arrival came news of the discovery of X-rays, and then of mysterious uranium radiation.

Rutherford spent some time working on the power of X-rays to confer electric charge on gases; then he turned to the problem of the rays emitted by thorium, the element next heaviest after uranium. By then he had moved to Montreal as Professor of Physics (at the age of twenty-seven) and on the strength of this had married Mary Newton, daughter of his landlady at Christchurch. While working on thorium and its emanation in collaboration with Frederick Soddy, they were able to isolate a substance, thorium X, which was chemically distinct from thorium (it is actually an isotope of radium) yet produced from it. So thorium is transformed into another element; the alchemist's dream of transmutation really takes place in nature and at a regular rate. Other radioactive products from uranium and radium were investigated, and it could be shown that each product has a definite half-life—when half a given amount has been turned into the next stage. Much of the next few years was spent in tracking down the various disintegration products and emanations—and relating them to their family trees. For this work he was awarded the Nobel Prize in 1908. The year before this he had returned to England, and in Manchester he built up a school of research into fundamental physics, the equal of any in the world.

But Rutherford was also keen to establish the true character of the radiations themselves. They could be classified into two groups depending on their power to penetrate matter. The less penetrating were more massive and more strongly charged electrically. He called them *alpha* and *beta*

Above: Ernest Rutherford (on the right) at the Cavendish Laboratory in Cambridge. The sign, put up because some of the thyratrons and other vacuum devices were sensitive to sound, was aimed at the loud-voiced Rutherford as much as at anyone else.

Below: Rutherford's lab at the Cavendish. After his retirement, the university authorities, fearful of radioactive contamination caused by 'splitting the atom', sealed it up until the end of 1977. When it was subsequently examined by men in protective clothing, it was found to be perfectly safe; in any case, Rutherford achieved his atomic distintegration in Manchester.

rays respectively. After some years he was able to prove that the former were atoms of helium, but without their negative electrons, and so had a double positive charge. These alpha particles became the missiles he used to bombard various targets.

When he investigated the way they scattered, as revealed by the scintillations they made on hitting a fluorescent screen, he concluded that each alpha was diverted by a single collision, so he was curious to see how widely they could be deflected from their path. It proved that a few could be turned through a much wider angle than expected: some actually reversed. 'It was as if a shell fired at a sheet of paper bounded back and hit you,' he commented.

In order to explain this effect, he proposed the idea that almost all the mass and all the positive electricity in an atom was concentrated on a tiny nucleus at its heart. The electrons circled round it like planets around the Sun.

World War I interrupted all this research; he worked instead on echo sounding to detect submarines. But in 1918 he resumed his work, and for the first time artificially transmuted a few atoms of nitrogen by artificially disrupting their nucleus. Rutherford became famous as the man who had 'split the atom'.

In 1919 he returned to Cambridge to head the Cavendish Laboratory. There he presided over the new style of physics, the investigation of the nucleus. He was supremely successful as a leader of a research team. Forthright, encouraging, enthusiastic, sociable, he left his 'young men' with a fund of Rutherford stories about his loud voice, gentle teasing and his cheerful exuberance—with no time for humbug, he always remained, as he said of himself, a simple man.

SMEATON, John (1724-1792)

Smeaton was among the first to determine the efficiency of the various energy sources of his day, water, wind and steam, demonstrating his conclusions by precisely measured experiments. He was no less renowned as a civil engineer; his masterpiece was the Eddystone lighthouse off Plymouth in the English Channel.

The son of William Smeaton, attorney of Austhorpe near Leeds, John Smeaton was intended for his father's profession, and was sent to study law in London at the age of eighteen. But even as a boy he loved to construct model machines, made his own tools and even built a little steam engine—then quite a novelty—which drained a fish pond in the family's garden. Rather to his father's annoyance, he became so interested in scientific instruments as to bind himself apprentice to an instrument maker. By 1750 he was ready to set up in trade for himself, and soon began to devise improvements to a wide variety of instruments, mainly for navigation. He submitted these to the Royal Society, of which he was elected a Fellow in 1753 at the age of twenty-nine. The next year he visited the Netherlands to study methods of canal and harbour construction there. Soon after his return, his reputation for mathematical and engineering skill earned him the contract to erect a new lighthouse on the Eddystone rocks. Two earlier wooden lighthouses had already been destroyed by fire and storm. He resolved to build a stone structure, despite the immense difficulties of construction work on such a site, and devised a system of dovetailing the stone blocks to provide mutual support.

It took three years to complete the job; Smeaton supervised on the spot with great courage. The new lighthouse stood up to severe gales, and Smeaton's name was made. The year of its completion, 1759, he began his experiments on the power of wind and water to turn mills; this was the first time a prolonged series of tests had been carried out to discover the most efficient form of windmill and waterwheel. Each particular component and element was varied in turn and the result of the alterations carefully measured, so as to arrive at the ideal shape and size of each part, and calculate effects on output. In 1769 he set about doing the same for steam power, studying the efficiency of the Newcomen engine. Where Watt, soon after, was to invent a revolutionary new machine, Smeaton sought rather to make

Left: John Smeaton, who is regarded as the first fully professional civil engineer, combining good construction techniques with economy.

Below: Smeaton's apparatus for measuring the power of various designs of windmill. Pulling the rope caused the column and model to turn, creating a breeze from the windmill's point of view. As its sails turned, they wound the weight up the column, giving an indication of the work done by the design. He also devised testing methods for watermills and steam engines.

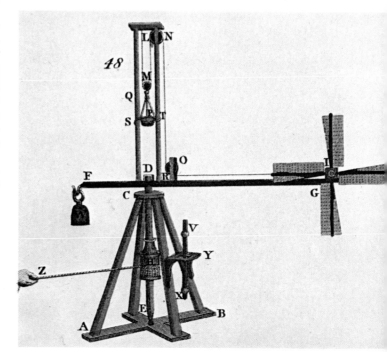

existing types more effective, again measuring the variations of each of the parts of the engines then in use.

Meanwhile, he was equally busy as a civil engineer. He designed three segmental arch bridges in Scotland and one, his only failure, in England. Most of the 1760s he spent in Scotland—his family had Scottish connections, and claimed descent from a well-known Scottish reformer. He was consulted on very many projects: harbours, bridges, drainage schemes, and designed much of the machinery of the famous Carron iron works. But his major work there was Scotland's first important canal, the Forth and Clyde, to link up the two estuaries which were the main highways of the country's commerce. Financial problems held work up; although begun in 1768, it was not completed for over twenty years, when Smeaton was well past sixty. In the south, his main undertaking was Ramsgate Harbour in 1774. But he continued his theoretical work and gathered around him in London a group of engineers interested in the development of their profession, nicknamed the 'Smeatonians', the nucleus from which the Institute of Civil Engineers later grew. But his home was always in his family's house at Austhorpe, where he had married; a shy reticent man, his chief diversion was astronomical observation which he found time for by raising his fees to fifty guineas a week to discourage the many clients who hankered after his services.

SMITH, Adam (1723-1790)

Adam Smith, regarded by many as the father of modern economics, was born in Kirkaldy, Scotland, the son of a Scottish Judge Advocate and Comptroller of Customs. He remained a bachelor for most of his life, and stayed for the most part in his native country.

However in 1740, after receiving his MA degree from Glasgow University, he worked for six years as a Fellow of Balliol College, Oxford. He then returned to Edinburgh, where his reputation as a public lecturer led to his election to the Chair of Moral Philosophy at Glasgow. In 1759 his first major work, *The Theory of Moral Sentiments*, was published.

It was to be another seventeen years before he published *The Wealth of Nations*, a book which dominated the teaching of political economy for half a century or more, and which earned him the reputation as a great economist. During those years Smith had spent some time in France talking to the Physiocrats, then the dominant French political economists; he had also acted as adviser to the Chancellor of the Exchequer; and he had developed his lectures on economics. So his most important book was the culmination of years of thought and experience. *The Wealth of Nations* was the product of the mind of the first systematic academic economist. It was received slowly at first, but by the end of his life it was becoming widely read by the public.

For the last twelve years of his life Smith was engaged as a commissioner of customs at Edinburgh; he never again produced anything of importance for publication.

Coming as it did at the very beginning of the industrial revolution in Britain, *Wealth of Nations* appropriately set out the theory of how the economy of a society works when conditions of free enterprise prevail. Smith developed the idea of the 'invisible hand' of the market. This was the mechanism which ensured that the economy did not degenerate into chaos, and that order prevailed.

According to Smith mankind was endowed by the 'Author of Nature' with certain natural characteristics—examples are a tendency to exchange goods with others, and a natural 'desire of bettering one's condition'. More importantly, man was naturally self-interested, and knew best his own interests. But if, in society, everyone pursued their own self-interest, why did not people's conflicting interests result in the breakdown of the economy? The answer lay in the 'invisible hand', which by adjusting the prices at which goods exchanged in the market ensured that all the people's urges to exchange were satisfied. Thus the economy thrived on self-interest. In a well-known phrase Smith argued that 'it is not from the benevolence of the butcher, the brewer, or the baker that we expect our dinner, but from their regard to their own interest'.

Having answered the question of why the economy with prevailing free enterprise did not degenerate into chaos, he then went on to explain how it was likely to develop. For this purpose he had to extract and develop from all the complex relationships of an actual society a system which contained what he thought to be the most important forces. (This is a bit like explaining how a car engine works. Initially, we ignore the nuts and bolts and concentrate on explaining the principles of the four-stroke engine. Only later are the details filled in.) In Smith's system, the development of the economy was governed by three interlocking laws of human nature. First, the law of the tendency to exchange goods gives rise to the market. Second, the law of the 'desire of bettering one's condition' leads to savings and investment. Thirdly, there was the law of population, which said that the population would naturally expand.

These three tendencies interacted with each other through the economy. But the principal mechanism through which they interacted was what Smith called the 'division of labour'. This is the name given to the fact that productive processes are divided up into many different parts, so that several workers are employed, each of them specializing in one particular task. Smith gave the example of the manu-

Below: Adam Smith, from an engraving by C. Picant, after a drawing by J. Jackson.

facture of pins, which involves several separate tasks between the initial stage of acquiring the wire and the final production of the pin. The total output of pins can be much greater if many workers are employed.

According to Smith, this principle of the division of labour was by far the most important in accounting for the development of the economy. And the expansion of the division of labour was related to the three laws. The greater the population the greater the possible division of labour. But the division of labour could only be extended as far as the size of the market would allow, and this was related to the law of the tendency to exchange. Finally, the greater division of labour enabled greater profits to be made by businessmen which, with the law of the 'desire of bettering one's condition', enabled greater savings and investment.

This was how the economic machine worked. But Smith was aware of the way governments tended to intervene in the economy and, according to him, governments generally tended to hinder rather than help it, by preventing the operation of the 'invisible hand'. Although he saw a role for government, such as in the provision of education, he was a strong advocate of the principle of *laissez-faire*, which meant that governments should leave well enough alone in the economy. The institution of private property and the pursuit of self-interest would see to the benefit of all. Smith was very much an advocate for the rising capitalist class.

This portrait of Smith was captioned 'The Author of the Wealth of Nations'.

SOSIGENES of Alexandria 1st century BC

Sosigenes of Alexandria was an astronomer and mathematician who was employed by Julius Caesar to devise a more accurate calendar, which became known as the Julian calendar.

The old Roman Republican calendar had 355 days in the year (roughly 12 lunar months). It had once had 10 months, but very soon January and February were added to the beginning—this is why, for example, October (Latin *octo*, eight) is the tenth month. Every two years, 27 or 28 days were *intercalated*—added to the year after 23 February, the remaining five days of that month being dropped. This gave an average of $366\frac{1}{4}$ days, more than a day longer than the true solar year. As a result, by 47 BC the year was four months out of phase with the seasons. The problem was how to have the months in line with the phases of the moon, while at the same time keeping the year even with the seasons.

At the suggestion of Sosigenes, the old lunar calendar was abandoned altogether, the months were arranged on a seasonal basis, and a *tropical* (solar) year was adopted, similar to that of the Egyptian calendar but with $365\frac{1}{4}$ days instead of 365. To repair the discrepancy between the calendar date and the equinox, two intercalations were made in the year 46 BC: the one due that year of 23 days, and an insertion of two months between November and December, making 90 days in all for the year. There was to be an extra day every four years to keep the average at $365\frac{1}{4}$.

Unfortunately, the Romans practiced inclusive numbering, which meant that they counted each leap year as the first in the next four-year period. As a result, in the next 36 years 12 days instead of nine were added. The Roman Emperor Augustus made a correction by eliminating the extra days between 8 BC and 4 AD, so that it took a total of 48 years for the Romans to get their calendar straightened out.

Not much is known about Sosigenes himself. His writings are all lost, except for fragments. The most interesting fragment which survives mentions his belief that Mercury revolves around the Sun, more than 1500 years before Copernicus (*q.v.*) demonstrated the plausibility of a Sun-centered system.

Further corrections to the calendar were made. February in the Julian calendar originally had 29 days, but in 44 BC the Roman Senate re-named the month of Quintilis, calling it July in honour of Julius Caesar, and in 8 BC Augustus re-named the month of Sextilis after himself. He increased it to 31 days, taking a day away from February, so that his month would have as many days as Julius'. More importantly, the solar year has 365.242199 days in it, rather than exactly 365.25; in October 1582 a Papal Bull of Pope Gregory XIII corrected the calendar by 10 days, and decreed that henceforth centennial years would not be leap years unless divisible by four. For this reason, 1700, 1800 and 1900 were not leap years, but the year 2000 will be a leap year.

The new calendar is known as the Gregorian calendar. For various political and religious reasons it was not immediately adopted everywhere; in 1752, when it was adopted in Britain, legislation was carefully drafted to avoid various injustices, but there were still riots, because the people thought they were being cheated out of eleven days (not ten, because 1700 had been a leap year under the Julian system). The Gregorian calendar has still not been accepted by the Russian Orthodox Church; after the Revolution of 1917, however, the new Soviet government adopted the new calendar. Books about Russian history often give dates of events before 1917 in both 'old style' and 'new style'.

A Russian Orthodox calendar marked with saints' days. The church still uses Sosigenes' Julian calendar.

SPERRY, Elmer Ambrose (1860-1930)

Elmer Ambrose Sperry was born in Cortland, New York on 12 October 1860, and is perhaps best known as one of the early pioneers in the application of Foucault's (*q.v.*) gyroscope to navigation, stabilization and control of ships and aircraft. This was not, however, his only interest and more than 400 patents on a great variety of subjects were issued in his name.

Sperry attended the State Normal School at Cortland and later was a special student at Cornell University studying generators and arc lamps.

In 1887 he married Zula Goodman, daughter of the Deacon of the Baptist Church in Chicago, and subsequently had four children. Elmer Sperry's aptitude for electrical devices was soon apparent and his early inventions in the period 1883 to 1890 include generators, arc lights, mining machinery, electric locomotives, trams [streetcars] and an electric automobile. All his inventions included innovations which were the subject of numerous patent applications.

Several companies were started bearing Sperry's name to exploit the different devices, and one by one the majority of the patents and companies were assigned or passed to other companies.

In the early 1900s Sperry's interest was taken by the gyroscope and the possibilities of using it to stabilize automobiles and then ships and also its use in the gyrocompass.

In 1911 he was awarded a naval contract to fit his stabilizer to the USS *Warden*. The installation consisted of two electrically driven 50 inch (1.27 m) diameter wheels, each weighing 4000 pounds. Other installations for naval and merchant ships followed, culminating in a massive three gyro wheel installation in the Italian liner *Conte di Savoia*. Each wheel weighed 110 tons and was 13 ft (4 m) in diameter. Although it effectively stabilized the ship, the problems of expense and weight associated with this type of stabilizer were such that no further installations were made.

During this same period, Sperry turned his attention to the gyrocompass. By 1911 his gyrocompass was undergoing sea trials on the USS *Delaware*. The United States Government placed orders for six compasses and within a month this was increased by a further ten to sixteen compasses.

By 1913 Sperry had set up an office in London and the Sperry gyrocompass was being tested by the Admiralty on a battleship, the HMS *St Vincent* and HM Submarine E1. The successful results of the test led to the Royal Navy adopting the new compass. Orders were also received from the Russian, Italian and French Navies.

To meet an enormous demand for the gyrocompass created by the onset of World War I, not only was production speeded up in America but the Sperry Gyroscope Company Ltd was incorporated by 1914 in London to manufacture gyrocompasses for the British and other world navies. After the war, the compass was taken up by the world's merchant marine, and it was followed in 1922 by 'Metal Mike', a device that enabled ships to hold course automatically; the forerunner of today's gyropilots. Also at this time, Sperry returned to his earlier work and developed a high intensity searchlight five times brighter than the previous best searchlight available. The new searchlight was widely used during World War I and after.

During this time, the new technology of powered flight was progressing, and again Elmer Sperry applied himself to its problems. In 1909 he had started work on an aircraft stabilizer based on similar principles to his ship's stabilizers, but this was later abandoned in favour of a more advanced system where four gyroscopes provided the basic references for stable flight and the control surfaces of the aircraft were operated by compressed-air servo-motors.

The stabilizer was first fitted to a Curtiss seaplane in 1912. Both Sperry and his son Lawrence, who had by then joined him in business, became deeply involved in the development of the stabilizer, which was to tax their skill to the utmost. Development continued with assistance from the US Navy.

Success finally crowned Elmer and Lawrence's efforts when in 1914 a spectacular demonstration flight in a French War Department competition on air safety proved the effectiveness of the Sperry Aeroplane Stabilizers. During and after the war Elmer Sperry turned his attention to attitude and azimuth flight instruments, but it was not until the late 1920s that a successful directional gyro and an artificial horizon were achieved. During this period, Elmer Sperry spent a great deal of time on developing a compound diesel engine for use in aircraft and for a diesel-electric engine for locomotives. After several years, however, the project was finally abandoned, owing mainly to the lack of materials that would withstand the high pressures and temperatures generated in his engine.

The last years of his life were mainly taken up with the development of rail track recorder gyros to check the level and alignment of rails, and a rail flaw detector. Both designs were highly successful and widely used in America.

Zula, Sperry's wife, died in March 1930 after contracting pneumonia during a voyage on the SS *Mauretania*. Three months later, Sperry died after surgery in a Brooklyn hospital on 16 June 1930.

Elmer Sperry's invention of the gyrocompass led to the development of the inertial guidance and navigation systems now used in a wide range of vehicles.

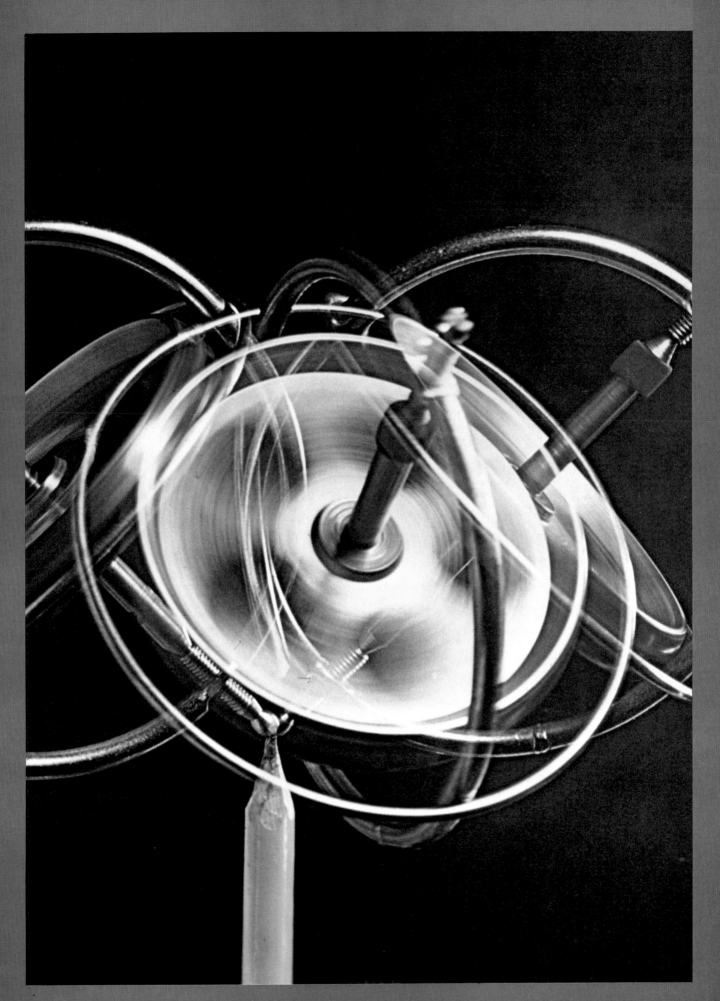

STEPHENSON, George (1781-1848) and Robert (1803-1859)

Even if they did not actually 'invent' railways and steam locomotion, it was the combination of George Stephenson's stubborn vision and pertinacity with his son Robert's intellectual skill which turned the tentative suggestions of their predecessors, confined to heavy hauling for the mines, into an engine that brought about a transport revolution in a few years.

Born in Wylam near Newcastle on the river Tyne in north east England, the son of a colliery engine fireman, George spent his early life within sight of the collieries he was destined to work in and to improve. From his first job as a cowherd at twopence per day—a job which gave him time to build clay models of the stationary steam engines then in use in the pits—he followed his father into the pits and at the early age of seventeen was put in charge of a new steam engine for pumping at Water Row. It was not until he was eighteen that he started to learn to read and write, and he never had any formal education.

To save enough money to get married, he learned to mend shoes, and in 1802 he wed Fanny Henderson and settled at Willington Quay. There he attempted to build a perpetual motion machine which, although a failure, whetted his inventive appetite. His son Robert was born in 1803 but two

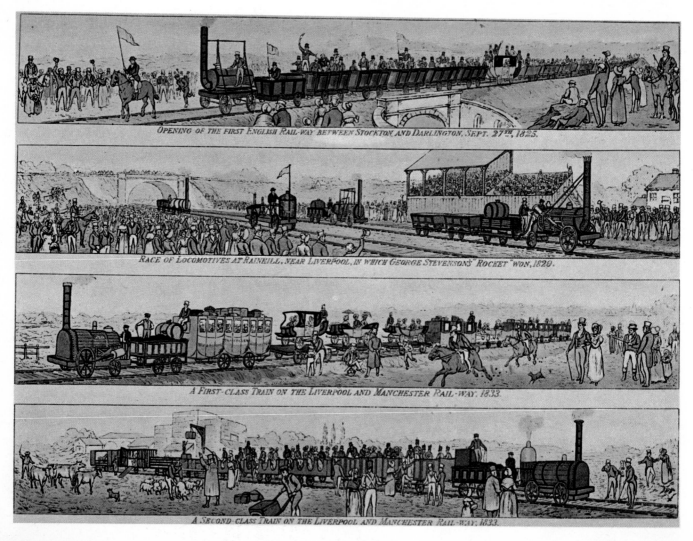

OPENING OF THE FIRST ENGLISH RAIL-WAY BETWEEN STOCKTON AND DARLINGTON, SEPT. 27TH, 1825.

RACE OF LOCOMOTIVES AT RAINHILL, NEAR LIVERPOOL, IN WHICH GEORGE STEVENSON'S ROCKET WON, 1829.

A FIRST-CLASS TRAIN ON THE LIVERPOOL AND MANCHESTER RAIL-WAY, 1833.

A SECOND-CLASS TRAIN ON THE LIVERPOOL AND MANCHESTER RAIL-WAY, 1833.

years later, now at Killingworth, disaster struck. His wife and daughter died and his father was blinded in a colliery accident. He considered emigrating, but had no money.

Because George had been self taught he decided to ensure his son had a proper education, sending him first to Newcastle by pony and then for a year in Edinburgh, and his son's education gave him new interest in life. By 1812 he had risen to being in charge of all the local collieries' machinery. He introduced stationary steam engines to replace horses and experimented with moving engines. He developed an underwater lamp and produced a miner's safety lamp in 1815, which brought him into great controversy with Sir Humphry Davy (q.v.).

Having gained knowledge of experimental locomotives at other collieries he was commissioned to build a locomotive for Killingworth and in 1814 *Blucher* entered service. Other locomotives followed and in 1822 he completed an eight mile (13 km) long railway at Hetton Colliery, helped by his son.

Up to this time all locomotives, except for Trevithick's (q.v.) short-lived demonstrations, had been intended only to take heavy loads of coal or ore to nearby river moorings,

Above left: a Stephenson family group. George holds a miner's lamp and looks up at Robert; their Killingworth house is in the background.

Below left: print commemorating early railway history, including the Stockton and Darlington Railway, which was opened by a train hauled by George Stephenson's Locomotion No. 1, *and the famous Rainhill Trials, won by the* Rocket.

Above right: George Stephenson's improved miner's lamp (first three drawings) was brighter than Davy's original (fourth drawing). It would not ignite mine gases because it drew in air faster than the flame would spread; Davy's relied on a gauze shield.

Below right: Robert Stephenson's High Level Bridge over the Tyne at Newcastle. Trains ran above and road vehicles below.

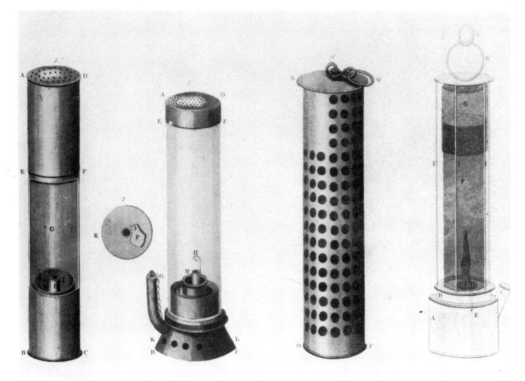

along the railways which had been laid down for horse transport since the 18th century. Now it was proposed to lay a railway to link two expanding towns, and open the service to public hire.

The world's first passenger railway was completed between Stockton and Darlington, about 30 miles (50 km) south of Newcastle, in 1825 after a fifty year argument over the possible construction of a canal to link the two towns, ten miles (16 km) apart. The first train on the line was hauled by Stephenson's *Locomotion No 1* (still to be seen at Darlington) on the by now well established 4 foot 8½ inch (1.43 m) guage. *Locomotion* ran at up to 12 mph (19 kph), and a challenge race between it and a stagecoach resulted in a win for *Locomotion* by 100 yards. One important side effect of this line was the creation of the now important town of Middlesbrough.

Before the Stockton and Darlington line was completed, an even more ambitious project was put forward—a railway to link Liverpool and Manchester. Never having been trained as a surveyor, Stephenson ran into many difficulties —his own lack of patience with civil engineers who knew plenty of mathematics but had less practical experience made the task worse. Still, he managed to get his railway across the bog of Chat Moss. The directors of the new line decided to hold public trials to see whether steam locomotives would really be the best mode of traction—and to see whose engine would best serve their purpose. These were the famous Rainhill trials which proved a great success for the Stephensons.

Meanwhile Robert had spent three years managing gold mines in South America. On the return voyage he was shipwrecked before reaching New York but survived to take up a post as locomotive works manager in Newcastle. His first engine was *Lancashire Witch*, in 1828, which had inclined cylinders (most earlier locomotives had vertical cylinders, like stationary steam engines), with direct drive to crankpins on the wheels, and was a precursor of the more famous *Rocket*, built the following year for the Rainhill Trials. This subsequently pulled trains on the newly opened Liverpool–Manchester railway at speeds up to 30 mph (50 kph).

By 1830 Robert, still only 27, had evolved in the *Northumbrian* and the *Planet* the basic type of locomotive which so rapidly conquered Europe and the Americas. On his appointment as engineer-in-chief for the London–Birmingham line three years later Robert moved to London. Through his railway exploits he became involved with bridge design and had great success with bridges of a tubular wrought iron design. Previously, the longest span of this type had been 31 feet (9.5 m). For the Britannia Bridge over the Menai Straits, between Wales and Anglesey, Stephenson built four spans, the middle two each of 459 feet (140 m). After the success of this bridge and a similar one at Conway on the same line, he was commissioned to build bridges in Egypt and Canada.

His father meanwhile had also been playing a leading part in the development of both British and continental railway systems. But he was essentially an engine designer rather than the kind of civil engineer that was now needed, and he retired to Tapton, near Chesterfield, in Derbyshire, where he could overlook the Midland Railway. Here he was invited to become President of a new 'Mechanics' Institute which was the predecessor of the Institution of Mechanical Engineers. In 1845 at the age of 64 he retired from active work to market gardening and died in Tapton three years later.

The year before (1847) Robert had become Member of Parliament for Whitby. He surveyed the route for the proposed Suez Canal and declared it impracticable, for which statement he was challenged to a duel by the Canal's eventual builder de Lesseps. He held the presidency of the Institution of Civil Engineers for two years from 1855, the year he was awarded an honorary degree by Oxford University.

He died at the age of 56 and was buried alongside Telford (*q.v.*) in Westminster Abbey.

Robert Stephenson also designed locomotives: this is his Northumbrian *of 1830, influential in having horizontal cylinders.*

STEVIN, Simon (1548-1620)

The illegitimate son of Cathelyne van der Poort, who had other such children by different fathers, Simon Stevin was born in Bruges and progressed from an unpromising start to become tutor in mathematics and adviser on engineering matters to Prince Maurice of Orange, the commander-in-chief of the Dutch armies during their struggle for independence.

His first job was as a book keeper; evidently his mathematical skill had already won him a better position than he might otherwise have expected. He soon left, however, and travelled to France, Germany and perhaps as far as Poland and Norway, working as an engineer. In 1577, at the age of 29, Stevin returned to Bruges and obtained a post in the city's administration, but he was soon on the move again. At that time Flanders was not distinguished from the Netherlands, so when Stevin moved in 1581 to Leyden, he may have simply wanted a suitable place to study. In 1583 he entered the new university there, a very progressive establishment which was the first to hold classes for engineers.

At the same time he was busy publishing his own books, including tables of interest suitable for book keepers such as he himself had been, a book on the elements of arithmetic and geometry, and a book which expounded for the first time the advantages of a decimal system, not generally adopted until long after. In the same decade he brought out his treatise on statics and hydrostatics. In statics, he discovered the law of inclined planes relating the proportions of two connected forces on two opposed inclined planes. He imagined a continuous chain of such forces, in the form of weights, suspended over the planes which were joined together horizontally at their base to create a triangle. He reasoned that the whole system of weights, or 'crown of globes' as he put it, would have to be in equilibrium or else they would be in perpetual motion, 'which is absurd'. If the weights below the triangle were removed, the condition of equilibrium would remain, in other words a smaller number of weights on a steeper incline will balance a larger number of weights on a gentler incline. His hydrostatics too contained many original ideas, all the more useful because the theory of the subject had been comparatively neglected since the work of Archimedes (*q.v.*). He gave a demonstration of the hydrostatic paradox later developed by Pascal (*q.v.*), and analyzed the forces exerted by a fluid on the base and sides of a containing vessel.

Besides theory, he tried to find applications for his ideas. In mechanics he suggested a new type of winch to haul boats over a slipway, a pivoted sluice-gate for canals and harbours, and a mechanical turnspit. While at Leyden he began to patent his embanking and draining inventions, and entered into partnership with Jan de Groot, the mayor of Delft, to build windmills for pumping off water according to Stevin's principles. Stevin had used the methods of mathematical mechanics to investigate the scoop wheel that drives the water out in these mills, and the teeth of the gears that turn them. He concluded that the teeth must engage on the face not the rim, and so developed, or perhaps invented, bevel gears.

The partnership with de Groot was not just for business; they also performed together Galileo's falling weights experiment a dozen years before Galileo (*q.v.*) himself. Some time after this Stevin entered the service of Prince Maurice, who became commander of the Dutch army in 1589. Stevin now became a military engineer; he devised a combined pick, shovel and axe, like a modern entrenching tool, to help in tasks of fortification. He also lectured on the theory of fortification, navigation and on politics. He believed that the 'Golden Age of Wisdom' could be restored if men of good will would band together to research the secrets of nature, rather as Francis Bacon was to propose.

In 1603 he was appointed quartermaster to the army in the old sense of laying out the army's quarters. He instructed the Prince in mathematics and all its applications. His lectures were soon published, first in Dutch which Stevin considered the perfect language for scientific reasoning, then in French and Latin translations.

In old age he set up home at The Hague with Catherine Cray, a young woman who bore him four children, but he seems to have inherited a certain carelessness in these matters, for his marriage was not notified until three of their children had been born.

Two engravings from Simon Stevin's works: explanation of the fallacy of perpetual motion, headed 'a wonder, but it is no wonder' and demonstration that the pressure exerted by a column of liquid is unaffected by its width.

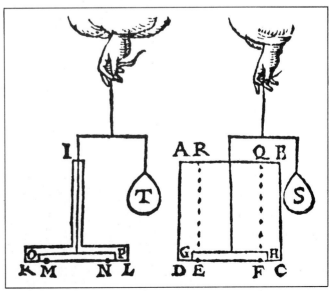

TALBOT, W H Fox (1800-1877)

Talbot was born in Dorset, England, the only son of an army officer, and was educated at Harrow and at Trinity College, Cambridge. He is most famous for the invention of the positive/negative process in photography, and as a photographer.

In 1833 Talbot entered Parliament, but retired the following year. He used the *camera obscura* for sketching; this was essentially a box with a hole in one end which allowed an image to be projected in colour in the end of the box opposite the aperture. (*Camera obscura* means 'dark room' in Latin.) Like many others, Talbot began to think of ways to fix the image permanently, using chemicals. In 1835 he took a one-inch square photograph of a window at his home, Lacock Abbey.

When a photographic process was announced by Daguerre (*q.v.*), Talbot described his own process to the Royal Society in 1839. He used paper coated with silver chloride, and fixed with sodium chloride.

Next he experimented with silver bromide and silver iodide, and patented in 1841 a process of developing a latent image with gallic acid. The process was faster than others, and allowed the contact-copying of the paper negative using silver chloride paper to make a positive print, the first modern photographic process.

He published *The Pencil of Nature*, the first book to be illustrated with photographs. By 1851 he had greatly reduced the necessary exposure time for photographs, and began to experiment with flash photography using electric sparks. In 1852 he patented a method of photo-etching on metal plates, and in 1858 an improved half-tone process, using gauze as a screen. He held so many important patents that the progress of photography was held up in Britain, until it was decided in 1854 that his patents did not cover the collodion process of Frederick Scott Archer.

Talbot was elected to the Royal Society in 1831, and delivered a total of 59 papers, mostly on mathematics. He won the Society's Royal Medal in 1838 for his paper called *Researches on the Integral Calculus*, and won the Rumford medal in 1842 for his photographic process. He was also one of the first to decipher the cuneiform inscriptions discovered at Nineveh.

Talbot's negative-positive process is the true ancestor of modern photography. He is on the right in the large picture, one of the first self-portraits ever made.

162

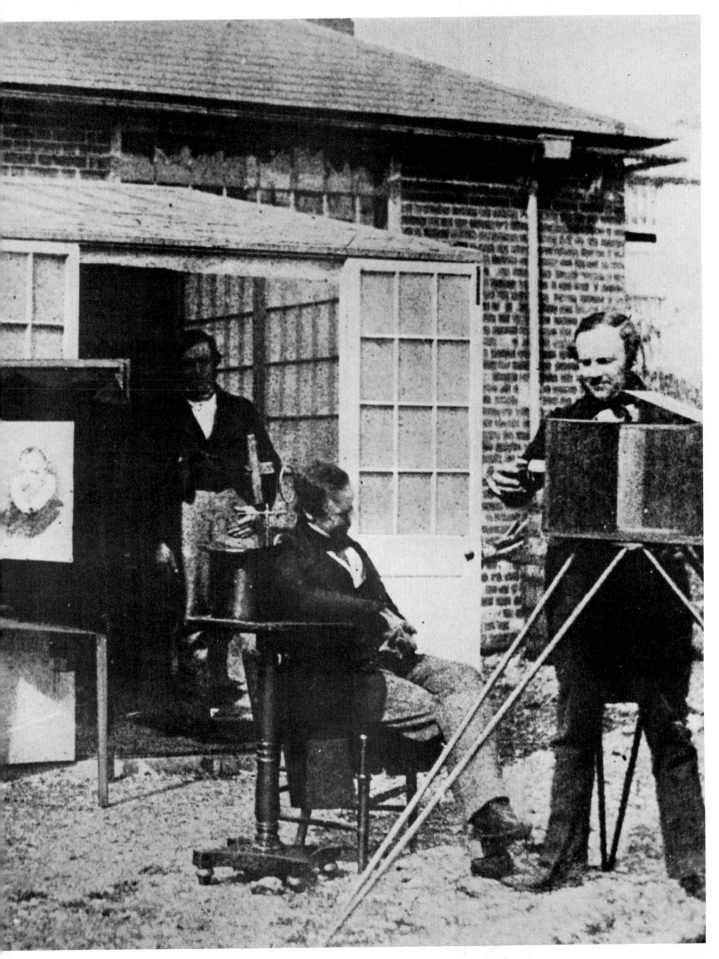

TELFORD, Thomas (1757-1834)

Thomas Telford was born the son of a shepherd in a remote valley near Langholm, across the English-Scottish border from Carlisle. From this unpromising start, Telford went on to show the world new techniques in civil engineering, leaving behind many impressive roads, canals and bridges. More important even than these, he started the modern system of contracting, where an employer undertakes to construct part of a road, for example, for a fixed cost and by a definite date. He was also responsible for the establishment of civil engineering as a definite profession.

Telford was apprenticed to a stonemason in Langholm, and became an avid reader of English literature before he went to Edinburgh and then to London, where he worked as a stonemason on Somerset House. He soon showed his

Thomas Telford built the road in North Wales from Chester via Conway (now Conwy) to Bangor, where it joins his Holyhead Road. He designed the towers of Conway Bridge to match the nearby castle, built in about 1284 during the reign of Edward I. These wrought iron chains are Telford's original ones, installed in 1826.

worth, for his next job was to superintend the building of the Commissioner's House in Portsmouth Naval Dockyard. By now he was well regarded by William Pulteney, Member of Parliament for Shrewsbury, and Telford was appointed Surveyor of Public Works for the County of Shropshire by the time he was thirty years old.

He wanted to become an architect, but opportunity arose to become the engineer to two canals, and this changed the course of his life. The Shrewsbury Canal was only a small work, but he built the first substantial cast iron aqueduct in the world for it. This was only to be expected, perhaps, since Shropshire was at that time, in the 1790s, the centre of the iron trade. Nonetheless, he showed that he could command iron as well as stone, and went on to build the big aqueduct at Chirk from both materials, and his most impressive aqueduct at Pontcysyllte, near Llangollen in Wales, with a cast iron trough over 1000 feet (305 m) long and 125 feet (33 m) above the river Dee. This was opened in 1805, and made him famous.

He built other major canals besides the Shrewsbury and the Ellesmere. The Caledonian Canal, linking Inverness with Fort William, was opened in 1822 as part of a Government scheme to develop the Scottish Highlands, and is still a very impressive waterway. He made linking roads all over the Highlands, still in use towards Skye and further south. His bridges at Craigellachie and Dean Bridge in Edinburgh itself are good examples of his work, but probably the most famous are those associated with the Holyhead Road.

His suspension bridge over the Menai Straits, and the smaller one at Conway, are very important engineering achievements. Not only the design but also the details of construction are impressive, for the hoisting of chains to support a span of 579 feet (177 m) was no easy task in 1825. The roads laid out by Telford would be a monument in themselves to any man, but in addition his work on Scottish harbours, his planning of the Gotha canal in Sweden, his part in the draining of the marshy fens of East Anglia, his design of St Katharine's Dock in London, and his many other major works, combine to increase Thomas Telford's status still further.

Although he designed the last major canal to be built in Britain, the Birmingham and Liverpool (nowadays called the Shropshire Union), in the same way as railway engineers laid out their tracks—with cuttings and embankments to avoid change of level—Telford never became a railway engineer. This is not because he was against railways, but because he thought he should be true to the canal proprietors who had given him their work in the past. This is typical of the upright character of the man, in devoting himself wholeheartedly to his undertakings for as long as his health lasted. He never married, but devoted himself, often without fee where the challenge far outweighed any other reward, to his work until his health finally failed. He died in 1834 and was buried, against his wishes, in Westminster Abbey.

Although his engineering works remain in impressive abundance, his real monuments are the Institute of Civil Engineers (of which he was the first President), and his system of stringent specification and methods of contracting for engineering works. They are still the basis of all such construction all over the world.

Above: Pontcysyllte acqueduct was opened in 1805, the year of Trafalgar, and is still in use. The cast iron trough has a towpath cantilevered out of the water to prevent spillage caused by the passage of boats. It is more than 300m long, and the water level is 33m above the river Dee, which it crosses.

THOMSON, Sir J J (1856-1940)

J J Thomson was the discoverer of the electron. Although the idea that electricity is composed of individual units of electric charge had been suggested earlier, he was the first to see that these were units of mass far smaller than any atom, and to realize that they were components of the atoms of all elements.

Born at Cheetham Hill in Manchester, the son of an anti-quarian bookseller, Thomson was educated at Owens College which he entered at the age of fourteen, and in 1876 he won a scholarship to Trinity College, Cambridge, where he remained for the rest of his life. His early investigations followed on from the electromagnetic work of James Clerk Maxwell (*q.v.*).

On the strength of his theoretical explorations into electricity, he was appointed Cavendish Professor of Experimental Physics at Cambridge at the early age of 28. He began to work on the effects of electrical discharges in rarefied gases, and notably on the problem of cathode rays. Were they a form of electromagnetic radiation, or minute particles? Thomson believed that they were particles, mainly on account of their deflection in a magnetic field. This lin e of research was interrupted in 1896 by the discovery of X-rays, which 'J J' immediately began to explore. He demonstrated their power to make a gas electrically conductive, and explained the laws that govern this process of ionization. After this diversion he returned to the study of cathode ray particles (electrons). In 1897 he determined that the particles were negatively charged by observing the deflection of a cathode ray beam in an electric field, and by measuring the strengths of electrical and magnetic fields needed to give equal deflections of a cathode ray beam he was now able to calculate the ratio of mass to charge for an electron.

Similar particles with the same mass to charge ratio were given off by metals exposed to ultra-violet light and by carbon heated to incandescence. In the case of the 'photoelectric' discharge under ultra-violet light, the charge could be measured, and it became clear that the mass of the electron was more than a thousand times less than that of the lightest atoms. As the cathode ray particles behaved in the same way however they were generated, Thomson supposed that they were universal constituents of matter, and that their number and arrangement, in the form of rings within a neutralizing sphere of positive electricity, would determine the chemical characteristics of each element. In recognition of his research into cathode rays he was awarded the Nobel prize for physics in 1906.

Although Thomson's ideas about the internal organization of the atom did not survive the discovery of the atomic nucleus by Rutherford (*q.v.*) (who had been his student at Cambridge), they set the scene for the later concept of atomic number (the number of electrons in a neutral atom and characteristic of the element). Meanwhile he continued his researches into ionization, and also into the positive rays which complement the negative cathode rays. Under magnetic and electric deflection they spread into parabolas whose shape depends on the atomic weight of the element from which they come. In this way he found in 1913 that neon had two forms, called isotopes, differing only in weight. These were the first isotopes of a light element to be discovered.

During World War I he was active on the Board of Research and Invention, and then President of the Royal Society and Master of his college, so once the war ended he decided to retire from his professorship. During his 35 years in office, the Cavendish laboratory had grown into a major international centre for physics research, largely because of his prestige and inspiration.

Left: Sir Joseph John ('J J') Thomson (left) with Rutherford, discoverer of the atomic nucleus.

Below: J J Thomson's cathode ray tube, with which he proved that Crookes' negatively charged 'atoms' were in fact very fast moving, extremely light particles, common to all chemical elements. At first he called them 'negative corpuscles,' but later changed to the word by which we know them today – electrons. They are the basis of all electric charge and current.

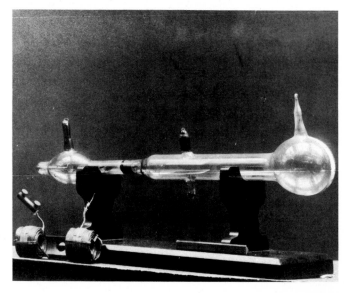

TORRICELLI, Evangelista (1608-1647)

Torricelli was an Italian physicist in a century that saw a great flowering of experimental science. He did much valuable research work in his short life, but his greatest contribution to science was the invention of the mercury barometer, and hence the measurement of atmospheric pressure.

There is uncertainty about Torricelli's childhood. It is believed he was born in Faenza, in the north east of Italy, and was probably orphaned. He is known, however, to have had the advantage of an education in a school run by Jesuits, the Roman Catholic order that has traditionally been their greatest contributor to scholarship and science. At the age of 19 he went to Rome to study, but did not write his first scientific treatise, *On the Motion of Heavy Bodies*, until he was 32. In this he dealt with the laws of falling bodies formulated by Galileo (*q.v.*) and reported ingenious experimental verifications of them. He also applied them to the case of fluids flowing from apertures in vessels and derived a law, now named after him, relating the rate of escape to the depth of the opening beneath the fluid surface.

The young man's work was drawn to the attention of Galileo himself, who engaged him as his personal assistant at Florence. Only a few months later Galileo died, and Torricelli took his place as court mathematician.

In this ideal situation Torricelli pursued his studies energetically. Some of his labours earned him a reputation in pure mathematics. As was normal at that time, he was several times engaged in controversy over questions of priority in discovery. But Torricelli also had a strong practical bent; he ground lenses for his own telescopes and made microscopes employing small glass spheres as lenses.

Galileo had speculated on the reasons for the well known fact that a suction pump was unable to raise water more than about 32 feet (9.7 m). He had decided that it was because the column of water in the pump's piston broke under its own weight when it reached this height, and had guessed that a denser liquid could be raised through a correspondingly shorter distance.

Torricelli followed up the idea, by taking a long narrow tube, filling it with mercury, which is over thirteen times as dense as water, and then inverting it in a bowl of mercury. The liquid fell in the tube, but only until the surface of the column was about 30 inches (76 cm) above the surface of the mercury in the bowl.

Although this was what Galileo had predicted, Torricelli did not adopt his explanation. He believed, correctly, that the mercury column was being supported by the downward pressure of air on the mercury in the bowl; above the mercury column was a space devoid of air. Torricelli had brought experiment to bear on a controversy that had been carried on for thousands of years: the question of the existence of a vacuum, which Aristotle had declared to be impossible.

After Torricelli's death, at the height of his powers, the mercury barometer became an indispensable item in the physical laboratory, and it remains the most accurate method of measuring atmospheric pressure. The evacuated space above the mercury column is still described as a Torricellian vacuum.

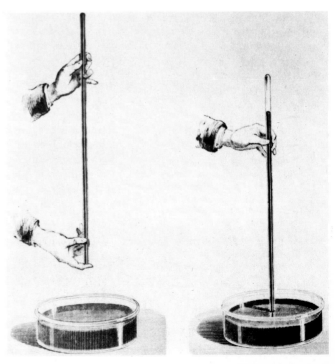

Evangelista Torricelli showed by his simple experiment (right) that a vacuum could exist, whatever the ancient Greek philosophers said.

TRÉSAGUET, Pierre (1716-1796)

At the beginning of the eighteenth century, Europe's roads were in a dire condition. The fine network of Roman roads had long since fallen into decay and disrepair (although the basic routes survived) and virtually nothing had been done to replace them. But military needs and growing commercial aspirations within and between the countries of western Europe were demanding improvements and it was in France that the problem was first tackled. The famous French Corps des Ponts et Chaussées (Bridge and Highway Corps), the first body of civil engineers in the world, was formed in 1716, the year of Pierre Marie Jérôme Trésaguet's birth.

P M J Trésaguet was the youngest son of a family in which his father and brothers were all engineers of sorts, though none was famous. Pierre Trésaguet served for many years in the Corps des Ponts et Chaussées. For a time he was a sub-inspector of roads in Paris and from that post he was promoted to chief engineer in the area around Limoges. Subsequently, in 1775, he was appointed inspector general of French public works.

Evidently Trésaguet's greatly improved method of road-building was developed initially during his time in Limoges and the first major route to feature his techniques was a highway from Paris to Spain by way of Toulouse. Once Trésaguet was inspector general he was able to introduce his ideas more widely.

A Trésaguet road was a simple proposition. Supported on a cambered foundation, the base layer consisted of long stones packed close together and set vertically. Above them a second and thinner layer of smaller stones was hand-placed and hammered down. The third and top layer, three inches (7.5 cm) thick, was of walnut-sized stones beaten into place. Because this layer provided the running surface, very hard stone was used. Consolidation was aided by the passage of iron-shod wheels whose grinding action also helped to seal the cambered surface against the weather.

The typical Trésaguet road was about ten inches (25 cm) thick; it was relatively cheap to build and flexible enough to transmit a large proportion of the superimposed loadings right through to the sub-soil. This helped to prolong the life of the road surface, as did Trésaguet's introduction of a road patrol system which allowed defects to be identified and repaired promptly.

By 1788 France had rebuilt some 12,000 miles of roads on Trésaguet's plan. It was by far the best road system in Europe and Trésaguet's influence was already reaching out to central Europe and Sweden. Whether or not his concepts ever reached Great Britain, there to shape the roadbuilding ideas of Thomas Telford (*q.v.*), is uncertain. On balance it is unlikely. The eruption of the French Revolution in 1789 effectively ended Trésaguet's career and he died in Paris in obscurity and poverty in 1796. Trésaguet's own description of his roadbuilding techniques was first written as early as 1775, but it was not to be published until 1831.

Above: Pierre Trésaguet, a little known figure, even in France, where McAdam is much more famous.

Left: early French roads, built by the 'corvée', a system of forced labour, were solid but ill drained (above) and often became waterlogged. This and public discontent led to the withdrawal of the system in 1776, the year after Trésaguet took over. Trésaguet's roads had upright foundation stones for better drainage (below), and a surface which was fairly impervious.

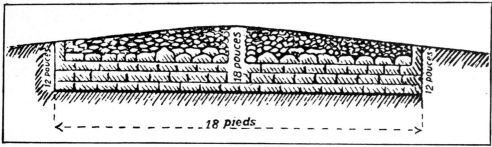

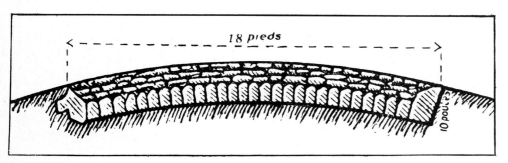

TREVITHICK, Richard (1771-1833)

Richard Trevithick was one of the greatest inventors in the history of the steam engine, but his talents were rather wasted. Like many inventors he was not a good business-man, and whereas James Watt (*q.v.*) had a hard-headed partner in Matthew Boulton, Trevithick had no such friend.

Richard Trevithick was born in Cornwall on 13 April 1771 the son of a mine manager, but as a boy Richard developed an interest in practical engineering rather than in academic or managerial subjects. By the time he was 18 he was a well paid engineer at one of his father's mines. He was a large and colourful character with an impulsive nature and great physical strength. He is reputed to have picked up a Captain Hodge, turned him upside down and marked the ceiling with the Captain's footprints.

For a while Trevithick worked with Edward Bull. Their pumping engines infringed Watt's patent, but Trevithick was continually improving the design and performance of his engines until they were superior to Watt's. In 1797 Trevithick married Jane Harvey, whose father ran a large foundry at Hayle near St Ives. Jane was a very patient and understand-ing wife, which was fortunate in view of Richard's reckless-ness. They lived for a year in Redruth then moved to Cam-borne and eventually to London. They had six children: two of their sons became well-known engineers in later years.

Trevithick's high pressure engines, which produced more power for their size than earlier machines, made the use of steam power for transport a feasible proposition. In 1801 Trevithick, with the help of his cousin Andrew Vivian, built a full-size steam road carriage which ran for a short distance before it overturned. A second steam carriage was built and demonstrated in London during 1803 but it too crashed due to a bad road surface; Trevithick turned his attention to the railways. The following year his now famous Pen-y-darren locomotive hauled a train of loaded wagons. Another of his locomotives called *Catch-me-who-can* gave joyrides near Euston Square in 1808. But Trevithick's stationary steam engines supplying power for factories were proving more

Right, top to bottom: Richard Trevithick, inventor of the high pressure steam engine; a handbill for his steam powered joyrides; and a paddle steamer design from a letter to a friend – asking for help with the calculations.

TREVITHICKS,
PORTABLE STEAM ENGINE.

Catch me who can.

Mechanical Power Subduing
Animal Speed.

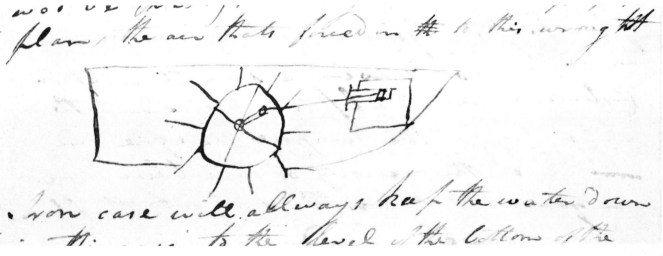

successful than his ventures into transport.

Trevithick never settled down with his own works; instead, he designed engines for other people to construct and his business affairs were never very stable. He worked on the Rotherhithe tunnel in London during 1809, but it was flooded. His attention turned to iron tanks which could be used to raise sunken ships, then to a steam threshing machine, but in 1811 he and his partner Robert Dickinson went bankrupt. Trevithick returned to Cornwall and developed a very efficient steam engine known as the 'Cornish' engine.

At the age of 43 Trevithick's career took a new turn when he was invited to install steam engines in the rich Peruvian silver mines. In 1814 engines and engineers departed, but Trevithick had to follow two years later as things were not going too well. Trevithick spent some ten years abroad and the account of his exploits with fortunes made and lost reads like an adventure story. It ended with him being rescued from an alligator-infested river by a Venezuelan army officer, and assisted financially by Robert Stephenson (*q.v.*), the locomotive engineer, who happened to be in South America. Trevithick continued with his inventions, but died penniless in 1833.

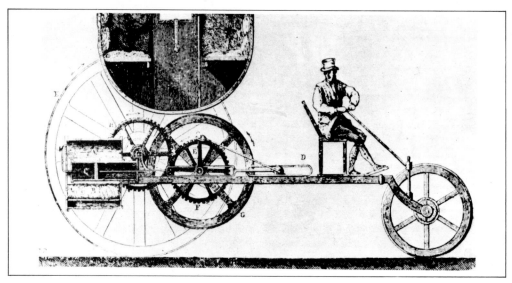

Above right: Trevithick's steam road carriage, showing how the cylinder was located within the boiler. The flue from the firebox also ran through the boiler in a U shape. The effect was to keep heat losses to a minimum; this and the high steam pressure – about 3½ times atmospheric pressure – made his engine three times more powerful than Watt's for the same piston size. The carriages suffered from instability, but the design of the engine was successful.

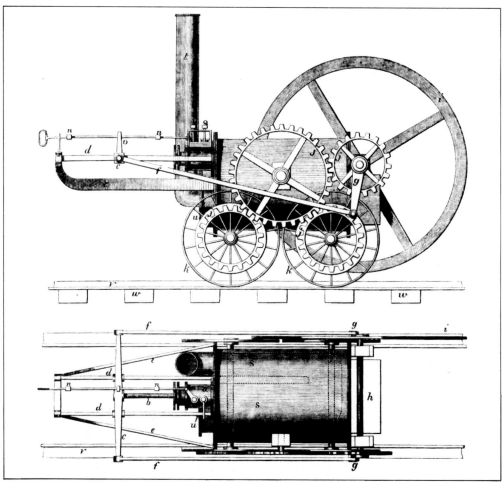

Below right: Trevithick's colliery locomotive, also with the piston inside the cylinder, which accounts for unusual drive linkage. The largest wheel is a flywheel; the drive wheels are 1.14m in diameter.

TSIOLKOVSKY, Konstantin (1857-1935)

Nowadays Russian schoolchildren learn of Konstantin Tsiolkovsky. This man, who was for most of his life an obscure peasant schoolteacher, and is still comparatively unknown in the West, is now rightly acclaimed as the pioneer of Russian rocketry. Completely self-taught, working alone, without encouragement or financial resources, Tsiolkovsky investigated the problems that were to be encountered in man's conquest of space, making many of his discoveries 10 or 20 years before Goddard (*q.v.*) in the USA and Oberth in Germany.

He was born in September 1857, and his childhood was marred by an attack of scarlet fever when he was nine which left him almost totally deaf and condemned him to many years of isolation. His father, himself an inventor, recognized the child's genius and encouraged Tsiolkovsky's learning at home.

Later, when he was 22, he became a schoolteacher in Borovsk and here managed to convert a small room into a laboratory in which he performed as many experiments as he could afford. Flight fascinated him, and he constructed a glider in the shape of a huge mechanical bird, which flew over his village. With a metal horn as a hearing aid he communicated better and during this time he married the daughter of a fellow schoolmaster, Varvara Sokolova. His solitary researches had a touch of irony about them, for without books or scientific contact he had to produce his

Konstantin Tsiolkovsky, below in schoolmaster's gown, and on the right at work on a model of his early rocket design. He popularized his theories by writing a science fiction story, 'Outside the Earth'.

own laws and more than once he painstakingly proved a well known scientific theorem. His papers show the diversity of his interests. He worked on balloon and airship flight, the development of jet aircraft, aerodynamic theory, studied the flight of birds and insects and developed and built his own wind tunnel, returning often to the study of rocketry.

Tsiolkovsky was probably the first scientist to outline the important difference between aircraft and rockets, that is, when travelling outside the Earth's atmosphere, flight can no longer be produced by the energy of combustion alone. Instead, the rapid release of chemicals at the rear of the vehicle produces forward motion, a direct application of Newton's law that for every action there is an equal and opposite reaction. Early on he proposed the multistage theory of rockets and he suggested the use of liquid fuels rather than powder in 1903, long before Goddard's first experiments in this field in 1919. He discussed the problems of living in a zero gravity environment, the necessity for sealed spaceships and space helmets and the construction of space platforms to break long journeys. When criticized for this apparent escapism he replied, 'The Earth is the cradle of the mind, but one cannot live for ever in a cradle'.

In 1919, when he was 62, Tsiolkovsky was elected a member of the Soviet Academy of Sciences, and eventually became well known in the Soviet Union. He addressed a May Day rally when he was 78, just before his death, and is today revered by the Soviet people. He lived long enough to know that the first rocket had been successfully launched from Russian soil in 1933; the first Sputnik was launched just 100 years from the date of his birth.

VEBLEN, Thorstein (1857-1929)

Thorstein Bunde Veblen, sociologist and founder of the 'Institutionalist' school of economics, was born in Wisconsin, in the United States, ten years after his parents had migrated there from Norway. The sixth of twelve children, Veblen was brought up in an age of economic upheaval. Immigrants of his parents' generation were unwilling to adapt their habits to the ways of the new world; Veblen and others like him were unable to mix easily with other farmers and townspeople. Veblen acquired a certain intellectual detachment from the changes that were going on around him, as the farming communities reacted with hostility to the onset of business dominance and of modern capitalism, so that as the structure of the American economy underwent profound changes, he was able to perceive the importance of these changes better than other contemporary writers. In addition, the alienation he suffered in his childhood days probably prepared him for the comparative isolation to which the economics profession subjected him for most of his life, due to his unorthodox views.

In 1884, Veblen gained a PhD. in philosophy at Yale, but then was unable to find a job. He returned to academic life in 1891 as an economist, spending 14 years at the University of Chicago from 1892 till 1906. Subsequently he had spells of academic life, notably at Stanford and at Missouri Universities, but his tenure in post was always precarious. In 1926 he retired, and the last years of his life were spent in obscurity and poverty, and in disillusionment with the triumph of business.

Veblen was one of those nineteenth century thinkers who were accomplished in many different fields. His books ranged over many of the social sciences—economics, sociology, psychology and anthropology. His most striking originality is in the area of economic sociology.

Veblen was highly critical of nineteenth century economic doctrine. In 1899 he published his most famous book *The Theory of the Leisure Class: An Economic Study of Institutions*. In this, he explains the motives behind people's consumption habits in the industrial age. According to Veblen, people tend to indulge in 'conspicuous consumption', whereby the value of consuming goods lay not in the goods themselves but in the socially beneficial effect this has for the consumer in the eyes of other people. Thus it was important to be seen to be consuming particular goods. This theory of status consumption is of course well known to any modern marketing expert. But Veblen's book does not merely assert its importance; he relates the concept of conspicuous consumption to the historical evolution of human nature and human societies. Thus, for example, 'conspicuous consumption' is the modern equivalent of 'conspicuous leisure' which in pre-industrial societies was indulged in by the ruling classes as a mark of their superiority. This perception of history is essentially that of Marx (*q.v.*).

In a series of essays collected and published in 1919, *The Place of Science in Modern Civilization*, Veblen shows how these ideas conflict with the utility theory of economists such as Marshall (*q.v.*). Whereas the orthodox economist always stressed rational actions by consumers, Veblen emphasised how human conduct was affected by habituation, by 'cause and effect', and by 'institutions' which orthodox theory excludes.

In the place of the theories he criticised he substituted his own theory of the development of the economy and of society. Rather like Marx, Veblen saw that the development of society was never smooth but proceeded through conflict. As technology developed, the habits and modes of thought (which Veblen called 'institutions') developed also, but more slowly. The 'instinct of workmanship' was always driving technology on, but social habits lagged behind. In the modern age there developed a conflict between industry and business: the former represented all those involved directly in the productive process, from engineers and scientists down to the industrial working classes generally; the latter represented the absentee owners of a society based on the corporate institution. The businessman's interest lay in the maximization of pecuniary gain, while the working man's interests lay in the satisfaction of the instinct of workmanship. Veblen's theory was thus highly critical of the business community.

The business world would always tend to inflate the value of capital. But with the progress of technology the decreasing cost of making capital would continually make the real value lower. The pecuniary value and the real value could diverge for only so long. Inevitably the pecuniary value would periodically have to be devalued, and this Veblen saw as the source of economic crises in modern society.

In later years, he became increasingly pessimistic because of the apparently successful resolution of the conflict in favour of industry, and foresaw that the instinct of workmanship would continue to be suppressed in the modern working man.

Veblen is said to have founded a school of 'Institutionalist' economists, but no such school actually exists. Rather, there are many economists who have followed some of his ideas, while no one has ever further developed all of them systematically. What these economists have in common is a rejection of the abstract methods of pure neoclassical economics and an emphasis on the importance of institutions for individuals and for the economy.

VINCI, Leonardo da (1452-1519)

'No other man has ever been born into the world who knows as much as Leonardo,' said Francois, king of France and Leonardo's last patron. His contemporaries marvelled at him, but could not really make use of his boundless talents. The thousands of pages of his sketch books carried engineering projects, mechanical inventions, studies in anatomy, botany, and hydrodynamics. But only his ideas on the theory and technique of painting were absorbed into the common stock of knowledge.

Leonardo was the illegitimate son of Piero da Vinci, a notary in the town from which he took his name: little is known of his mother but her name, Catherina. But Leonardo was brought up by his father's family, and moved with them to Florence when he was twelve. Two years later he was apprenticed there to the painter Verrocchio. In 1472 he was accepted into the painters' guild. Through painting he was introduced to perspective and anatomy which the artists of his time were beginning to explore for their own purposes. But he was never content to limit himself to what was necessary for his art. He learnt of the new inventions conceived by earlier 15th century scholars and architects such as Valturio, Brunelleschi and Francesco di Giorgio. For the

Renaissance architect was an engineer too, concerned with fortification, canals, bridges, and the machines needed in construction or in war. As with his predecessors, most of the first machines he drew were pumps, hoists and cranes, or mills.

After ten years as a Florentine artist, he decided to seek out the court of a prince with the ambitions and wealth to realize his projects, and wrote to Lodovico Sforza, effective ruler of Milan, offering his services. He could provide many novel weapons of war; collapsible bridges, novel guns, mines, instruments for destroying hostile ships—his work as architect and artist is listed almost as an afterthought. So, at thirty-one Leonardo moved to Milan. He was consulted on completion of the cathedral there, and began to design war engines, including armoured vehicles and firearms such as he had promised Sforza. It is not known, however, whether any were actually made.

Always Leonardo turned each problem into a comprehensive examination of the principles involved, seeking to arrive at the perfect form. He wished to derive the operation of machines from mathematical theory, and analyzed every possible type of bearings, linkages, gears and other modes of mechanical transmission. He was employed as a hydraulic engineer, and may have been first to mitre the gates of locks (construct them at an angle against the water pressure), when he designed them for the Martesana canal. He was always impressed with the immense power of moving water,

and in sketches and writings portrayed his fantasies of a mighty deluge. But he was no less fascinated by small scale variations in the flow of water; he was the first to build apparatus to study them, and worked out a theory of water's motion which anticipated many of the conclusions of later hydrodynamics. He studied how to make watermills more efficient, and toyed with steam and gunpowder as sources of power.

He was active too in designing a model city for Lodovico —with roads on different levels—or buildings for his country estate. He found new uses for machinery—cutting files or screws, grinding nails, rolling and slitting mills to make the rods which were then welded together to make iron cannon, even a new kind of mechanical musical instrument. Although it has been claimed that Leonardo anticipated the invention of submarine or tank, it should be said that his apparatus for going underwater and his armoured chariots differ less than most of his devices from notions in the books of earlier 15th century inventors. But he began one thing which was completely new: research toward a mechanical flying machine.

Those who before him had dreamt of flight thought only

Among the 5000 surviving pages of Leonardo's notebooks are many remarkable devices, including these diabolical weapons. The notes are in his 'mirror writing' – he was left handed, and it also helped maintain secrecy.

of flapping wings on their arms. Leonardo saw that the human frame was incapable of this. He worked out means whereby a man could work vanes or bat-like wings through different arrangements of levers and drew a helical aircraft like an outsize whirligig, designing a parachute in case of mischance. He had understandable hopes of the glory he would win as the first man to fly.

There is a story that he tried and failed, but it seems unlikely. Realizing that he would first need to know how bats and birds fly, he opened a new line of enquiry which meant fresh studies in comparative anatomy: he had already started to investigate the workings of the heart, musculature and organs of sense and locomotion of various animals.

In 1499, Lodovico's rule was overthrown by French invasion. Leonardo returned to Florence and was commissioned to paint a fresco for the city's council chamber. The Florentines were engaged in a long war with Pisa, and it had been proposed to divert the river Arno and so ruin Pisa alto-

gether. Leonardo converted this into a plan for a great new canal from Florence to pass along the north side of the Arno basin bringing water and commerce to towns away from the river. While investigating this project he began to study the geology of the region. He realized that the geomorphology of its structure and the strata of the rocks, with fossils they contained, were evidence of a long history, and not simply the results of Noah's flood. But he soon found a new lord of the calibre of Lodovico—Cesare Borgia, the Pope's son and military commander.

For several months during 1502–3 Leonardo toured the Papal territories, mapping and inspecting fortifications and planning canals and harbour improvements. Then the Pope died, and Borgia fell from power. Leonardo went back to Florence.

In connection with his canals he also designed a whole new range of mechanical cranes and shovels to remove earth from the diggings. But although he even calculated the costs,

Left: this self portrait is the only genuine likeness of Leonardo da Vinci to survive.

Below: design for an automatic file cutter, not used till 200 years later, when the idea was taken up by a Frenchman, Verger.

Right: a wing intended for human flight.

such a scheme was more than Florence could undertake. In 1506, now fifty-four, he went back to Milan and took service with the French conquerors as canal and military engineer, while continuing his anatomical researches and studies of flight. But he had to leave yet again when the French were driven out by a descendant of the Sforzas in 1512.

Leonardo found a new patron in Rome, Giuliano de' Medici, the brother of Pope Leo. The original Mona Lisa may have been a mistress of Giuliano. But Leonardo only stayed there three years, until Giuliano left Rome to get married. Fortunately for Leonardo he then found at last a master who appreciated him even if he could not realize Leonardo's schemes—Francois I, who invited him to France. Leonardo was now sixty-four; his handsome and impressive face now wore the full beard which gave him the look of a seer, as he appears in his self portrait.

In France, he made studies for a canal that would join the Loire to the Saône, which would have linked the Atlantic to the Mediterranean. But there seems to have been more interest at the French court in a mechanical lion which walked across the floor: its breast opened to reveal the arms of France. Leonardo's manuscript wealth of discovery and invention was known, but no attempt was made to publish any of it. In his thoroughness, in his imaginative power, in his fables and images, and above all in his immense variety—for there is hardly a single craft which he did not study and suggest ways to improve—nobody indeed has come anywhere near Leonardo.

Yet apart from modifications to a few existing devices, none of his designs were ever built. Within his notebooks there lay hidden a one-man industrial revolution—not to speak of his work as naturalist, writer and artist. This is the tragic side to Leonardo. He could quench his own insatiable thirst for knowledge, yet although he was just as keen to be useful to others, he could not communicate his ideas and his discoveries.

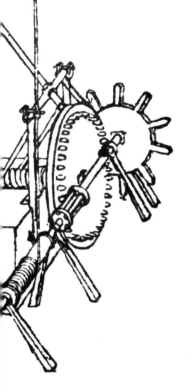

Overleaf: 'The Last Supper', one of the world's most famous paintings, is also one of the worst preserved. The reason for this is that Leonardo was impatient of the haste imposed by the conventional fresco wall painting method, which involved working on fresh, damp plaster. He devised a method of oil painting for walls, but it was not successful.

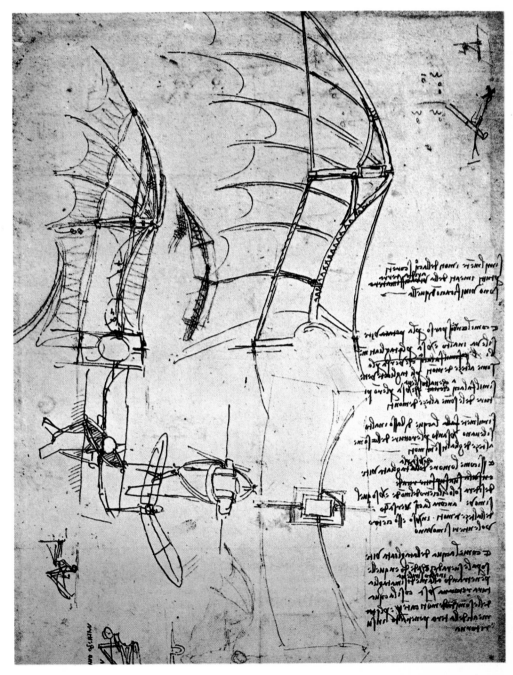

VOLTA, Alessandro (1745-1827)

Volta's invention of the voltaic pile, the earliest form of battery supplying continuous current, was the climax of many years' research into electricity, always with the idea of detecting weak charges, and reducing these elusive phenomena to measurable quantities.

He was born at Como into a family of local nobility fallen on hard times—his father left Volta a burden of debts. In childhood Volta began to speak only at the age of four; still, he went quite successfully through the local school system. He became interested in the rapidly developing sciences of chemistry and electricity; his earliest work was a long poem in praise of Joseph Priestley, the chemistry pioneer. Soon he began research on his own account, hoping to find laws of electric attraction comparable to Newton's laws of gravitation. To this end most of his inventions were devised to accumulate weak charges, or to help in measuring them.

An example of the first is his *electrophorus*, in which a resin plate was charged by friction, and this charge transferred to an iron plate upon it. This he designed in 1775, the same year as his appointment to teach experimental physics at the Como Gymnasium (high school). Three years later, aged thirty-three, he became Professor of Physics at Pavia university, where he remained until his retirement at the age of seventy-four. While there he modified his electrophorus, so that it could be used (with a weakly conducting alabaster plate) for detection and measurement of weak charge as a 'condensing electroscope'.

He also turned his attention to gas chemistry, notably that of methane, and studied the composition of the atmosphere. He wished to use electrical methods—testing the humidity of the air by leakage of charge, or using sparks to explode mixtures of gases. He even devised an 'electric pistol', in which a spark ignited methane, and suggested it could be utilized for signalling at long distances.

Most of these researches were published in the form of letters to better-known scientists, and while professor at Pavia, Volta set out on three extended tours to make the necessary contacts. Yet it was a fellow Italian, Galvani, who made the great discovery, the electrically stimulated twitch of a frog's leg, interpreted as evidence of 'animal electricity'.

This inspired Volta to embark on a series of researches into the electric stimulation of our senses of sight, taste and hearing, which involved placing two different metals in contact, pinching the relevant sense organ—a tricky and often painful business. As a result, he decided the metals were the source of this ever available electricity. He was able to arrange them in an electrochemical series from positive to

Below: Alessandro Volta, by Luigi Rados.

Bottom: Volta's 'pile', or battery, consisted of numerous cells connected in series with metal hoops.

WHITTLE, Sir Frank (1907-)

It is often said that Sir Frank Whittle invented the jet engine, and in a sense this is true, but the bare statement does need qualification. The aircraft jet engine is a variant of the gas turbine—a form of power which had been under development since the early years of this century. The first aircraft to fly using a jet engine was the German Heinkel He 178 in August 1939—some two years before Whittle's first engine was ready for flight testing. The Heinkel engine was not developed for production aircraft, however, whereas many of the early British and American jet engines were derived from Whittle's design.

Frank Whittle was born at Coventry on 1 June 1907, and after attending Leamington College he enlisted in the Royal Air Force as an apprentice. He qualified as a pilot and became a flying instructor, but he also developed a deep interest in the technical problems of aircraft propulsion. The idea of adapting the gas turbine engine to power an aircraft seemed a logical development to Whittle, and in 1929 he tried to persuade the Air Ministry that his engine was feasible. They turned it down. Nevertheless he took out a patent in January 1930, then concentrated on his flying career, in the same year marrying Dorothy Mary Lee. A few years later, at the age of 27, Whittle went to Cambridge University to study engineering and carry out research. In the meantime a new company called Power Jets Ltd had been set up to develop Whittle's jet engine.

By 1937 Whittle and his colleagues from Power Jets had built the world's first turbojet engine, and on 12 April it was run for the first time in a test bed. Whittle was still an officer in the RAF, but permanently attached to Power Jets, where he remained throughout World War II except for a short time at the RAF Staff College. When Air Ministry officials saw a jet engine working for the first time they were still a

Sir Frank Whittle, shown below (on the right), and the W1 turbojet engine; hanging above it is the Gloster E28/39 aircraft on which it was installed.

little apprehensive but they gave financial support, and in March 1938 an order was placed for a new engine. This engine was to power the Gloster E28/39 experimental aircraft, specially designed to take Whittle's engine.

The Gloster E28/39 made its first flight on 15 May 1941 with Flight Lieutenant P E G Sayer at the controls, although it had made a very short hop previously during taxying trials. The engine on this historic flight was a Whittle W1 fitted with a centrifugal compressor, ten combustion chambers and a turbine to drive the compressor. Both aircraft and engine are preserved in the Science Museum, London. As tests continued they demonstrated that the jet engine became more efficient at high speeds and greater altitudes, whereas the conventional piston engine became less efficient under these conditions. These facts had been Whittle's argument from the beginning, but it had been a long struggle to overcome both the technical difficulties and the lack of interest in some official circles.

In 1948 Whittle retired from the RAF with the rank of Air-Commodore and received a knighthood. After holding several advisory posts Sir Frank Whittle started a new line of research, this time into equipment for the oil industry.

WHITWORTH, Sir Joseph (1803-1887)

Whitworth's name has been used, perhaps unwittingly, by generations of engineers, since he was the originator of the notion of standardization in the size and pitch of screw threads. Although his system has now been officially replaced, the 'Whit' classification of nut and bolt sizes is still in popular use, particularly in Britain.

Joseph Whitworth was born in 1803 at Stockport, Cheshire. He was educated in his father's private school until the age of 12, and then sent as a boarder to a private academy for a further two years. He was then placed with his uncle, a successful cotton manufacturer, to learn the trade and establish himself in the business. At the age of 18, however, he broke away from the family influence and went to Manchester to become a mechanic in an engineering workshop.

At the age of 22 he married Fanny Ankers, a Cheshire farmer's daughter and then went to London to work in the workshop of Henry Maudslay (*q.v.*). Eight years later, and after gaining further experience in the workshops of Joseph Clement and John Jacob Holtzappfel, he returned to Manchester to set up in business on his own. He commenced operations in a rented room as 'Joseph Whitworth, toolmaker from London'. This modest start was to be the beginning of the machine tool industry, where machine tools were manufactured for sale.

Hitherto manufacturers had built their own, limited, machine tools to satisfy a particular requirement in a specific manufacturing process. Whitworth set out to develop and sell more adaptable general purpose machines which could be used throughout the metal forming industries. To this end he designed and improved lathes, metal planing and shaping machines, drills, gear cutting machines—in fact the whole range of basic tools required in production engineering. He developed automatic devices and mechanisms in all his machines to replace manual skill and to speed production. His own design skill and the high standard of craftsmanship he obtained in his workshops guaranteed operational precision and accuracy to his customers. Ultimately he became recognised as the foremost machine tool builder of the 19th century.

Whitworth also served mechanical engineering in other ways. Just as each manufacturer had had his own idea about machine tools, the same attitude held regarding screw threads. There were as many screw threads as there were workshops. In his early thirties Whitworth examined as many screw threads as possible and suggested a compromise form of thread based on the average measurement of those he had investigated. By 1860 the Whitworth system was in general use in Britain. By this time also Whitworth had advised government committees up to Royal Commission level on engineering matters, had been made President of the Institution of Mechanical Engineers, and had been elected to the Royal Society.

More honours were to follow from universities and institutions both at home and from overseas and, in 1869, Whitworth became Sir Joseph Whitworth, Bart. His firm continued to prosper and this, together with his sound business sense, made him a millionaire. After his retirement he occupied himself in landscape gardening and farming, and eventually died in 1887, at the age of 83. He had no children, but his name survives today in the Whitworth Scholarships and awards he founded in 1868. These are given, fittingly, to outstanding students of engineering.

Sir Joseph Whitworth, pioneer of standardization, and the standard screw thread which he devised.

WILSON, C T R (1869-1959)

C T R Wilson's cloud chamber, by means of which so many key discoveries in physics have been made, was originally invented not so much for the purpose of basic physics, as to re-create in the laboratory some of the phenomena of electricity, light and water vapour in the atmosphere. For Wilson was attracted to physics through meteorology and his great love for the beauty of nature and the Scottish outdoors. He was the son of a progressive and successful sheep farmer in the Pentland Hills who died when Charles, his youngest child, was only four.

At fifteen he went to Owens College, Manchester, to get a scientific education, and then on to Cambridge, where he remained all his working life. There he began to specialize in physics—then still unusual. After his graduation in 1892 he was appointed demonstrator in physics, later lecturer and finally Professor of Natural Philosophy in 1925. In the summer vacations he would return to Scotland, and in 1894, when 25, spent some time in the meteorological observatory which had been set up on Ben Nevis. 'The wonderful optical phenomena shown when the sun shone on the clouds surrounding the hill top, especially the coloured rings surrounding the sun, or surrounding the shadow cast by hill top or observer on mist or cloud, greatly excited my interest and made me wish to imitate them in the laboratory,' he said later.

It had already been established that condensation of vapour requires nuclei around which droplets can form. Normally these will be dust particles. But Wilson showed there could be some condensation even when all dust is removed—a kind of condensation which did not diminish as the nuclei settled on the base of his apparatus. In his instrument, air is contained in a cylindrical glass chamber, whose base is formed by a piston. If the piston is suddenly drawn down, the volume in the cylinder is enlarged accordingly, the air is cooled and any water vapour in it will condense. With greater expansions, the condensation became cloud-like, and change of colours like those in nature could be seen.

Wilson thought these few nuclei always present might be charged atoms—ions—and after J J Thomson (*q.v.*) and J S Townsend had shown that X-rays would ionize air, he borrowed one of the new X-ray tubes, and carried out an expansion of his cloud chamber with air exposed to X-rays. A dense cloud was produced. This showed that his instrument could make individual ions visible, and could be used widely in ionization research.

Wilson was renowned for his perseverance and care in designing and constructing his own apparatus. Rutherford (*q.v.*) once remarked that when he returned after many years absence from Cambridge 'the first thing I did was to look up my old friend C T R—I found him still grinding a large glass joint.' He returned to his cloud chambers in 1910 to show how alpha and beta particles produce ions which act as centres of condensation. With improved apparatus he could photograph the track of these particles as they passed through the cloud chamber, leaving a vapour trail behind them. In this way individual particles of atomic dimensions could be recognised as plainly as a horse by its hoof-prints.

All this while, he had been devoting as much time to the study of atmospheric electricity as to his cloud chamber. While walking in the Highlands in 1895, he had been nearly struck by lightning. 'This experience,' he said, 'drew my attention very forcibly to the magnitude of the electric field of a thundercloud and to its sudden changes' and throughout his life he continued to work at theories as to how thunderclouds develop their immense electromotive forces. In 1927, Wilson, now 58, received a Nobel Prize for his cloud chamber work, although by now he was concentrating again on electricity in natural clouds on which he kept working through his long retirement. He is said to have been the oldest person to have contributed to the Royal Society's proceedings, with a paper he wrote when 87 on thunderclouds. The year before he learnt that 'students of meteorology' could request to be taken on weather research flights of the RAF, and for the first time he had an opportunity to go up in an aircraft and enjoy looking at thunderstorms from close quarters.

Cavendish physics students, 1898: C T R Wilson is third from left, middle row; on his left, Ernest Rutherford.

WRIGHT, Wilbur (1867-1912) and Orville (1871-1948)

The Wright brothers are now generally accepted as the first men to fly in an aircraft, but recognition of their achievement was not universally accepted for many years— even in their home country, the United States. One reason for this lack of recognition was perhaps due to the Wright brothers' reluctance to let anyone see their early flights in case an unscrupulous inventor should steal their ideas. A further problem was the definition of what constituted a 'flight'; several people claimed to have made a flight before the Wrights, but these 'flights' were really short uncontrolled hops. There is no doubt that the Wright brothers made the world's first practical powered aircraft.

Wilbur and Orville Wright were the sons of a minister of the United Brethren Church and the family moved from place to place. The boys were interested in mechanical devices, and their father gave them a model helicopter which convinced them that this was not the way to fly. Later their father became a bishop, but the boys went into the newspaper and printing business before turning to the booming bicycle trade, first selling, then manufacturing bicycles of their own design.

The Wright brothers were interested in the gliding experiments carried out in Germany by Otto Lilienthal (q.v.), and his death due to a gliding accident in 1896 seems to have started them thinking seriously about the problems of flight. Wilbur was then 28 years old and Orville just 25. They had a thriving bicycle business in Dayton, Ohio, and could afford to finance their experiments themselves. Throughout these experiments thoroughness was the key to their success, for

Above: the Wright brothers built their original engine of 1903 themselves. It was a simple four cylinder design, made as light as possible; even so it weighed a total of 81kg and only developed 12hp.

Below: 17 December 1903 at Kitty Hawk: Flyer No 1 *gets into the air for the first time.*

Above right: although Cayley, Henson and others had designed aircraft with a 'conventional' layout (not surprisingly, because that is how birds are designed) the Wrights' Flyer had a 'tail first' arrangement. The rudder was an afterthought when they found that wing warping would not steer an aircraft, only tilt it. The contrarotating propellors were chain driven.

Below right: Wilbur Wright at the controls of a later Model A in 1911. The pilot is now seated, and the wing warping and rudder controls separate, though worked by one (right hand) lever; the other is for the elevators.

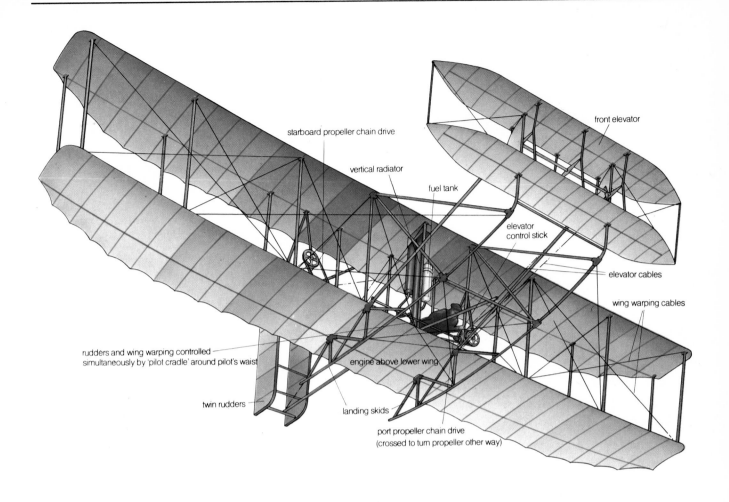

starboard propeller chain drive

front elevator

vertical radiator

fuel tank

elevator
control stick

elevator cables

wing warping cables

rudders and wing warping controlled
simultaneously by 'pilot cradle' around pilot's waist

engine above lower wing

twin rudders

landing skids

port propeller chain drive
(crossed to turn propeller other way)

59 seconds covering 852 feet (260 m).

A new *Flyer* was built in 1904 and this made about 80 flights, including simple manoeuvres and a complete circuit of the field. The longest flight achieved was 5 minutes 4 seconds. During the following year *Flyer No 3* made several long flights, including one lasting over 38 minutes. The Wright brothers had produced a practicable aircraft.

For a period of $2\frac{1}{2}$ years the Wrights did no flying, but instead concentrated on building improved aircraft and engines. In 1908 they were ready to fly again and *Flyer No 3* reappeared with several improvements. A passenger was carried for the first time. It was not until April 1908 that their nearest rival exceeded 5 minutes, so when Wilbur demonstrated their new model A in France, observers were astonished by its performance—one flight lasted 2 hours 20 minutes. Considerable numbers of the model A were built and this was followed by the model B and the model R racer.

From about 1910 the Wright brothers' influence on aviation began to decline, and Wilbur died of typhoid fever in 1912. Orville retained an interest in aviation and lived until the age of 77 in 1948.

YOUNG, Thomas (1773-1829)

'Phenomenon' Young, as he was known at Cambridge, was most aptly nicknamed. His contributions to Egyptology made him as well known in this as in his professional fields of medicine and physics, and, such was his degree of expertise at almost everything, he was even able to dance on a tightrope.

Born in Milverton, Somerset, on 13 June 1773, Young gave a good indication of his future achievements by learning to read at the age of two, and had read through the Bible twice by the time he was four. At school, he was encouraged in his interest in optics by one of his masters, and succeeded in constructing a telescope, but at the same time he continued his interest in the written word. By the time he left school, he had mastered not only several Middle-Eastern languages but had also read and understood the *Principia* and *Opticks* by Sir Isaac Newton (*q.v.*).

He chose the field of medicine for a career, and, with the view of taking over the practice of his great-uncle, entered St. Bartholomew's Hospital, London, in 1793. His literary leanings were maintained by contacts with his uncle's circle of friends, which included such eminent men as Samuel Johnson and Sir Joshua Reynolds. But he was very soon making contributions to medicine, and at the age of 21 was made a Fellow of the Royal Society for his first paper, which described the way in which the lens of the eye changes shape when focusing on objects at different distances (*accommodation*). In the same paper, Young also described the phenomenon of astigmatism, which he discovered from experiments on his own eyes.

His medical studies took him to Edinburgh and Göttingen

they approached the problem of flight methodically stage by stage. They studied the work of their predecessors, especially their fellow American Octave Chanute, and learned from their mistakes. For instance Lilienthal controlled his glider by shifting his body to change the weight distribution, but the Wrights decided this was no way to control an aircraft. They studied bird flight more closely and noticed that the buzzard twisted its wing tips to retain its balance. By twisting the wings of an aircraft the same effect could be achieved; wing warping was a major step towards controlled flight.

The Wright brothers decided to start with a glider and they favoured a biplane—as had Chanute. Before venturing into the air, however, they tested their glider by flying it tethered like a huge box kite at Kitty Hawk, North Carolina. In October 1900 they made several manned flights, but the results were disappointing; realizing that much of the existing information they had used was wrong, they decided to carry out their own research. They built a wind tunnel to test new wing sections and made many other experiments. By October 1902 they had produced a glider which was readily controlled: the next stage was a powered aircraft.

The Wrights decided that a petrol [gasoline] engine was the most suitable source of power, but existing examples did not meet their requirements, so they designed and built their own. They then had to design a suitable propeller. During the summer of 1903 the Wrights built their first aircraft, the *Flyer*, and transported it to Kill Devil Hills near Kitty Hawk. Wilbur won the toss and attempted a take off, but ploughed into the sand and damaged the *Flyer*. On 17 December they were ready again and it was Orville's turn—he flew for 12 seconds. A further three flights were made including one of

Below: Thomas Young, an engraving after the portrait by
Sir Thomas Lawrence.

radiation, shows both characteristics, and in his 1801 paper, Young demonstrated the ease with which the wave theory could explain reflection and refraction. On his appointment as Professor of Natural Philosophy at the Royal Institution in 1801, his Bakerian Lecture included not only an account of the principles of superposition and interference of light waves, but also a determination of their wavelength. Newton was so highly esteemed, however, that Young's work was not widely accepted, and not until 1816, when the Frenchman Auguste Fresnel (*q.v.*) published very similar results, including an account of the transverse motion of light waves, did he receive support.

Young resigned his Professorship in 1803, finding difficulty in lecturing to popular audiences, and resumed his career in medicine. But his interest in linguistics was as strong as ever, and he produced outstanding contributions to the understanding of Egyptian hieroglyphics, starting in 1814 with his almost perfect translation of some of the symbols on the Rosetta Stone. This he followed with a monumental (and anonymous) article on Egypt in the *Encyclopaedia Britannica*.

The later years of his life were occupied with committee affairs; among other responsibilities he was Foreign Secretary of the Royal Society. His original output still continued, however, one particular example being his establishment of the *three colour theory* which described the mechanism of colour vision. Applications of this principle are used in colour television and photography today.

His other contributions to science include measurement of the size of molecules, investigations into surface tension and a scientific formulation of the meaning of energy. His studies in elasticity are commemorated by the name of the constant in the equation describing elasticity: Young's Modulus.

Universities (1794 and 1795) and finally, Emmanuel College, Cambridge, in 1797. Here he spent two years before entering medical practice in London, pursuing original research and publishing *Outlines of Experiments and Enquiries respecting Sound and Light* in 1801. At the time Young wrote this paper, it was generally accepted that light was composed of a stream of *corpuscles* (particles). This conclusion had been reached by Newton, whose reputation gave weight to the theory. The alternative hypothesis, that light was a wave motion, advanced by Christiaan Huygens (*q.v.*), was not as popular. We know now that light, and indeed all electromagnetic

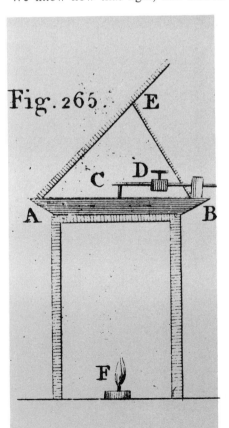

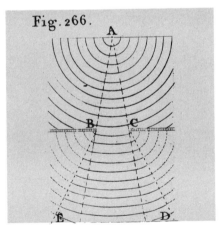

Thomas Young worked out his wave theory of light in 1801 with the help of a model, far left, consisting of a tray of water, a vibrating device to make waves in it, and a movable wall with one or more gaps. This allowed him to observe diffraction, near left, and interference effects, below, both of which occur (on a much smaller scale) in light waves.

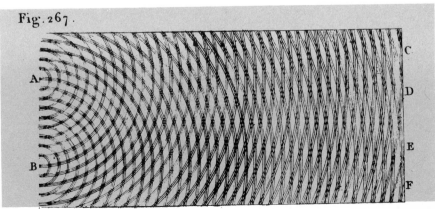

ZEPPELIN, Count F von (1838-1917)

The name Zeppelin is known world wide as a highly successful range of German airships but less well known is the man after whom the airships were named. Ferdinand was born on 8 July 1838 at Constance in Germany, the son of Count Frederick von Zeppelin. As was the custom in Germany, he joined the army as a volunteer in the American Civil War. On reaching the rank of lieutenant-general he left the army and started a new career in aviation.

For several years Zeppelin and his staff worked on the design of a rigid airship, but they received little support. Most of the airships built previously had been of the non-rigid type which consisted of a sausage-shaped balloon with a cabin suspended below containing the crew, engines and control surfaces. These non-rigid airships became rather unwieldy when their size was increased—some were 290 feet (88 m) long—and Zeppelin was convinced that the answer was to house separate gas-bags inside a rigid framework. The framework was to be made up of a lightweight metal structure covered with fabric.

Zeppelin formed a company and built a huge floating shed on Lake Constance. Then he built his first airship, the LZ1, which was 420 feet (128 m) long and powered by two Daimler engines of only 16 hp each. On 2 July 1900 the LZ1 made its first flight. The method of control, using a rudder and moving weights, was not adequate and modifications were made before the next flight in October. The improvements were still not sufficient, and a new Zeppelin, LZ2, was planned with two 85 hp engines. After a poor first flight, LZ2 took off in January 1906 with the Count at the controls. She was flying reasonably well when both engines failed and a forced landing had to be made. LZ2 was moored for the night but a strong wind got up and she was wrecked. LZ3 followed in a few months and was a great success, and in 1908 the Count made a spectacular 12 hour flight over the Swiss Alps in LZ4.

The next great milestone in Count von Zeppelin's life was the founding of a new company to operate a passenger carrying service using Zeppelins. In 1909 this company, with the

abbreviated name DELAG, was set up by Zeppelin, backed by the rich Colsman family. The first airship to be delivered was LZ7, *Deutschland*, and in June 1910 the service began with flights from Düsseldorf. The network expanded and in four years DELAG carried over 34,000 passengers without a fatal accident—a remarkable achievement for these early days of aviation.

Count von Zeppelin was more interested in building military airships than running an airline, and he devoted much of his time to this end. After a long hard struggle he convinced both the German army and navy to operate Zeppelins. After two of his naval airships crashed in 1913 with heavy casualties the 75-year old Count took a less active part in the Zeppelin company's day-to-day operations. He did not actually retire, and even developed a new interest in large heavier-than-air craft. Zeppelin's airships were widely used to drop bombs during World War I, but by 1917 (the year of his death) the old Count is reputed to have said: 'Airships are an antiquated weapon. The aircraft will control the air'.

Above right: Count Friedrich von Zeppelin talks to Kaiser Wilhelm II during World War I.

Left: advertisement for the ill-fated Hindenburg.

Below: after the Hindenburg *crashed in 1937, killing 97, her successor,* the Graf Zeppelin, *never entered service.*

ZWORYKIN, Vladimir Kosma (1889-)

Although many people, particularly in Britain, believe the Scot John Logie Baird (*q.v.*) to be the inventor of television, the credit must largely go to the Russian-American Vladimir Zworykin. As early as 1923 he had demonstrated a television system, and his invention of the *iconoscope* formed the basis of the first true electronic television cameras.

Zworykin's father was a merchant in the town of Murom, on a tributary of the Volga between Moscow and Gorky in Russia. Vladimir was sent to the Institute of Technology at Petrograd (now Leningrad), where he graduated with a degree in electrical engineering at the age of 23.

His professor at Petrograd, Boris Rosing, was very interested in the possibilities of cathode ray tubes, which were commercially available around the turn of the century. At a time when even movie pictures were hardly known, the cathode ray tube was a unique means of displaying moving images, even if at the time they only consisted of the single lines of an oscilloscope. Many people realized that it ought to be possible to use the system for displaying images, but the electronic techniques of the time were not equal to the task.

Rosing's ideas used mechanical scanning of the original scene, but he and Zworykin realized the limitations of such a method. The notion that a complete electronic system should work remained in Zworykin's mind, however.

After World War I, when he served in the Russian army's radio corps, Zworykin emigrated to the USA. He joined Westinghouse, who were working on radio research, where after some difficulty in managing to persuade people that pictures could be transmitted by radio, he was able to continue his research. In 1923 he was able to demonstrate not just a cathode ray tube receiver but also an electronic television camera.

Vladimir Zworykin, the true inventor of television, is shown here holding an early version of his kinescope – what is now called a picture tube. The equivalent component in the camera was called an iconoscope; below is a later development of it, the Emitron, which is very similar in function and appearance.

The problem with mechanical scanning devices, apart from the obvious disadvantages of requiring whirling discs of lenses, was that the amount of light transmitted for each picture element was very small. The photoelectric cells of the day were insensitive, and the amplifiers weak. The iconoscope, however, used the principle of charge storage: the action of light builds up a charge on a signal plate until it is 'collected' by scanning the plate with an electron beam. The light can thus build up the charge for a much longer time than the instant in which that part of the picture is scanned.

Although a system had been demonstrated, it was very far from being a saleable proposition. Zworykin managed to interest David Sarnoff, then the vice-president of RCA, in the system, as a result of which Zworykin went to RCA and was given a team to work on the development of television. By 1939, they had produced the circuits and apparatus for a complete system which would operate commercially over the long distances necessary for American television.

In Britain, a team working for EMI under another emigrant Russian, Isaac Shoenberg, took the basic idea of the iconoscope, which had been patented in 1923, and developed it into the Emitron. They had a working system operating by 1935—a system which, with modern equipment, is still giving excellent pictures in Britain today though a higher definition colour system operates alongside.

Zworykin continued his work on electron image systems, and played a part in the development of the electron microscope. He has contributed to many fields of science, being particularly interested in the application of electronics and engineering in medicine.

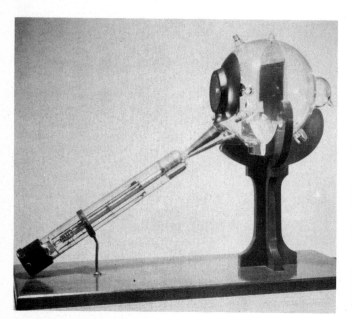

Index